RELIGION FOR SKEPTICS

A Theology for the Questioning Mind

RELIGION

FOR

SKEPTICS

A Theology for
the Questioning Mind

WILLIAM B. SILVERMAN

JONATHAN DAVID *Publishers Inc.*

RELIGION FOR SKEPTICS

Copyright 1967

by

WILLIAM B. SILVERMAN

JONATHAN DAVID PUBLISHERS

131 East 23rd Street, New York, N. Y. 10010

Religion For Skeptics appeared originally in a cloth edition, published by The Macmillan Co., and was entitled, *God Help Me.*

Library of Congress Card Catalogue No. 67-17071

Printed in the United States of America

To my sons:

Joel and Eldon

Whose questioning minds insist upon a rational, dynamic and living faith.

Introduction

This book has been written for questioning minds. It is dedicated to those who insist upon the free and critical evaluation of religious beliefs and theological concepts that are generally accepted as "sacred" and "unquestionable." It offers an invitation to skeptics and doubters to consider "what not to believe," as well as "what to believe," about religious concepts that are rationally feasible and tenable.

If you are a skeptic and a doubter and you are smugly content with your skepticism, and complacently satisfied with your doubts, it would be unwise to read this volume. There is enough misery, discontent and unhappiness in this world without subjecting a happy skeptic to the possibility of doubting his doubts.

If you are inclined, however, to reject superstition and magic in religion, to accept the conclusions of science, archaeological research, behavioral psychology, astronomy, biochemistry and nuclear and astrophysics, and you are searching for a faith that is predicated on reason, groping for a theology that is in consonance with science, then hopefully this volume may challenge your thinking and motivate an interest in pursuing in greater detail the questions that are considered.

Modern man, like Robert Frost's "Poor Bear In a Cage," fights his inward, nervous rage. He paces back and forth, caged in ,by frustration, yearning to be free. He turns to the burgeoning wonders of science, and his mind encompasses galaxies in space beyond imagination, but he cannot encompass or control the tempestuous feelings that surge through him, that drive him, goad him, and allow him no peace.

He looks at an unseen world through his microscope as the infinitesimal looms in gigantic proportion. He yearns to wrest the secrets of the universe from their esoteric hiding places; he hurtles down the bastions of morality, boldly shaking the acceptable mores of his society, tearing at values clothed in sanctity, clawing at the very entrails of respectability, to shock, appall, dethrone, disgust, challenge, defy, resist, rebel and throw off the shackles of restraint—to be free. Only to be free—

As a consequence of this thrust to freedom, religion is being demythologized, analyzed and frequently paralyzed. We are told that God is dead. Some believe that God is not dead, but missing in action. Others contend that our archaic, kindergarten and juvenile concepts of God are dead. The requiems have been intoned, the *kaddish* recited, and man is free from the mandates of divinity. Hugh Heffner and his "playboy" philosophy have replaced Socrates and Spinoza, morality is dead; man is free of the responsibilities of love, free to become a slave to sex. The birth-control pill is outselling aspirin, tranquilizer tablets have been substituted for the tablets of the moral law, and LSD is replacing geritol, castoria and vitamins. Hail to the goddess bunny! Sing praises to the chemically induced illusion!

Modern man did not discover skepticism. Twentieth century man did not innovate rebellion, non-conformity and revolt against the institutions and ideologies of society.

In the biblical tradition, Abraham questioned God, asking: "Shall not the Judge of all the world do justly?" Moses asked about the essence of God and was told: "I will be what I will be." Moses was excoriated, mocked and repudiated. The prophets of Israel were condemned, harassed and castigated. Elijah was called a troubler. Jeremiah was lowered into a pit. Amos was driven away by the priests of Beth El. The Psalmist questioned and doubted. Ecclesiastes, the gentle cynic, articulated his confusion, his perplexities and his skepticism. When the questioning Job finally resolved his religious torment by saying: "Though He slay me, yet will I trust in Him," he adds in a final assertion of theological independence: "But I will argue my ways before Him." The Jewish rabbinic tradition goes so far as to have God say: "Let my children doubt Me, and not believe in Me,—if only they keep My Commandments."

It is claimed that Jesus was crucified. Spinoza was excommunicated. A heroic parade of rebels, skeptics and non-conformists march through history: Socrates, Marcion, Martin Luther, Descartes, Copernicus, Galileo, Newton, Pasteur, Curie, Darwin and Einstein; Thomas Paine, Ghandi, Louis Brandeis, Karl Marx, Sigmund Freud and Margaret Sanger. Troublemakers, agitators, deviationists, heretics, skeptics all—who directed their rebellion into channels of creative discontent; who offered alternatives to the status quo. What do we have to offer besides intellectual arrogance, ideological contempt, and a negative rejection, without any something positive or meaningful to replace what we have rejected?

As the universe becomes larger and more complex in our thought and comprehension, as science adds new knowledge to our understanding of the nature of life, there is a commensurate growth of our ignorance. The more that is known, the more there is to know. This is equally true in the field of religion. We struggle, grope and aspire to religious truth, only to find that new insights open up greater and more perplexing areas of religious thought and endeavor. Skepticism and creative doubt should be encouraged in religion as well as in science. It is difficult, if not impossible, to attain to a rational, dynamic and sustaining faith without skepticism and doubt.

There are many today who would paraphrase Wordsworth, saying: "Great God! I'd rather be a pagan than be sucked into a creed outworn." They reject theological cliches and religious dogmatism, as they search for "reason to believe."

St. Thomas Aquinas, Maimonides, Spinoza and Hegel believed that God can be found through reason and logic. Many in our generation also believe that if religion is to survive, man must pioneer and advance to new frontiers of a rational faith— a faith that is not regarded as a substitute for reason but is postulated as an extension of reason, from the known into the unknown. If religion is to survive it must be made rational and relevant to the problems of contemporary society.

As we consider a theology for the questioning mind, it isn't necessary to make skepticism a religion, but it is essential to provide a direction, an opportunity for honest dissent, creative doubt and rational inquiry, which are the definitive requisites of a religion for skeptics.

W. B. S.

April, 1967

"Come now, and let us reason together, Saith the Lord."

—Isaiah I.18

Contents

RELIGION FOR SKEPTICS

A Theology for the Questioning Mind

I

Kindergarten Religion

《 》

1

Man in Search of an Answer

From whence shall my help come?
—PSALM 121.1

Somewhere Behind Space and Time

A college student sought the advice of a religious counselor in dis-
entangling what he called his "social maladjustment and morbid
tendencies." When the counselor asked the youth about his belief
in God, he reacted with immediate hostility. "I'll tell you what I
believe," he said. "I believe with the poet that 'somewhere behind
space and time, there is nothing but wetter water and slimier slime.'
We fool ourselves if we think there is anything else. Religion is a
pious fraud, and all this talk about God, immortality, and a purposeful, moral universe is just so much theological gibberish meant for
naïve and infantile minds."

The religious counselor replied, "If these are your convictions, why
did you come to me?"

"That's just it," replied the student. "I want to have a religious
faith. I want to believe. I need help, but I don't know what to do or
where to turn."

That student symbolizes twentieth century man, hurling his impre-
cations at the universe, defiant of God, hostile to religion, and yet
compelled by a desperate need for help. In quest of a simple and infallible cure for the sickness of his soul, he seeks a guaranteed prescription for happiness, the formula for peace of mind, and the secret
of a sustaining and healing faith. Echoing the cry of the psalmist, he
asks, "From whence shall my help come?"

Why should we expect to discover the prescription for happiness
when we don't really know what happiness is, and might not recog-

3

nize it even if it came our way? Stubborn in our conviction that it can be found, we are like the Oriental monarch who was told by his counselors that if he would wear the shirt of a happy man he would discover the secret of happiness. After a long and desperate search, a happy man was found, but, alas, he didn't own a shirt. More plausible solutions for the secret of happiness have been advanced only to provide the same disappointment. But, undaunted and undismayed, man continues his quest despite the warning of John Dewey that any single-hearted search for happiness is doomed to failure, and that life's happiness comes unheralded to people who invest all of their energies in each developing experience so as to distill its full and unique meaning.

As for peace of mind, how can man obtain it without isolating himself from the problems and realities of the world in which he lives? How can a sensitive individual enjoy peace of mind in today's turbulent world? How can he nurture complacency and feed his smugness with high-caloried selfishness when millions of people are starving for want of bread? Is it possible for man to achieve peace of mind when justice, exploitation, and evil add up to a staggering total of human misery? Let him ask himself with Richard Beer Hoffman:

"Could I be happy in a suffering world?
By day, by night, in dreams I feel the touch
Of every living thing; to me, man, beast,
The stones and grasses of the field, all cry.
With mute imploring eyes they cry
To me, and yet the answer must be His." [1]

Peace of mind may be a vice and not a virtue—a palliative for the intellect and a barbiturate of the spirit that dulls our sensitivities and renders us indifferent to our moral and human responsibilities. A selfish and callous person may acquire peace of mind. The apparent piety of such an individual is superficial and deceptive. He has confused indifference with tranquillity and has succeeded in shutting out the "still small voice" that summons him to heed the requirements of a dynamic religious faith.

It is well for us to be vigilant against the seductive allure of catch-

[1] Translated from "Jacob's Dream," Jewish Publication Society, Philadelphia.

words, phrases, and patently simple solutions. There is no single prescription or formula, no matter how palatably and ingeniously compounded, that will guarantee happiness and peace of mind. There is no theological pill dispensed from a celestial pharmaceutical laboratory that will guarantee a cure for our dissatisfaction, offer complete healing for our spiritual sickness, and provide the answer to our appeal for help.

Handouts from Heaven

Just as there are no miraculous means to achieve happiness and peace of mind, neither is there a simple and infallible formula for faith. Many of us mistakenly regard the God-seeking personalities of the Bible as men and women who were congenitally endowed with faith, unearned and unlearned, a gift of God like heavenly manna, available for the asking. Even a cursory reading of the Bible demonstrates the fallacy of such a conclusion.

Abraham was forced to leave his homeland and family, and grope through endless hours of torment before he glimpsed a vision of the living God. Jacob had to writhe and wrestle through a long night of fear to win a blessing of faith. Moses endured forty years of suffering in the wilderness. The prophets of Israel were driven from their homes, reviled and mocked, subjected to hatred and contempt, and were called revolutionaries and traitors! Elijah, a fugitive from the wrath of Jezebel, alone in the wilderness, prayed: "It is enough; now, O Lord, take away my life" (I Kings 19.4). Amos narrowly escaped death from the vicious enmity of the priests of Beth-El. Jeremiah was cast into a dungeon to starve and rot. A man of faith? Yes, but it was this man of faith who once said, "My heart within me is broken, all my bones shake" (Jeremiah 23.9). It was this same man of faith who protested: "I am become a laughing-stock all the day, every one mocketh me. . . . For I have heard the whispering of many, terror on every side: 'Denounce, and we will denounce him'; even of all my familiar friends" (20.7, 10). Bereft of his wife, his children, and his possessions, Job cursed the day that he was born. Scraping his festering sores with a potsherd, he earned his faith through suffering and doubt. These men had to find their way to a sustaining faith. It was not given to them as a handout from heaven. They had to earn their faith, struggle for their blessing. In the hour of their need, they cried out, *God help me!* But they did something more than articulate their despair. Emulating the action of the author of the 121st Psalm, each turned in the direction of God, saying:

> "I will lift up mine eyes unto the mountains:
> From whence shall my help come?"

In the hour of their need, they cried out, *God help me!* but even as they asked for help they lifted their eyes on high. They turned their thoughts from futility to hope, and found the strength to rise above despair to a supreme affirmation of faith.

I Will Lift Up Mine Eyes unto the Mountains

We, too, need help, but instead of lifting our eyes to the mountains and turning to God, we turn to our checkbooks and say, in effect, *I lift mine eyes unto my material resources.* I lift up mine eyes unto my stocks and bonds, my savings account, my property, insurance policies, and collateral, only to discover that faith cannot be financed even at 3¼ per cent interest. The president of the local bank makes a poor substitute for God.

In 1920 the British economist R. H. Tawney, in his volume *The Acquisitive Society*,[2] which significantly enough was originally published under the title *The Sickness of an Acquisitive Society*, tried to teach us that, far from being the cure, money is frequently the cause of the sickness of our souls. Thirty-five years later the psychiatrist Erich Fromm, in his book *The Sane Society*,[3] contended that our society is sick and that man "is alienated from himself, worships the products of his own hands, the leaders of his own making, as if they were above him, rather than made by him." He concludes that society will not be restored to health and sanity until spiritual values are substituted for the market-place orientation that dominates our way of life.

Dr. Kenneth McFarland, educational consultant to General Motors,

[2] New York, Harcourt, Brace Co., 1920.
[3] New York, Rinehart and Company, Inc., 1955, p. 356.

recently stated that we have never had so much wealth per capita or been so physically comfortable. Despite all this, we live under tension, experience insecurity, and suffer more mental breakdown than ever before. Never have we been so close to a general failure of the human spirit, or so close to moral bankruptcy.

We needed neither Fromm nor McFarland to tell us. We know that those who worship the golden calf seldom receive an answer when, spiritually impoverished and morally bankrupt, they ask the mute and glittering beast, From whence shall come our help?

Perhaps, then, we may say, *I lift up mine eyes unto the bookshelves.* But contemporary literature is paragraphed with pessimism and punctuated with doom. Wherever we turn—to art, music, politics, to the philosophers, psychologists, to the scientists and sages of our age— we cannot escape dire predictions of catastrophe, ominous messages of disaster suggesting the futility of life and the imminence of death.

In a pessimistic volume called *Road to Survival,*[4] William Vogt makes the startling announcement that within a short time our planet will be unable to provide sufficient food for its inhabitants, and he advises curtailment of population. This twentieth century Malthus suggests: No more babies—for an increase in population will reduce the earth to starvation. Another contemporary author, Isabel Leighton, has edited a book, with the graphic title *The Aspirin Age,*[5] that attempts to show the headaches, the pain, the migraine of an era.

We turn to music to find that Leonard Bernstein, the talented composer and conductor, offers a Symphony Number Two called *The Age of Anxiety.* One critic wrote: "And so Leonard Bernstein commences his Symphony with neither the excitement of Beethoven, nor even the abortive hopefulness of Tschaikowsky. He starts with a wail of despair, uncertainty, insecurity, frustration." This is hardly a promising outlook for our future. Our planet is starving. Our age is sustained by aspirin. And the dominant theme of our civilization is one of anxiety.

We lift our eyes to the poets. Perhaps they have a word of hope for our society. So we read George Barker's "Elegy Number One" and discover that "Time is a tragedy. There is nothing left to celebrate but death. This is the only dignity left, the single death without

[4] New York, William Sloane Associates, Inc., 1948.
[5] New York, Simon and Schuster, Inc., 1949.

purpose: . . . and so we are perfect sacrifices to nothing." The poet Jeffers maintains that the life of mankind is "a pilgrimage from birth to death, a journey from darkness to darkness." W. H. Auden beholds the world as a madhouse: "Man is trapped in the tenement of flesh, incapable of loving anything but death." These are not poets of faith, but authors of defeatism and ghost writers of death.

We turn from these literary pied pipers of doom, leading man in a rat race to oblivion, to the philosophers and sages of our era, hopeful that they can provide the help we need. All too soon we discover the pessimism of the Existentialists, with the high priests Sartre, Camus, and Heidegger intoning the conviction of the futility of human endeavor, the delusion of progress, the mockery of a purposeless universe, and the emptiness of a generation of men garbed in the raiment of intellect, will, and emotion—all dressed up for life, but with no place to go.

These are the literary and intellectual spokesmen of our age, penning an obituary for the future and intoning a solemn requiem over the demise of our civilization. But we are not asking, "From whence shall come our doom? From whence shall come our destruction?" We are asking, demanding to know, *From whence shall come our help?*

So, *I lift mine eyes unto the General Assembly of the United Nations,* only to behold confusion, conflict, divisiveness, spheres of influences, charges and countercharges, with great powers vying in a dangerous contest for supremacy. We look upon the representatives of the United Nations struggling to find the answer to the problems of starvation and war. With an ample food supply for the earth's population, countless millions hunger and starve for lack of bread. The nations talk of peace at the very time they create new and more devastating nuclear weapons of destruction. As satellites are sent to chart and conquer outer space, the problems that beset us on earth multiply. We harness the energy of the cosmos to pulverize the world into atomic dust, but can't generate enough spiritual energy to create a family of nations living together in justice, brotherhood, and peace. That may be what led George Bernard Shaw to assert that our world is the one to which other planets in the universe send their insane.

I lift mine eyes unto the scientists and beg them, "You learned scholars, you men of intricate, technical knowledge—you help us!" *I lift mine eyes unto the test tubes. I lift mine eyes unto the isotopes—* but the scientists just throw up their hands in despair because of the atomic jinni they have let loose. They realize that one cobalt bomb exploded in the middle of the Pacific Ocean can produce 7.5 tons of radioactive cobalt, equal to nearly five million pounds of radium. It could require only one day for this radioactive dust to reach California, and three more to reach New York, and all life would be destroyed in its path. It is estimated that 499 one-ton deuterium-cobalt bombs could release enough radioactivity to destroy the total population of the earth. We look to the scientists for help, but they are terrified of the Pandora's box of nuclear evil that may spring open at the touch of a pushbutton and shower the world with radioactive death. Banded together into the "league of frightened men," they plead with religious teachers and educators to find a way, to implement the religious values and ethical ideals that will enable our civilization to survive. The question, From whence shall come our help? remains unanswered.

And so modern man, in desperate need of something to fortify himself to meet the impact of fear, crisis, tension, frustration, and insecurity, continues his search for help. His desperation makes him susceptible to the appeal of fads, panaceas, cults, organizations, pseudoscientific programs and utopian dreams. He is the prospect for the peddlers of panaceas, the gullible customer eager to buy each new commodity that promises salvation.

In recent years psychiatry has beckoned as the answer to man's quest for help, and the cure for the sickness of his soul. Reluctantly at first, and then with an increasing eagerness, man has forsaken his upright posture to recline hopefully on the couch as he lifts his eyes to the psychoanalyst.

It is manifestly unfair to equate psychology and psychiatry with dubious fads and questionable panaceas. The trained analyst serves an important purpose, especially for the disturbed and emotionally maladjusted individual. Man is better able to understand himself, and to get along with himself, because of the new and valuable insights provided by dynamic psychology and psychiatric research. Psychology and religion are co-partners in the endeavor to educe the inherent strength for an individual to achieve his greatest potential for wholesome and healthy living. But man deceives himself when he substitutes psychology for religion—the couch for the pew—and makes the psychiatrist a surrogate for God. Seduced by a new idolatry, he bows before the libido and prostrates himself in worshipful obeisance before a new psychological trinity: the id, the ego, and the superego. He cries out, From whence shall come my help? and then lifts his eyes to the ink blots with hopeful anticipation that a Rorschach test will provide the answer. A few are helped, but psychology alone cannot fill the vacuum of a generation described by T. S. Eliot as

". . . the hollow men
. . . the stuffed men
Leaning together
Headpiece filled with straw. Alas!

. . . .

Shape without form, shade without color,
Paralyzed force, gesture without motion."[6]

Psychology alone cannot cure the sickness of our world.

It cannot be that God has placed man upon the earth, endowed him with a soul, given him the ability to perceive beauty, quest for holiness, and create a society of justice and peace upon earth, only to have His greatest masterpiece, blessed with freedom of will, the power to move and build and hope, gaze upon his world—beaten and defeated by his own will.

There is no condition more terrible than that of men crushed by life who in their weary desperation await the end with no one to help or care. Such hopelessness is more dangerous to the universe than the explosive potential of a cobalt bomb. But man is not without hope. Man is not alone. There is a power that can help us if we make the effort to avert our gaze from the ground and reach for the stars.

We have turned to literature, economics, philosophy, psychology, and science seeking an answer, but the only response has been the mocking echo of our own voice pleading for help. Now, even though reluctantly and with no alternative, we must turn to God, and go beyond ourselves, from the finite to the infinite.

We have lifted our eyes to our material resources, to the bookshelves, and to the General Assembly of the United Nations. We have lifted our hopes to the test tubes, the isotopes, and the ink blots of a Rorschach test. Will we be daring enough to lift our hopes and our eyes unto the mountains, and then, even higher, beyond the stars?

[6] "The Hollow Men," *Collected Poems 1909-1935*, copyright 1936, by Harcourt, Brace and Company, p. 101.

What we see will depend upon what we seek. If it is only a prescription for happiness, the secret of peace of mind, or a formula for faith, then, with H. G. Wells, we shall look at the stars as we look at "the pattern of wallpaper on a railway station waiting room." If it is God we seek, then we shall look beyond the stars and know that somewhere behind space and time there is more than wetter water and slimier slime—the awesome mystery, the infinite power, the supreme and compassionate Being we call Divinity.

Our help is not packaged in the word we call "religion," but in the quest for a living religious faith. Our salvation is not in finding, but in seeking. Our answer is not in the discovery, but in the effort to discover the presence of God in every aspect of life. Therefore, when modern man lifts his eyes to the mountains and begins a journey of faith in the direction of the Most High, he learns with the Psalmist:

"My help cometh from the Lord,
Who made heaven and earth."

2

The Danger of Respectable Religion

The dogmas of the quiet past are inadequate to the stormy present. We must think anew, we must act anew. We must disenthrall ourselves.

—ABRAHAM LINCOLN, in an address given on December 1, 1862

Faith Without Magic

If man is to derive help and strength from God, he must advance from a puerile, infantile kindergarten conception of religion to a rational, ethical, prophetic, mature, and radical faith devoid of magic, miracles, and theological anachronisms. The religious obscurantism that equates religion with cultural lag, reactionary political doctrines, fundamentalist theology, resistance to science, and antagonism to progress must give way to a revolutionary attitude—a radical approach that will identify religion with cultural change, liberal political thinking, modernist-rational-ethical theology, a *rapprochement* with science, and the will to create and further "the good society" dedicated to the dynamics of progress.

To activate this approach, faith must be divorced from miracles, magic eradicated from ritual, and superstition expurgated from creed, and the irrational "I believe because it is absurd" must be banished from theology. In short, religion must be made disrespectable.

Respectability has been inimical to man's effort to achieve a mature religious faith. The demands of social acceptance and the requisites of religious conformity have impeded man in his quest for God and his search for intrinsic and abiding religious values. The criteria for contemporary religious acceptability are frequently in conflict with the moral and ethical requirements of the mature faith, compelling man to ask himself, "Is it condoned by the Church or the Synagogue?" rather than, "Does it bring me closer to God and my fellow man in love?" "Is what I believe in compliance with the established creed?" rather than, "Does my belief sensitize and compel me to moral action?" Just as a man seeks group approval and acceptance, so religion has pursued acceptability and resisted nonconformity. In consequence, it has in large measure degenerated into a cult of the respectable, thus repudiating its primary responsibility of bringing man to God and God to man.

Religious respectability encourages us to take refuge in religious clichés and bask in the warm and the comforting assurance that "God's in his heaven: all's right with the world." Reason, however, dictates the conclusion that God is not restricted to heaven and that there is much that is wrong and evil in the world. We claim that there has been a revival of religion because of the phenomenal sale of religious books, the return to the Church and the Synagogue, and the mass attendance at revival meetings that compete with television spectaculars in vulgarity and odious theatricalism. Gallup, Roper, and other public-opinion analysts poll the American people and announce that the overwhelming majority believe in God. Respectable religionists nod happily but neglect to ask, How does this belief in God affect the thoughts, attitudes, and actions of the American people?

Is There a Revival of Religion?

With church membership at an all-time high of 100,000,000, and despite the talk of religious revival in America and a mass return to God in time of international tension, public-opinion analysts insist that surveys completed among maturing young people in the seventeen- to twenty-two-year-old group throughout the country indicate that most young people, both boys and girls, know very little about their religion—or any other religion. Few could manage a passing mark on a grade-school-level Bible test. A majority of young Protestants and young Jews and a minority of young Catholics do not attend church regularly. Few of the Protestants and few Jews look upon themselves as "religious persons." An overwhelming majority of young adults of all faiths said they would never think of turning to a clergyman for help in solving life's problems. Certainly these facts do not indicate that youth is experiencing a spiritual or religious renaissance.

Because literary titles are taken from Scripture, because movies and plays abound in biblical themes, and because church attendance is breaking all records, we conclude that there is a resurgence of religion. But who asks whether religion is meaningful to our youth or vital to their parents? How many who call themselves religious are struggling with the ubiquitous problem of how to narrow the dichotomy between belief and action? Who is assessing the moral significance of this so-called religious revival? To question is to risk the danger of nonconformity. To doubt is to invite the charge of religious disrespectability.

The word "religious," for all its respectability, may be a mask for deception, hypocrisy, and falsehood. Let a man call himself "religious," and he is regarded as an acceptable, approved, respectable, and worthy member of society. Let a man honestly state that he is "irreligious," and we look upon him as suspect, different, nonconformist, and potentially dangerous.

The fact that we put the motto "In God we trust" on our coins does not necessarily make us a God-seeking or God-trusting nation. To amend the pledge of allegiance to make us "one nation *under God*" does not perforce make us Godlike in our national behavior. We may believe in the Ten Commandments without practicing them, honor the Bible without translating it into our lives, belong to a church or a synagogue, and yet separate ourselves from its preachments and teachings.

We demand religion in our public schools without agreeing on the doctrines or the tenets that we so urgently advocate. We place the Ten Commandments on the blackboard of a classroom, hoping that the reading of them will make our children honest, and we trust that the Decalogue will deter juvenile delinquency. Meanwhile we ignore the danger of slums, the poison of prejudice, the evil of broken homes, the necessity of parental love and care, the instruction of religious values, and the inculcation of moral discipline. Many of us think that all we have to do is take refuge in the labels, forms, and institutions of religion, stamp our lives with the imprimatur of Divinity, and we have "got" religion. This is what one churchman called so much "theological rubbish."

College students particularly are questioning the pious platitudes of respectable religion. In a survey of the religious attitudes of college men and women, one student replied: "In high school I attended church regularly—twice every Sunday, plus Sunday school. I wanted to believe. Before I finished high school I was aware of the logical paradoxes which riddle religion, and I was saturated with doubt about the existence of God. I still don't know—and I doubt whether religion can offer me any answers."

This student is but one of many who are questioning the existing beliefs about God, prayer, Scripture, and immortality. The usual answers of respectable religion did not satisfy. "I wanted to believe," he said; but there were no answers that provided him with a meaningful faith.

Recently a college student came into my study for help. He began with the statement: "God is a despicable and pious fraud!" His words exploded with startling rapidity: "God is a myth foisted upon the ignorant to exploit the underprivileged! The belief in God is a device to rob man of the incentive to solve his own problems. God is the cruel, vengeful, bloodthirsty war lord we use to justify and give sanction to our own desire for violence. What we call religion is really magic supporting the belief in a supernatural magician, an all-powerful jinni who will give us what we want, if we use the right formula in asking. Religion isn't for me. I don't go for that antiquated nonsense, although I hunger and yearn to believe in something. Help me. Help me to believe!"

What shall we do? Shall we castigate this young man as a blasphemer or shrug aside his comments as the rebellious nonsense of youth? His charges must be considered seriously and objectively, not as an indictment of God, but rather as an indictment of man's primitive kindergarten conception of God. Intoxicated by his own daring, exhilarated by the intensity of his emotional "binge," the student gave uninhibited expression to doubts that are usually repressed in the interest of respectability. Is there any truth in the young man's strictures?

Respectable religionists will aver that this is the talk of a callow youth who hasn't had time to grow up. They may also contend that he is too ignorant of life to understand the true meaning of religion and that with the proper religious indoctrination he can be made to "see the light."

How is one to answer the claim of Dr. Nathan M. Pusey, President of Harvard University, in his baccalaureate sermon at Cambridge, Massachusetts, in May, 1958: "When one considers how inadequately churches have served the needs of people in this new technological and secularly attractive age it is not so surprising that many have withdrawn from or remain outside churches to the advantage of the growing secularization." He lists among the churches' shortcomings: "Juvenile conceptions of God, primitive notions of a large-size man who exists to be pleased like an old-style father, or a stern, perhaps even petulant judge, or at best of some kind of anthropomorphic figure whose conduct could be compared to that of our own more virtuous human beings only to His disadvantage, as Homer's gods with Homer's heroes."

The answer to Dr. Pusey is not an outcry of protest against this seemingly blasphemous excoriation of the respectable God worshiped by respectable religionists. The answer to Dr. Pusey and to all who question the validity of our present stereotypes of religion is to re-examine our concepts of God, prayer, religion, social justice, and immortality in the light of a mature, radical, rational, and questioning faith. Religion must withstand the scrutiny of reason. If it cannot, it is not worthy of survival. If it can, then it must be directed to the sanctification of life and the moral reverence for God.

The Indictment Against Modern Religion

It takes but a quick and cursory appraisal of present-day religion to note the bibliolatry that pays obeisance to Scripture without any effort to apply its teachings to life. A superficial analysis will point out the prevalence of stock religious answers being given perplexing problems relating to values and ideals; the religious double talk that condones bigotry, prejudice, ignorance, and evil even as some professional clergymen preach eloquently and persuasively against sin. Know-nothingism, specious rationalizations, and ecclesiastical immorality sanctioned and promulgated by the Church and the Synagogue are contributing to the moral degeneration of man and the bastardization of the God-seeking ideals of a mature faith. "Keep the Church out of politics," "Resist the findings and discoveries of science," "Venerate the past," "Conform or be confounded," "Believe without questioning," "Be saved or be damned"—these are some of the slogans bearing the imprimatur of respectable religion.

The indictment against our modern religion could be documented with detailed evidence to make the God-hungry look to secular causes to nurture the yearning for spiritual fulfillment. The nonconformist, the questioning mind, the rebellious in spirit, the seekers after truth, and the lovers of God are finding it more and more difficult to combat the power and influence of respectable religion. The revolutionary spirit of religion that characterized the prophets of Israel and the teachers of Christianity is anathema to those who would retain a spiritual status quo and who would make all deviationist thinking conform on the procrustean bed of religious orthodoxy.

The thinking youth of our nation, sensing the seeming futility of revolt, find it more acceptable to reject religion than to revolutionize and purify it of its superstitious pollution. Though the intellectuals, despising the authoritarianism and dogmatism of modern religion, find it fashionable to excoriate the ignorance and stupidity of respectable religion, to blue-pencil truth as well as error, and to spew forth venom against the institutions and teachings of religion, they scarcely consider the possibility of correcting the evil with love and consecrated resolve. It seems to them to be too formidable a task, too futile and fruitless an ambition.

As for the believer, weariness enervates the will to combat the popular and accepted Church or Synagogue. It is easier to withdraw politely from the struggle. The great mass of those who call themselves religious are satisfied to settle into a nominal approval of socially acceptable institutional affiliation, even as they "don't observe, don't believe, and don't participate"—maintaining the correct posture of piety even as they succumb to the norm of indifference.

Secularists rise eagerly to attack religion, pounding away with sledge-hammer blows at the weaknesses and the hypocrisies that characterize respectable religion. Unfortunately, there are few men and women identified with the Church or Synagogue who call themselves "religious" who out of love and reverence will venture to examine critically the institutions of religion with the objective of strengthening mature religious insights.

C. Wright Mills, Professor of Sociology at Columbia University, is an example of the secularist who attempts to sound a literary alarm to arouse the exponents of religion from their dogmatic slumbers. Lamenting the lack of moral response, in the March 8, 1958, issue of *The Nation* he offers "A Pagan Sermon to the Christian Clergy," stating: "Religion today is part of this sorry moral condition; to understand the crucial decisions of our pivotal times, it is not necessary to consider religious institutions or personnel or doctrine. Neither preachers nor laity matter; what they do and what they say can be readily agreed with, and safely ignored. I am aware that there are exceptions, but the average output is correctly heard as a parade of worn-out phrases. In the West, religion has become a subordinate part of the overdeveloped society.

"As a social and as a personal force, religion has become a dependent variable. It does not originate; it reacts. It does not denounce;

it adapts. It does not set forth new models of conduct and sensibility; it imitates. Its rhetoric is without deep appeal; the worship it organizes is without piety. It has become less a revitalization of the spirit in permanent tension with the world than a respectable distraction from the sourness of life. In a quite direct sense, religion has generally become part of the false consciousness of the world and of the self."

Professor Mills is scathing in his strictures. He denounces "the religion of good cheer and glad tidings . . . a getting chummy with God." He asserts that "with such religion, ours is indeed a world in which the idea of God is dead. . . . Men and women, in brief, are religiously indifferent; they find no religious meanings in their lives and in their world. . . . Men of religious congregations do evil; ministers of God make them feel good about doing it. Rather than guide them in the moral cultivation of their conscience, ministers, with moral nimbleness, blunt that conscience, covering it up with peace of mind. . . . As a mass medium, religion has become a religiously ineffective part of the show that fills up certain time slots in the weekly routine of cheerful robots."[1]

We may not like to read what this self-styled pagan writes, but whether we like it or dislike it is not important. We must ask ourselves: "Is there truth to his criticisms? Has religion become a pious fraud? What can we who identify ourselves with religion as seekers of God do to restore religion to its primary purpose? How may we make religion disrespectable, sacred, radical, and meaningful again?"

The Mistake of Taking Religion Seriously

Respectable religion expects its adherents to pay lip service to its ideals, to accept its teachings theoretically and theologically, but looks askance at those who would dare to apply the teachings and implement the ideals of religion through personal piety or social action. The command of the Bible to "love thy neighbor as thyself" is respectable and revered. What if one should take this literally and actually love his neighbor with unselfish devotion? His actions would arouse suspicion, and his unselfish devotion to his neighbor would be regarded as anomalous, unnatural, and peculiar. Theories would

[1] The Causes of World War III (New York, Simon and Schuster, Inc., 1958).

abound more numerous than the seeds of a pomegranate as to his reason and intent. Moreover, if it should be ascertained that his devotion to his neighbor is without guile or deceit or selfish purpose, then such a person would be categorized with some subtle malevolence as "too saintly to be human."

Respectable religion teaches that man must be concerned with the welfare of his fellow man. He must be his brother's keeper. If a religionist should take this seriously and dedicate himself wholeheartedly to the plight of his fellow man, circulating petitions, raising funds, organizing protests, joining picket lines, advocating humane and social legislation, and supporting unpopular causes in behalf of the oppressed and the afflicted, would he not risk the opprobrium and displeasure of those who do not like to be disturbed? Is it likely that he would escape the hostility of those who would call him "crank, troublemaker, and radical"?

What would be the attitude of respectable religion toward a man who would literally accept the moral mandate to love his enemies by first loving his business competitor, rejoicing in his prosperity, and by assisting him to increase his sales and expand his business? Such a man would be regarded as a "psychotic" and in all likelihood would be committed to an institution for the mentally ill.

Assuming that a religious man regards the Russian Communists as the enemies of America, and is nevertheless compelled by the literal application of his faith to assist, support, and love them because they are his enemies, how long would it take before he was investigated by the FBI, indicted for treason, condemned as a subversive, vilified as a "Red," and subjected to the calumny, hostility, and abuse of his family, friends, and neighbors? It is manifestly dangerous to take the moral teachings of respectable religion too seriously. Contemplate the reaction to an Amos speaking from a soapbox in Times Square, an Isaiah proclaiming peace before the General Assembly of the United Nations, a Jeremiah protesting slum conditions before a City Planning Commission, a Jesus demanding that we regard all men as of one blood before a prosegregationist White Citizens Council. It is reasonable to assume that the opposition from respectable religion would be most formidable.

We must conclude, therefore, that what is so frequently and erroneously called religious is in our day nothing but modernized magic sanctioned by a theological abracadabra that relegates the ethical objectives of higher religion to secondary significance. Quasi-witchcraft is elevated to the status of God-sanctioned ritual. Bigotry and ignorance are dressed up in the verbal garments of ecclesiastical doctrine. Cults and crackpots exploit the faith-hungry. Devils, demons, and angels alike are honored in our litany. Faith is demonstrated in one American cult by the handling of snakes. The fires of hell are fanned by the preaching of eternal damnation. Blood transfusions are regarded as a sin against God. Vaccines are evils compounded by the devil. Ghostly apparitions of saints and martyrs are given credence by hundreds of thousands. Miracles are adduced at will by so-called faith healers who call upon the Lord and bestow a blessing with a background of maudlin music provided by an orchestra of fifty pieces. All of this, tolerated and frequently condoned, constitutes part of the threat and danger of respectable religion.

We Must Disenthrall Ourselves

It is becoming increasingly evident, therefore, that the comfortable, popular, respectable concepts of religion must be challenged. If religion is to have any meaning and relevance in the lives of thinking people, it must be made disrespectable and revolutionary. What Abraham Lincoln said on December 1, 1862, is even more applicable to our own generation; namely, that "the dogmas of the quiet past are inadequate to the stormy present. We must think anew, we must act anew. We must disenthrall ourselves."

Thirty years ago, Dick Shepherd, Rector of St. Martin's in the Fields, London, wrote that Christianity needs rash men who will not shrink from the crispness of religion or fear the results, for surely there is nothing more dangerous than to avoid danger, and nothing so annihilating as timidity. This challenge to Christianity is equally valid for Judaism and the other world faiths. Religious men and women must challenge, doubt, question, and sometimes oppose the accepted doctrines of respectable religion as they search for God. The devotees of the true religious spirit must be prepared to accept danger, suspicion, rejection, and vilification. They must behold religion as the vocation of the strong, the courageous, the adventurous, and the bold destined to pioneer into new social, political, and spiritual frontiers. They must determine to exorcise the demons from religious thinking, eradicate superstitions, contest dogmas and doctrine, assess ritual, evaluate attitudes, and reconsider ethical goals and moral objectives in order to purify religion of the cumulative errors and accretive superstitions it has embraced through the centuries. In order to accomplish this, it may be necessary to subject themselves and their faith to a traumatic ordeal. The religion thus acquired will inevitably become unpopular, disrespectable, and radical because of its commitment to dynamic and revolutionary change.

If a man is to find a meaningful answer to his query, "From whence shall my help come?" he must divest himself of archaic concepts and meaningless clichés and proceed to liberate himself from the tyrannical and authoritarian domination of respectable religion.

3

What Not to Believe About God

For I am God, and not man.
—HOSEA 11.9

The Kindergarten God

A character in a recent play by Tennessee Williams called *Suddenly Last Summer* says that we are all children in a vast kindergarten trying to spell the name of God with the wrong alphabet blocks.[1]

[1] This same thought has been expressed by John Foxe in *The Book of Martyrs'* wherein he says that the world is a vast nursery and men are children engaged in trying to spell God with the wrong blocks.

If man is to seek and find the help that comes from God, he must have the courage to eradicate outmoded superstitions and archaic stereotypes of divinity and advance from a "kindergarten" concept of deity to a mature consideration of a supreme and spiritual "being." To accomplish this it will be necessary to divest God of anthropomorphic attributes, and destroy the orthodox stereotypes of respectable religion.

During the past twenty years the author has been conducting a survey of the God-concept of children of kindergarten age compared with the God-concept of adults. The results are as startling as they are disappointing. A typical answer of a five-year-old child to the question "Tell me about God" is as follows: "God is a man. He is good and strong. He wins battles for us. God gives us our food and everything we need. God makes miracles happen. God makes us well when we are sick. When we are good, He gives us things. When we are bad God is angry and will punish us. God is an old man. He has a long white beard and sits on a throne in heaven. He makes it rain. I love God. He watches over me and gives me things."

We may smile in good-natured indulgence at this infantile and whimsical theology expressed by a kindergarten child, but the answers given by adults are strikingly and unbelievably the same. The language used may be more adult, but the concept of a male grocer, military commander, maker of miracles, dispenser of medicine, man of magic, celestial shaman, angry policeman, and benevolent Santa Claus indicates a kindergarten concept of God.

This survey, made over a period of twenty years, was conducted by an amateur in the highly technical field of sociological research and statistical evaluation. Competent authorities in these areas have substantiated the author's conclusions and offer expert statistical evidence of kindergarten and child-like concepts of God, prayer, Bible, and immortality.

One of the most valuable empirical studies of the religion of the child was made by Ernest Harms. His conclusions and findings were reported in "The Development of Religious Experience in Children,"[2] which appeared in the *American Journal of Sociology* in 1944.

Dr. Harms asked several thousand children aged from three through

[2] September, 1944, pp. 115-117.

adolescence to imagine how God would look, then draw a picture of Him and give a statement of what the picture represented. The results indicate that the child evolves in religious growth through three stages.

1. THE FAIRY-TALE STAGE. From three to six years of age the child's conception of God is anthropomorphic, fantastic, and irrational.

2. THE REALISTIC STAGE. When the child enters school up to the threshold of adolescence, the child's idea of God indicates a greater realism. His image of God is now shaped and influenced by his church or synagogue and the instructions of his parents and teachers. The pictures of God resemble those of a priest, minister, or rabbi. The child's interest in symbolism prompts the drawing of the Cross or the Star of David.

3. THE INDIVIDUALISTIC STAGE. Children of the adolescent age reflect a high degree of sensitivity. They picture God with originality and emotion.

A more specific study of what children think of God was published by A. H. MacLean in *The Idea of God in Protestant Religious Education*.[3]

Interviews were held with seventy-five Protestant children eight years of age or younger living in New York City. The following responses were given by the children:

God is like a· man with long white robes. He looks very kind.
God is an old man and has long white whiskers all over his face.
God is a spirit and can get into places without being seen.
God is nature.
God is a man with power who uses his power in the right way.
God is as big as a cloud. He wears a long dress and a blackish beard.
God has a smiling face.
God is a king—the greatest king of all.

According to this study, the children thought of God as a man with flesh and bones and whiskers, a spirit, ghost, or fairy.

Between 70 and 80 per cent of the children believe that God has a

[3] New York, Teachers College, Columbia University, 1930.

face, hands, and feet like a man. He reveals Himself through dreams, miracles, inspired men, storms, earthquakes. He desires songs of praise, church membership, and unquestioning obedience to parents. He wants us to go to war whenever our government asks us to.

We should not be surprised at such a report. The textbook of religion, the Bible, abounds with anthropomorphic allusions to an anthropomorphic God. It is understandable that the God-concept of children should be influenced by biblical references to the hand of God, the finger of God, the face of God, God walked, God said, God touched, God smelled, God heard, the voice of God, the anger of God, God slew, God came down, God ascended. The concept of the anthropomorphic God is strengthened by a plethora of biblical citations, including Chapter 7, Verse 9 of the Book of Daniel:

> "And one that was ancient of days did sit:
> His raiment was as white as snow,
> And the hair of his head like pure wool;
> His throne was fiery flames,
> And the wheels thereof burning fire."

Because of an unquestioned bibliolatry, and the inherent resistance to change, respectable religion inadvertently encourages the perpetuation of the kindergarten concept of God beyond childhood. This is apparent in the God-concept of chronologically mature adults.

The evaluation of children's concepts of God also reveals three patently "juvenile" concepts of the Deity that must be altered to enable man to attain religious maturity. One is the concept of the Lord as a man of war; another is the belief that God is a superman; and the third is the concept of God as a divine magician who operates by sleight of hand, and conjures up miracles upon request.

1. *The Lord Is a Man of War*

During periods of crisis and decision, when many of our young men are called into the Armed Forces of our beloved country, we are disturbed by these questions: To what extent should we bring God into war? Is it proper to implore God, the Supreme Military Commander of the Universe, the Lord of Hosts, to destroy our enemies?

In 1904 Mark Twain wrote a short story called "The War Prayer." Without specifying the date or the nation, he imagined a time of great and exalting commitment when the country was at war. One Sunday morning, just before the battalions were to leave for the front, a minister proceeded to pour out a tremendous invocation: "God the all-terrible! Thou who ordainest, thunder Thy clarion and lightning Thy sword!" With all the passion of his heart, the minister prayed that God might watch over the noble young soldiers, make them strong and confident, invincible in the bloody onset, help them to crush the foe, and to grant to them, to their flag and country imperishable honor and glory.

As he spoke, an aged stranger entered, moved down the aisle and, with all eyes following him, made his silent way to the preacher's side, and stood there, waiting. The minister was concluding his fervent appeal, saying: "Bless our arms, grant us victory, O Lord our God, Father and Protector of our land and flag!" Then the stranger touched his arm, motioned the startled minister aside, and took his place. The stranger surveyed the spellbound audience with solemn eyes, and then, in a deep voice, told the unbelievable and uncanny story that he had just come from Heaven, bearing a message from Almighty God: God had heard the prayer of the minister, and God would grant it if such were the desire of the congregation after he, the messenger, explained it in its full import. The mysterious stranger continued: "God's servant and yours has prayed his prayer. Has he paused and taken thought? Is it one prayer? No, it is two—one uttered, the other not. Both have reached the ear of Him who heareth all supplications, the spoken and the unspoken."

The congregation trembled as if in the presence of some awesome messenger from on high as the stranger proceeded to interpret the implications of the prayer that had fallen upon the listening spirit of God. God had commanded the stranger to put into words the unspoken part of this prayer: "O Lord our Father, our young patriots, idols of our hearts, go forth to battle—be Thou near them! With them—in spirit—we also go forth from the sweet peace of our beloved firesides to smite the foe. O Lord our God, help us to tear their soldiers to bloody shreds with our shells; help us to cover their smiling fields with the pale forms of their patriot dead; help us to drown the thunder of the guns with the shrieks of their wounded, writhing in pain; help us to lay waste their humble homes with a hurricane of fire; help us to wring the hearts of their unoffending widows with unavailing grief; help us to turn them out roofless with their little children to wander unfriended the wastes of their desolated land in rags and hunger and thirst, sport of the sun flames of summer and the icy winds of winter, broken in spirit, worn with travail, imploring Thee for the refuge of the grave and denied it. For our sakes who adore Thee, Lord, blast their hopes, blight their lives, protract their bitter pilgrimage, make heavy their steps, water their way with their tears, stain the white snow with the blood of their wounded feet! We ask it, in the spirit of love, of Him Who is the Source of Love, and Who is the ever-faithful refuge and friend of all that are sore beset and seek His aid with humble and contrite hearts. Amen."

After a pause, the mysterious stranger added almost as a postscript: "Ye have prayed it; if ye still desire it, speak! The messenger of the Most High waits."[4]

There is nothing that illustrates more pointedly what not to believe about God than a letter written during the Korean conflict and addressed to the editor of a Nashville newspaper by a man who wrote: "God wants us to drop atomic bombs on China! What are we waiting for? It is the will of God to destroy the Chinese people and to grant us military victory." By what divine revelation does he offer this assurance? How can he be so certain that this is the will of God? To him, God is a man of war who sanctions the destruction of our enemies, and not the God of Love and compassion—the God we call our heavenly Father.

This concept of God as a man of war has biblical precedent in the fifteenth chapter of Exodus, when the children of Israel were liberated from the tyranny of Pharaoh in Egypt. After they had crossed the Red Sea, when the warriors of Pharaoh had perished, even as the lifeless bodies of the Egyptians were being cast upon the shore:

"Then sang Moses and the children of Israel this song unto the Lord, and spoke, saying:

"I will sing unto the Lord, for He is highly exalted; The horse and his rider hath He thrown into the sea.

. . . .

This is my God, and I will glorify Him;

[4] Mark Twain, *Short Stories*, "The War Prayer," from *Europe and Elsewhere*, pp. 861-863 (New York, Harper and Brothers, copyright 1928 by Clara Gabrilowitsch).

My father's God, and I will exalt Him.
The Lord is a man of war,
The Lord is His name."

In the full flush of victory, the children of Israel did not pause to consider the misery, the sorrow, the human wreckage and devastation co-existent with their victory. They were so ecstatically relieved of the years of bondage and slavery that they could now offer joyous praise to the God who gave them victory in battle. At that time the Lord was not a God of holiness; the Lord was not a God of truth, mercy, and love—*the Lord was a man of war.*

But in all the years that have transpired since that song of victory, have we really changed our belief in God to any appreciable extent? Isn't the Lord still a man of war?

By what authority do we bring God into our man-made wars? By what right do we identify God with human destruction, international butchery, and wholesale murder?

It is so easy for us to think of war as a vague and nebulous concept, erasing from our minds and souls the horrible realities that are concomitants of cruel conflict. When we read that our forces or the military unit of a friendly nation advanced ten miles into enemy territory, we thank God; but do we ever pause to think what those ten miles represent in terms of casualties, misery, of maimed bodies, stiffened corpses, telegrams to bereaved parents, fear-crazed refugees throwing themselves and their children into blood-soaked rivers, babies dying of hunger on the highways of human suffering? Do we have the right to rejoice, to thank God, or even mention the name of God as sanctioning the destruction of His children? Do we have the moral right to invoke the name of the Lord as a man of God?

Did that citizen who wrote to the editor of the Nashville newspaper ever stop to think, with all his certainty and knowledge of the Divine, that his Lord is a man of war willing to destroy hundreds of thousands of people; that his God is a God who sanctions the screaming of His children, burning alive, disintegrating into atomic dust by the cosmic energy He has created? A God responsible for the screams of pain, a God responsible for mangled bodies and distorted hopes— is this the God we worship? Is this the God about whom it is said, even in that same fifteenth chapter of Exodus: "Who is like unto

Thee, O Lord, among the mighty?/Who is like unto Thee, glorious in holiness . . .?" What is glorious or holy about such a God? What is glorious or holy about a Lord who is a man of war?

It is blasphemy and unspeakable irreverence to call upon God to destroy His own children. Any father who consciously and intentionally murders his children is regarded as hideously wicked, cruel, and loathsome. If we agree to that without question, then how can we, in the name of religion, implore a loving God, a merciful God, a compassionate Father in Heaven to destroy His own children? A prayer should ask God, implore God to help us blot out the scourge of war, but the blessing of human speech should never be exploited or perverted to beseech God to murder His children even if they are our enemies.

In a beautiful commentary, the rabbis of the Talmud could not reconcile the belief in the Lord of Hosts with a God of forgiveness, mercy, and love; and while they, too, were happy in the salvation of the Children of Israel, and were thrilled as they read the story of the liberation of their people from the slavery of Egypt, they could not conceive of their God rejoicing in the destruction of their enemies. Thus they taught: "When the Egyptian hosts were drowning in the Red Sea, the angels in heaven broke forth into songs of jubilation; they were elated because of the victory of the children of Israel; and while they were rejoicing, they looked up and saw that God was weeping. They said to God: 'Rejoice, Lord. The Egyptians have been thrown into the sea. Why do You weep? Rejoice.' And God answered, 'No! These Egyptians were cruel; they were tyrannical—but still My children. When My children perish, how can I rejoice at the destruction of the work of My hands?'" Which concept of God will you choose: The Lord as a man of war, or the concept of a heavenly Father weeping at the destruction of His children?

There are those who ask: "Where is God at a time of war? If there is a God, why must there be this killing, this maiming, this butchering, these torrents of blood and tears that flow from the bodies of human beings who want to live and love and dream?

It is man's primitive concept of God that makes Divinity seem responsible for the chaos and bloodshed, the hatred, injustices, and evil that exist. It is man that should be held responsible for war—not God. The guilt rests upon man, who refuses to apply his religious ideals to the realities of life. It is man who utilizes the psychological principle of displacement for his own failure and projects his crimes to his God. It is the God of the warring savage, and not the God of Isaiah, Hosea, and Jesus, who delights in bloodshed and sanctions mass killings.

If we are to enter into co-partnership with God to build His Kingdom, then it is imperative that Judaism and Christianity join together to blot out the concept of the Lord as a man of war, and substitute a God of love and compassion, a God who cannot delight in the destruction and suffering of His children, whether those children are Jewish or Christian, white, brown, black, or yellow—whether they are our enemies or our allies.

The primitive, savage, vengeful Lord of Hosts who exults in battle must be relegated to the kindergarten period of man's religious history. Those who listen to reason, the religiously mature, will seek a God who is merciful and gracious, long suffering and abundant in goodness and truth, keeping mercy unto the thousandth generation, forgiving iniquity, transgression, and sin. Only such a God, who weeps at the destruction of His children, can answer the appeal "From whence shall my help come?"

2. The Divine Superman

Although the Bible states that "man is created in the image of God," we have succeeded in creating God in the image of man. This is not entirely due to an arrogant, deliberate attempt at self-deification. Man's conceptual imagery is determined by the perception of his senses. As a result, any abstraction not experienced by the senses lends itself to false imagery. Thus, man developed the concept of a God who is a superman endowed with sex, body, temperament, inclinations, race, language, and culture, corresponding to the prevailing in-group characteristics of the dominant society.

Green Pastures dramatically illustrates the God-concept of the illiterate Negro. The patriarchs Abraham, Isaac, and Jacob are Negroes. God is a Negro. His skin is black. He speaks in the accepted dialect of the Negro. He is Uncle Tom elevated to the status of a deity. Hence God is created in the image of the Negro.

What is true of the Negro in Green Pastures is equally true among other races. The yellow man thinks of God in similar racial and ethnocentric terms. To the Caucasian it is unthinkable to regard God as anything other than white. The pigmentation of the worshiper determines the pigmentation of the God.

The language of the Bible and the prayer book specifies God as a sexual being. In a patriarchal society God is referred to as He, Him, our heavenly Father, King of the Universe, Lord of Hosts, Master of the World, divine craftsman, artisan, and creator. In a matriarchal society, God becomes a Goddess, He becomes She, heavenly Father becomes heavenly Mother, Queen of the World, Lady and Mistress of the Universe. What, then, is God's sex? If God is sexless, why impute male or female sexuality to Divinity?

Language, too, evinces the same anthropomorphisms and the same ethnocentrism. To one steeped in the Hebrew Bible, God speaks Hebrew. To the American and the Englishman nurtured on the King James and the Revised Standard versions of the Bible, God speaks English. Even the type of English that God speaks is dependent upon the literary tradition to which one is conditioned. As a result, those brought up on the King James Version would believe that God speaks in the style of "thee" and "thou." Regional dialects also enter into consideration.

Because God is created in the image of man, kindergarten religion regards the deity as one who walks, talks, sees, hears, smells, eats, and touches. These sensory skills require feet, mouth, eyes, ears, nose, stomach, hands and fingers. Despite the insistence that "God is not a man," we impute to "Him" the human weaknesses of anger, vengeance, pride, vanity, and the human virtues of love, kindness, humility, goodness, morality, justice, and mercy.

In answer to this the Jewish sages argued that "the Bible speaks the language of man" because that is the only way that man has to communicate. How do we give expression to our belief in a God that doesn't have a body? How do we give expression to and articulate concepts of something abstract, spiritual, and incomprehensible to the finite mind? Pagan religions solved the problem by creating idols. Christianity solved the problem for Christians by making God incarnate in Jesus. Judaism, insisting that God is not corporeal, that God is without accidents of matter or form, uses the "language of man" to describe God and communicate with God.

Harry Emerson Fosdick aptly writes that: "Man has read his vanities in God, until he has supposed that singing on themes to God's praise might flatter Him as it would flatter us. Man has read his cruelties into God, and what in moments of vindictiveness and wrath we would like to do to our enemies we have supposed Eternal God would do to us. Man has read his religious partisanship into God . . . and conceived Him to be a Baptist or a Methodist, a Presbyterian or an Anglican. Man has read his racial pride into God; nations have thought themselves His chosen people above all others because they seemed so to themselves. The centuries are sick with a God made in man's image."[5]

Man has created God in his own image from the time the primitive savage offered an animal on a sacrificial altar to a God who was hungry for the sweet savor of sacrifices, through Greek deities who drank and hated and engaged in sexual intercourse, to the present respectably religious concept of a God who manifests the physical and moral attributes of a superman.

Clarence Darrow once said that he didn't believe in God because he didn't believe in Mother Goose. Frequently modern intellectuals pursue the same fallacious thinking. To reject the superstitions and the childish man-made God-image of the past does not mean that we must relinquish our search for a mature faith in a mature concept of God.

3. The Lord as a Divine Magician

"In the beginning there was fear and fear was in the heart of man and controlled man." This is how Lewis Browne began his book *This Believing World.* Dominated by fear, early man sought to propitiate the nature spirits and gods to act in his behalf by means of incantations, rites, and magical formulas. He thought of the gods as workers of miracles, divine magicians ruling the universe with a heavenly bag of supernatural tricks. As the years went by, man came to believe in one God, but the attributes and skills of the magician still characterized Him. The fingers of God indulged in sleight of hand. "The outstretched arm of God" worked miracles and produced wonders. The irrefutable proof of God's power was His ability to manipulate the universe by a word or a glance—to divide waters, stop the sun in

[5] Harry Emerson Fosdick, *Christianity and Progress* (New York, Fleming H. Revell, 1922), pp. 220-221.

its celestial course, bring about plagues, revive the dead, heal the sick, feed the hungry, and otherwise indicate His power by effecting deviations of nature.

Even today, in an age of sputniks, color television, and guided missiles, when we worship God and offer our prayers on high, all too often we inadvertently reveal our belief in a God who is a divine magician. We invoke God's magic and call it prayer. We fear God's vengeance and call it reverence. We rub the cover of a prayer book and look for a heavenly jinni to appear and grant our requests. We still look for miracles as the undeniable proof of God's existence.

The credo of a second century Tertullian, "Credo quia impossible est" (I believe because it is impossible), still dominates our religious thinking. The more impossible the miracle, the greater the evidence of the wonder-working power of God.

It is imperative that religious fantasies, whimsical delusions, and childlike stereotypes of God be dissipated. The false and transitory euphoria induced by the happiness pills of respectable religion will not satisfy those who cannot accept the belief in the Lord as a man of war or God as a divine superman and heavenly magician.

The kindergarten concept of religion that subscribes to the belief in angels, demons, saints, and other categories of divine beings must give way to the mature faith that is predicated on the belief that there is but one God and that all other beings are or were human.

The questioning mind will not long endure facile phrases and simple answers to complex religious questions and Mother Goose explanations of perplexing problems of faith. The God-hungry soul will not be satisfied with the theological pablum spooned out by so many clergymen. Thinking, intelligent seekers after God are stirring with rebellion against the kind of God indicted by Mark Twain, as the God "who gave his angels eternal happiness unearned, yet required his other children to earn it; who gave his angels painless lives, yet cursed his other children with biting miseries and maladies of mind and body; who mouths justice and invented hell—mouths mercy and invented hell—mouths Golden Rules, and forgiveness multiplied by seventy times seven and invented hell."

Those who seek a mature faith recoil from the God of modern evangelists who invoke divine love but punctuate every sentence with God's hate; who speak of divine mercy but fill their messages with threats of God's vengeance. Those who quest for the mature concept of God must reject the scathing words of one of the most popular of the twentieth century revivalists: "The sins that you committed when you were twelve years old—God has them all marked down. No one can commit a sin in the sight of God and get away with it. God is holy—why? Because he punishes sin. . . . Your stealing, your lying, your immorality . . . all this is mounting as evidence in the book of heaven in anticipation of a terrible Judgment by this holy God on a corrupt way of life."

What kind of God do we accept with such childlike credence? Is it the God of Dante, a divine Specialist in torture, reveling in the pain of sinners as the theme of a Divine Comedy? Is it the God of the philosopher Fichte who gave the name Divinity to his own metaphysical concept which was the action of the pure Ego, or the absolute function of the moral world order? Is it the God of Emerson, Alexander Pope, or of his American counterpart, Charles Fleischer, who in 1911 founded the religious movement called "The Commoners" in order to promote a cult of American humanism dedicated to the worship of man, declaring: "Let us devote ourselves to the greatness and the glory of man. We believe that man is God."

The cemeteries of history are filled with the graves of dead gods: Astarte, Baal, Zeus, Isis, Osiris, Varuna, Jupiter, and Thor. It would be well for us to kill another God, the God of hate. It would be well for us to kill any God-concept that makes the Supreme Being a deity of vengeance and anger, a theological policeman whose beat is the universe, with hell as a club and heavenly pie in the sky as the reward for goodness. Mankind may well intone a solemn requiem for the petty, vengeful God who is, in colloquial phraseology, a celestial hatchet man, a heavenly trigger man whose sole purpose is to cut us down, punish us and destroy us because of our sins.

We cannot hope to find our help in such a God, nor can we advance to a mature, rational religion by conjuring up a divine bogyman to frighten grown-up children with threats of infantile punishment or coax them into moral conformity by the childish bribe and promise of eternal reward.

When we spell the name of God with the wrong alphabet blocks we form childish words and infantile concepts that impede the rational pursuit of the rational God. To progress to a mature faith, man must exorcise the devil from his theology, drive the demons from his liturgy, disassociate ignorance, sorcery, and magic from his concept of the God-idea. Above all, he must expunge the consonants and vowels of evil, hatred, anger, and supernatural caprice from the alphabet of Divinity.

4

What Not to Believe About Prayer

Yea, when ye make many prayers, I will not hear;
Your hands are full of blood.
—ISAIAH 1.15

The Kindergarten Prayer

The kindergarten concept of prayer is closely identified with the belief in God as a divine magician, celestial Santa Claus, and heavenly donor. Magic, theological hocus-pocus, and ritualistic legerdemain are liturgical concomitants of man's religious immaturity.

In this regard W. H. Auden attempted a poetic satire that indulges in literary fun at the expense of adults who exhort God with childish prayers, when he wrote the following:

"O God, put away justice and truth for we cannot understand them and do not want them. Eternity would bore us dreadfully. Leave Thy heavens and come down to our earth of waterclocks and hedges. Become our uncle. Look after Baby, amuse Grandfather, escort Madam to the Opera, help Willy with his homework, introduce Muriel to a handsome naval officer. Be interesting and weak like us, and we will love you as we love ourselves."[1]

Such a prayer makes God a winged superman, a benign and indulgent relative, baby sitter, male escort, director, geriatrical entertainer, and marriage broker. If we are repelled by the offensive irreverence, we should pause to examine the infantile nature of our own prayers, and reflect upon the manner in which we supplicate God as a divine jinni to grant us the benefits we request liturgically.

Murray G. Ross[2] made a questionnaire study of 1,720 youths who replied to the question "Why do we pray?" Their replies are summarized in the following table:

Reply	Per Cent
God listens to and answers your prayer	32.8
It helps you in time of stress and crisis	27.2
You feel relieved and better after prayer	18.1
Prayer reminds you of your obligations to man and society	10.7
It's a habit you have	4.0
All good people pray	0.9
One takes a chance if one doesn't pray	0.5
Other replies	5.8

Of the responses given, 89.3 per cent indicated the concern with self, and only 10.7 per cent revealed a concern for man and society. This suggests that the egocentric concerns of the child, which begin in infancy, are perpetuated in youth and, from every indication, continue through the mature years. There is apparently little evidence of the prophetic concept of prayer that will inspire the individual to go beyond himself to social justice in behalf of his fellow man.

Kindergarten religion encourages adults to set forth their personal petitions to a sacred magician with the expectation of being the beneficiaries of liturgical magic. Just as the child relies on verbalization of his wants, so kindergarten religion promulgates the assurance that participation in religious ritual and prayerful verbalization will induce the ever benevolent God to shower gifts from heaven.

[1] "Herod," from For the Time Being (New York, Random House, 1944), p. 122.
[2] Murray G. Ross, Religious Beliefs of Youth (New York, Association Press, 1950), p. 63.

Alexander Pope ridiculed the religious immaturity that is limited to ritual and verbalization when he wrote:

"Behold the child, by Nature's kindly law,
Pleased with a rattle, tickled with a straw;
Some livelier plaything gives his youth delight,
A little louder, but as empty quite:
Scarfs, garters, gold, amuse his riper stage,
And beads and prayer-books are the toys of age."[3]

We arrogate to ourselves the belief that through the centuries mankind has matured beyond those primitive and infantile concepts of prayer, and yet many of our prayers differ very little from the supplications of primitive man. We ridicule the religion of savages because of its link to superstition and magic. We look with contempt upon the anthropological evidence that early man utilized prayer wheels, sacrifices, homeopathic magic, and propitiatory rites to induce the nature spirits and gods to act in his behalf, operate in his favor, and accede to his demands. We smile with condescension at the religious antics of our primitive forebears who augmented their ritual with a verbal appeal of praise and adoration designed to cajole, coax, bribe, and flatter the spirits and gods into divine acquiescence. But, as we examine our own religious practices, we are forced to the conclusion that our alleged superiority is unwarranted. The respectable religion of modern man still utilizes superstition and magic, prayer wheels, sacrifices, homeopathic magic, propitiatory rites, and elaborate doxologies to induce God to favor our requests, accede to our wishes, and perform miracles upon prayerful request.

Holy Scripture reveals that the patriarch Jacob attempted to make a deal with God as he vowed: "If God will be with me, and will keep me in this way that I go, and will give me bread to eat, and raiment to put on, so that I come back to my father's house in peace, then shall the Lord be my God" (Genesis 28.20-21). Don't we still attempt to make deals and bargains with God, promising to accept Him, love and adore Him if he will grant us protection, sustenance, and favor? How different is this premium prayer that attempts to buy divine

[3] *Complete Works of Alexander Pope* (Boston, Houghton Mifflin and Company, Cambridge ed., 1902), p. 145.

insurance, from many of the supplications and petitions that we direct on high as we assume the posture of prayer and give our orders to a "cosmic bellhop"?

In some of our metropolitan communities there is an available service that enables a person to dial a number and listen to a recorded prayer, just as he receives a weather report or the correct time. This project met with overwhelming success. Thousands called in. The entire telephone system was jammed until the company hastily installed more equipment.

It was claimed that the public response to Dial-a-Prayer indicates the resurgence of religious faith in our country. If so, there is considerable doubt as to the maturity of our contemporary religious faith. Such a kindergarten concept of prayer indicates that the average man is so spiritually inarticulate that he cannot express the religious yearning of his own heart, but needs a liturgical automaton to communicate with God. How uncomfortably similar to the magical formulas of our primitive forebears who used prayer wheels! We, their allegedly civilized descendants, twirl the dial of a telephone.

The Clergyman Is the Sorcerer's Apprentice

Prayer is frequently and erroneously thought to be a means of changing or influencing the will of God to comply with the desires, hopes, and ambitions of man. The more pious the individual, the more effective his prayer is thought to be in terms of propitiating God. Since ministers, priests, and rabbis are thought to be closer to God, partaking of the spirit of God to a greater degree than laymen, the clergy is expected to offer prayers in behalf of the wishes of their congregants. This inadvertently imputes to God the nature of a divine sorcerer, and casts the clergyman into the role of the sorcerer's apprentice. The pious petition that is uttered implies that God's will may be altered and influenced by the magic of prayer.

Several years ago, the writer had to struggle through a very personal and trying problem of prayer. A woman whose husband was desperately ill called on the telephone, and pleaded, "Please go into the Temple sanctuary and say a prayer, asking God to save my husband." I suggested that she permit me to say a prayer with her husband. She informed me that her husband was in a coma and could not be remotely influenced by prayer. I said to her, "Let me meet with you, and let us pray together and implore God that He might grant you the strength of faith and the fortitude and the spiritual courage to accept His will." She refused to listen, and insisted that I say the prayer. Most reluctantly, I walked into the sanctuary, stood before the open Ark, and lifted my heart in prayer to God that He might save this man who was so desperately ill.

I worried about that prayer, and my troubled soul struggled with the question: "Did I pray to God, or did I plead with a divine magician, invoking a sorcerer?" In effect, was I a sorcerer's apprentice? I was asking God to permit a man to live when His own natural law decreed otherwise. Was it right for me to ask God to perform a miracle simply because I, a rabbi, had requested it? Why should God listen to me more than to any other man? Was I more holy than any other member of my congregation? Could my prayer have been more sincere than a prayer uttered by this man's wife who, out of her grief and agony, could have implored God with greater eloquence and greater sincerity to spare her husband? What kind of God would it be who would spare this man simply because I asked Him to do so? And what if I had not asked? Would God permit that man to die simply because a rabbi or priest or a minister had not uttered the prayer? Do we call such a god a God of love, of mercy, of compassion? Do we have the right to call Him Father? A god who would permit a man to die simply because a religious functionary had not recited the proper formula or the required petition might more correctly be called a capricious Devil. In such a case, isn't prayer to be equated with sorcery? Is it reverence, or unspeakable blasphemy, to worship God, and pray to God as a divine sorcerer, and to regard the minister, priest, or rabbi, as the sorcerer's apprentice?

May God's Will Be Changed?

During World War II the famous aviator Eddie Rickenbacker was cast afloat with his companions on a raft in the Pacific Ocean. During the agonizing days that followed they uttered desperate prayers to God for rescue. When a ship did appear, full credit was given to God for answering their prayers, and peforming a miracle of rescue in their behalf. I can't help wondering about all the other fine and good men, in similar plight, who croaked out words of urgent appeal to God through parched throats, and whose prayers were not answered. Why were no miracles produced to save them? Was it because they lacked the virtue and the merit of those who were saved? Was it because their prayers were less sincere? Grateful though we are that Rickenbacker and his companions were saved, it is extremely difficult to find justice and equity in such a capricious God when we think of other good God-seeking people who perished because no miracles were performed for them.

What happens to those who pray sincerely and passionately and whose prayers go unheeded? Are they to be content with the conclusion, advanced by some contemporary theologians, that God has answered but that the answer is "No"? One of the greatest deterrents to sound and cogent religious faith is the disappointment of those who appeal to a god of magic for miracles that are not forthcoming. Often they conclude that prayer is not efficacious and that God is a myth to be relegated to the archives of the past.

When prayer is a verbal appeal for a miracle, in effect, we are calling upon God to deviate from the natural laws of the universe, to alter His will, and to perform religious magic because of the merit, eloquence, and sincerity of the spoken plea. Both the answered and the unanswered prayer suggest that God is amenable to influence. Consequently, the Talmud[4] warns against praying for the impossible or supplicating God to alter His will. "A man whose wife is about to bear a baby should not pray: 'May it be Thy will that the child carried by my wife prove to be a boy (or a girl).' The man who hears a fire alarm sounding in his community shall not pray: 'May it be Thy will that the fire be not in my home.' " The result in these instances neither proves nor disproves the validity of prayer. An appeal has been made for God to effect a miracle, and the god addressed in such a prayer is no different from the deity of primitive man, a god of magic who may be bribed, enticed, influenced, and propitiated.

Faith healing raises a similar problem, for it implies that miracles may be performed for the faithful and that God's will may be altered and natural law superseded by the efficacy of prayer. Faith healers exploit the credulity of the afflicted by demonstrating miraculous cures. Utilizing the most advanced and tested methods of mass

4 A vast compendium of postbiblical rabbinic literature.

persuasion, religious confidence men merchandise healing and sell the promise of health, attractively packaged and popularly priced. Performances are promoted and advertised with all the acumen of Madison Avenue publicists. The "show" itself is designed to condition the prospect by the use of music, testimonials, hymns, and prayers. The necessary dramatic effects contribute to a theatricalism that emulates the standard techniques of Hollywood and the slickness of a television playhouse.

In mid-1956, most of some four hundred members of the Church of God, gathering in Missouri from fourteen states, drank water from a polluted well. It took many weeks for public authorities laboriously to track down seventeen cases of typhoid, including three in which there were deaths suspected to be due to the disease. As one of the church members said later: "We feel no need for earthly physicians. We believe the Lord can heal through our faith."

While faith is a vital factor in the promotion of health, ethical ministers and physicians are firmly allied against the "fake healers," whose huge fund-raising exhibitions exploit the superstitious and misinformed. For six years a Presbyterian minister from Atlanta, Georgia, the Reverend Carroll Stegall, Jr., has interviewed scores of invalids before and after they lined up at healing campaigns. He says, "I have never seen a vestige of physical change." So far not a single "healer" has submitted one of his "cures" to medical examination. And yet the flamboyant cultists are collecting millions of dollars from elaborate radio, television, and tent performances.

Shrines, holy places, and the celebrated faith-healing phenomena of Lourdes have elicited countless arguments affirming and denying the validity of curing illness by faith. Doctors, specialists and scientists attest to the so-called miracle cures. Psychiatrists insist that the infirmities cured fall within the category of functional hysteria. Regardless of the technical explanations offered, this basic question must be answered: Will God be induced and persuaded to change His will and effect a miracle because of prayer? If so, then how are we to account for the number of pious, God-loving people who pray for a divine miracle and receive no physical alleviation of their infirmities? A God so capricious as to heal some and permit others to suffer is hardly worthy of the attributes of love and compassion. A prayer that is thought to result in a miracle is to be equated with magic, sorcery, and superstition.

Faith can effect marvelous cures and promote healing. Those diseases that are caused by the mind may frequently be cured by the mind. The will to live and the will to health are tremendous factors in encouraging healing. However, when we pray to God for miracles we are asking God to violate His own laws of nature. The so-called supernatural miracles that allegedly take place at sacred shrines, instead of contributing to the compassion and mercy of God, quite to the contrary may suggest a capricious deity who plays favorites with his children and limits his divine power of healing to specific locations and places.

Such miraculous phenomena of healing also present some perplexing and tortuous theological problems about the mercy and love of God. What about those who do not have the funds to travel to Lourdes or other shrines of healing? Are we to assume that a God of compassion will permit a little child to go through life a cripple because the parents of the child lack the faith that persuades them to take their child to a shrine? Why should a God of love withhold healing from any of His children? If He will heal at Lourdes, why will He not heal in Nashville, Kansas City, Los Angeles, Paris, Moscow, or any other locality? Does a special supernatural magic attach to shrines because of the visitation of a saint or the apparition of the Virgin Mother? If God is the God of the Universe, then the healing powers of God should be available in the most remote village, in the most commonplace farm area, and in the most urban community as well as in the sanctified area where the miracles have supposedly been performed.

In the extremities of life, when confronted with danger, crisis, and fear, man does cry out for divine help and supernatural intervention. It is understandable that one whose wife is stricken with incurable cancer should pray for a miracle of healing. We can sympathize with the indescribable grief of a parent whose child is dying and who pleads with God to permit his beloved to live. If the wife dies does this mean that God has ignored the prayer? If the child dies does this mean that God is bereft of pity and love? When we ask God to answer our petitional prayers, we are appealing to a god of magic no matter what name we use to address the Deity. This concept of prayer fostered and perpetuated by respectable religion ultimately drives more people away from sincere and reverent worship than all the tracts and utterances of atheists, agnostics, and freethinkers, who openly claim to be enemies of religion.

In one of the most unusual speeches ever heard in the United States Senate, Senator Ralph E. Flanders of Vermont declared on August 2, 1950: "It has . . . been suggested that bombarding the throne of grace with 50,000,000, 150,000,000 or even 500,000,000 prayers would solve the world's problems. This assumes that with enough prayers God may be persuaded to work a miracle. With regard to this, Mr. President, may I make two suggestions? The first is that no miracle is necessary, for God in His law has already provided the means. The second suggestion is that these prayers would be better addressed to the opening of the blind eyes and closed minds of the petitioners themselves, who have neither understood the law of God nor worked in accordance with it."[5]

Senator Flanders was not being facetious when he used the militant expression "bombarding the throne of grace." Undoubtedly, he was aware of the organized efforts in many of our communities to sponsor "prayer raids." The following leaflet was distributed by the thousands:

"PRAYER RAID
"Twelve noon for one minute
"The defense siren will sound for a *prayer raid* not an *air raid*
"Everyone is urged to pause 60 seconds in prayer."

This is a graphic, childish example of the juvenile thinking that would have heaven raided by a bombardment of prayers to influence and coerce God into granting world peace. How does this differ from the effort of primitive man to influence the spirits by sending the savor of burnt offerings heavenward?

The Perfunctory Prayer

No less indicative of kindergarten religion is the crass and vulgar exploitation of prayer to inject a meaningless note of religiosity into

[5] *Congressional Record* (Washington, U.S. Government Printing Office, 1950), Vol. 96, Part 9, p. 11552.

otherwise secular meetings and functions. It is difficult to estimate the time wasted by ministers, rabbis, and priests who are asked to give perfunctory invocations and benedictions at countless meetings and banquets. Those who attend are not praying; they are waiting. The invocation is tolerated if it is brief. It is the socially sanctioned liturgical dinner bell that signals the approach of food. The benediction likewise has a purpose. It heralds the conclusion of the meeting, as the worn-out, speech-fatigued members of the audience bow their heads but brace themselves for the "amen" that will start them racing madly to the parking lot to beat the crowd.

The secular uses of prayer are many and diverse. A businessman recently disclosed that production has increased 20 per cent since he introduced "prayer breaks" into the daily schedule. Athletes are sent into the competition to triumph over their rivals with freshly blessed footballs and baseball bats. Fox hunts and greyhound races receive the invocation of divine grace, and new models of streamlined automobiles come off the motorized assembly line to be prayed over by resident clergymen. Countless are the so-called prayers enunciated for a winning poker hand, for success in catching streetcars and buses, for business opportunities, passing grades, victory in beauty contests, luck in raffles, lotteries and jingle competitions. The name of God is invoked. Words of supplication are uttered. Fervent yearning is articulated, but such childish prattling is not worthy of being called prayer.

Professor Abraham Cronbach summarized the urges that prompt prayer when he said: "Sometimes prayer amounts to nothing but a piece of conventionality. Sometimes it retains vestiges of primitive magic, operating as a kind of incantation imagined to be efficacious. Many a prayer is but an act of dull dead conformity tinged with superstition. That is one of the possibilities. By contrast, prayer can also be the voice of one's loftiest ideals. It can dramatize one's noblest aspirations. It can express one's love and devotion toward others. It can articulate one's profoundest yearning for the wise, the blessed, and the true."

There is a growing sense of weariness with kindergarten religion and infantile prayer. We are all desperately in need of a mature faith in God, not just an emotional tidbit that will stay us for the moment, not just a theological hors d'oeuvre or a pedantic appetizer. We want something that will satisfy us intellectually and emotionally, and appease the pangs of spiritual hunger that nag at our souls. We want to believe. We want to pray. We want to have faith in a God of holiness, not a phantom lifted out of the past to haunt us, not a divine mirage that evaporates in the desert of yearning when we approach with reason as well as with emotion. What we need is not a divine magician but a real, vital, living, loving faith in a vital and living God—a faith that expresses itself in the mature prayer that articulates our yearning for communion with that God—a mature prayer that enables us to voice our ideals and articulate our yearning for holiness. Mature prayer enables us to turn our thoughts and lives toward the divine. The central meaning of mature prayer is not to get something, but to be with someone; it is not to have more, but to be more. Prayer is not to change God, but to change ourselves.

Prayer Is Limited to Words

Popular in the minds of many people is the belief that the efficacy of prayer depends upon the right words and the proper verbalization of religious formulas. This is contradicted by a story from the tradition of the Chassidic rabbis who lived in the villages of eighteenth century eastern Europe. It is taught that an ignorant peasant once wandered into a synagogue. He approached the holy altar, and as he listened to the sages embellish their ornate prayers of adoration of the Most High he was crushed with humility as he recognized his own ignorance and incoherence. For a while he stood before God, bowed and silent, and then he began to recite the letters of the Hebrew alphabet over and over again. The erudite scholars of the law laughed contemptuously at this rustic who could not even express a simple prayer to his God. Then, ridicule and mockery froze on their lips. Shame suffused their beings as they heard him say: "O Lord God of the Universe, it is true that I am an ignorant man, a simple man. Alas, I cannot form beautiful prayers worthy of Thee. But hear me, O God, as I recite the letters of the alphabet, and then take these letters, my heavenly Father, and You form the words that express the sentiments of my loving and adoring heart."

Another homily from the Chassidic tradition tells of the saintly Rabbi Israel Ben Eliezer of Miedboziboz who tried to make his devotion a complete surrender as if he were offering his heart and his soul on high. It happened on the sacred Day of Atonement that he poured out his soul in yearning for God, hoping to recapture the spirit of true, unselfish worship that he knew was acceptable to God. Somehow, he felt that genuine heartfelt prayer was absent, that neither he nor any member of his congregation was able to offer it. The time for breaking the fast had long since passed. Yet he and all the devout around him were still searching their souls for the prayer that surely finds its way to Heaven, and it chanced that a little ignorant shepherd boy came down from the hills. Attracted by the chant that came to him from Rabbi Israel's synagogue, he entered it. There he saw a multitude of men and women engrossed in their devotions. The boy felt a sudden urge to join in the prayers. He wanted to thank God that he was alive. In his childish way he did the only thing he could. He put his fingers into his mouth, and gave out a long, shrill whistle. The congregation looked up, scandalized at the shamefaced boy who now realized what an awful thing he had done. Rabbi Israel, however, with a happy smile on his face, turned to the congregation and said: "Our devotions are over. At last we were fortunate enough to offer an unselfish, heartfelt prayer in our midst."

Prayer is not limited to words. The efficacy of prayer is not in the flowery language of scholars, garnished with adjectives and embellished with ornate terminology.

In the nineteenth century Ralph Waldo Emerson insisted that prayer transcends the spoken language and that the true prayer is spoken through the language of the heart:

> "The great Idea baffles wit,
> Language falters under it,
> It leaves the learned in the lurch;
> No art, nor power, nor toil can find
> The measure of the eternal Mind,
> Nor hymn, nor prayer, nor church."[6]

We are in error when we believe that prayer is limited to a verbal articulation of our desires and wants. Prayer is not only speaking—it is also listening to the still small voice of Divinity. The Danish

[6] "The Bohemian Hymn," *Poems* (Boston, Houghton, Mifflin and Company, Household ed., 1898), p. 298.

philosopher Kierkegaard contended that the true relation in prayer is not when God hears what is prayed for, but when the person praying continues to pray until he is the one who hears what God wills. Thus, prayer is not petition. Rather, it is man's submitting of himself to God that He may speak.

After All I've Done for God

A woman became angry with God because He did not comply with all her requests and petitions. She voiced her complaint, saying: "After all I've done for God, look at how He ignores my prayers. Prayer is a waste of time. I'll never pray to God again as long as I live!"

Prayer was not a failure. The woman was a failure in her prayer relationship. She really believed that because she had done so much for God that He was indebted to her because of her prayers and words of adoration and thanksgiving. Does God need our prayers of adoration and praise? Do we think that because we pray we are helping and serving God?

The prophets of Israel repeated over and over again that God is sated with the offering of fat beasts, with sacrifices devoid of ethical significance and moral purpose. God wants justice, truth, and righteousness from man, not his flowery phrases or the poetic cadence of liturgical chant. The most acceptable offering we can make to God is a life of personal piety and devotion to His commandments. The way we show our love of God is by service to His children.

A God of magic requires sacrifices and offerings. A God of justice requires justice from those who worship Him. It is not what God sends to us, but what we bring to God that makes our prayers meaningful. By faith Job could cry out, in a supreme affirmation of love, "Though He slay me, yet will I trust in Him." In such moral magic of faith, the wonder of the human heart elevates itself to a communion with holiness that provides the answering response to our supplications to God.

When Ye Make Many Prayers

We manifest the most childish naïveté, and an absurd, infantile credulity, if we believe that our rites, forms, and verbal prayers, unrelated to personal integrity and moral commitment, will permit us to commune with God. The prophet Isaiah was scathing in his condemnation of pseudoreligious hypocrites who divorced religion from morality. Speaking in the name of God, he asked:

"To what purpose is the multitude of your sacrifices unto Me?
I cannot endure iniquity along with the solemn assembly.
Your new moons and your appointed seasons
My soul hateth;
They are a burden unto Me;
I am weary to bear them."

—ISAIAH 1.11, 13-14

Is our modern ritual less deserving of the strictures of the prophet? We no longer place sacrifices upon the altar. We no longer offer oblations of oil. Respectable religion offers money, words, and ritual in place of sacrifices. We convene at new moons and appointed seasons to extol our God with pious declarations of love. Do we weary and burden God with the poetry and pageantry of our ceremonials? How long would an Isaiah last as a minister, rabbi, or priest in our congregations if he spoke in this manner today? Consider the fate of such a spokesman for God if he should be the guest preacher at one of our fashionable and respectable churches or synagogues. "Friend Isaiah," he would be told, "go and peddle your prophecies elsewhere. We don't like you or your preachments. You are a Communist, an agitator, troublemaker and a heretic. Damn you and damn your blasphemous denunciation of the ritual and forms that have been sacred to us through the ages! You don't speak in the name of God. You speak in the name of the devil!" But the Voice persists:

"And when ye spread forth your hands,
I will hide Mine eyes from you."

Unrest murmurs through the congregation, swelling into a dissonance of thunderous protest. The ushers look uncertainly at one another. People are leaving their seats and crowding to the doors. "This man must be insane. God does not hide His eyes from us when we spread forth our hands in supplication. God loves our praise and our ritual.

He has ordained our ritual with divine sanction." But the Voice
continues:

> "Yea, when ye make many prayers,
> I will not hear;
> Your hands are full of blood."

The women members of the choir retreat in hysteria at the mention of blood. A child screams in fright. An official phones frantically
for the police. Some sober and solemn people remain seated, trans-
fixed with the intensity of inner searching: "Are his words true? Have
we not stood by in passive acquiescence while mobs mauled the
innocent because of the pigmentation of their skin? Have we not
permitted our greed to dispossess others of their due? Have we not
contributed to the ugliness of prejudice, bigotry, and ignorance?" The
rising cadence of the Voice is heard demanding:

> "Wash you, make you clean,
> Put away the evil of your doings
> From before Mine eyes."

Only a few silent worshipers remain to ask themselves: "With all
our respectability, isn't it possible that our hands, washed, bathed,
immersed and rubbed with germ-repellent soaps, are not clean?

"We have prayed and praised, appealed, supplicated, confessed,
adjured, and petitioned for things, miracles, power, success, virtue,
health. We have said our amens and hallelujahs, repeated doxologies,
performed ritual, bowed and knelt. We have been sermonized and
exorcised, but have we really put away the evil of our doings from
before the eyes of God? We must not turn away. We must listen and
move our prayers into action." The Voice again, commanding:

> "Cease to do evil;
> Learn to do well;
> Seek justice, relieve the oppressed,
> Judge the fatherless, plead for the widow."

"The Voice! Will it ever stop?" Even the contrite few, awed by prophetic truth, retreat through the exits leading to the world of respectable indifference. Isaiah is left alone with God.

5

What Not to Believe About Man

Man is the incommensurable idiot of the universe
—JEAN-PAUL SARTRE

The Golem of Prague

According to Jewish legendary sources, a sixteenth century mystic, Judah Lowe of Prague, determined to create a golem, a robot-man out of clay.

In the year 1580, on the second day of the month of March, as the clock struck midnight, with his two associates, he went to the outskirts of the city to the banks of the Moldau River, where, after finding a clay bed, he proceeded to fashion the clay into the figure of a man. Chanting from the Sefer Yetzivah, the Book of Mystery, working with desperate haste, he formed the golem out of clay, and the robot lay before him with its face turned toward heaven.

Walking around the clay body from right to left, he looked, and behold, the clay body became red like fire. As he observed with a growing terror in his heart, the fire-redness faded, water flowed through the clay body, hair sprouted on its head, and nails appeared on the fingers and toes. But the golem was not alive!

The sages walked around the figure again, placed in its mouth a piece of parchment with the name of God written thereon, and, bowing to the east and the west, the north and the south, all three recited together: *And He breathed into his nostrils the breath of life, and man became a living soul.*

They looked, and behold, the golem opened his eyes. They said to him: "Stand up," and he stood up.

Three men had assembled at midnight to create a robot-man, a golem. At daybreak, four men walked homeward.

The place of the legendary event was Prague. The time: the sixteenth century. Almost four hundred years later, in Cambridge, Massachusetts, the Science Department of Harvard University created a modern golem, a robot, a machine that so closely resembled a human being that it was given a name: Mark II. Mark can calculate, compute, walk, think, respond to stimuli—but Mark cannot make moral judgments; he cannot determine the difference between right and wrong, good and evil. Mark seems to be a man in every respect except one—he lacks a soul. Mark was not created in the image of God, but in the image of a blueprint, in the likeness of a machine.

It is not enough for us to shrug aside the story of Judah Lowe and the Golem of Prague as a fantastic and imaginary legend. Nor is it sufficient for us to regard Mark II of Harvard University as an interesting experiment. We must pause to ask ourselves whether *we* look upon man, in terms of flesh and bone and sinew, as a combination of atoms and molecules, as a golem, as a machine, a robot that responds to stimuli, or whether we look upon man as a child of God, created in the image of God, endowed with a divine potential for beauty and holiness, and as a sacred personality that is more than clay, that is more than flesh, that is more than chemistry, that is more than a robot without a soul.

Is Man a Machine?

Respectable religion makes God a man, and humanism makes man a God. The materialist philosophy of life takes the man out of God, the God out of man and makes him a machine.

Ever since the Industrial Revolution of the eighteenth century, efforts have been made to demonstrate that man is a machine—an ingenious phenomenon to be sure, but nonetheless a machine that can be reduced to component parts, and then reassembled again into an integrated totality. Scientists, philosophers, and sociologists have endeavored to convince us that the machine resulted from some cosmic dust exploded from the collision of other cosmic machines in the traffic of a chaotic, unguided universe. Man was not created in the image of God, endowed with a soul. Man came into being as an accidental machine, and a machine doesn't have a soul; a machine doesn't need a God—just a productive environment to supply the gas, the oil, and the necessary parts to keep it functioning.

Thus, ever since the Industrial Revolution, instead of hearing the voice of God, the ears of man were conditioned to the vibrations of machinery. The test tube replaced the chalice, and religion became a dirty word on the lips of the intellectual. A machine doesn't need religion. A machine can't appeal for divine help. A machine isn't expected to search for God or meet the moral challenge of divinity.

Within recent years we have been introduced to a new science called "cybernetics." Professor Norbert Wiener, in *Control and Communication in the Animal and the Machine,* contends that the human brain functions very much like a mechanical brain and that there are common elements in the functioning of automatic machines and the human nervous system. While Dr. Wiener has indicated the military uses to which cybernetics may be put, it is not devoid of peacetime significance. For example, it seems possible that before long "a mechanical chess player may be constructed that might very well be as good a player as the vast majority of the human race." Man becomes a robot with a chessboard, a golem with a pawn, with only a suspicion of religion suggested by the bishop—an anachronistic symbol of the past.

This mechanistic doctrine that makes man a robot is reflected not only in science but also in a philosophy of education that would regard the child as a stimulus-response machine propelled along a pedagogic assembly line to be duly inspected, labeled with an academic degree, and sent out to function in a scientifically conditioned world. Man becomes a golem with a diploma, a robot with a cap and gown.

Educators must alert themselves to the danger of seeing children as mechanized robots, impervious to their hopes and fears, unresponsive to their apprehensions and tensions, callous to the unspoken prayers that well up in their hearts, estimating the worth of our children in terms of the elements on a valence chart. The Research Department of a prominent university recently assessed the worth of a child as approximately $3.94 in chemicals. According to the ruling of the Treasury Department, a child is worth at least a $600 exemption on an income-tax form. Modern education must behold the child as something more than a lovable mechanism or a mischievous unit occupying space. Unless we agree that there is a plus, a soul, a divine image inherent in man, then the child is an automaton in a gym suit, a conglomeration of atoms with homework, a calculated combination of molecules wearing bobby socks, a golem with a report card.

According to the mechanistic philosophy of life, human beings are reduced to things "whose hearts are rags and whose souls are chalk." As the writer Russell Davenport describes man, he is "winged and wheeled, wired, propelled, lighted, electronized." The noted psychiatrist Erich Fromm warned that the great danger of the future is not that man will become a slave but that he will become a robot.

What Is Man?

The ancient Hebrew psalmist experienced an overwhelming sense of awe and wonder at God's creative power, as he pondered the order and the majestic splendor of the universe, and then lifted his soul on high as he exclaimed:

"When I behold Thy heavens, the work of Thy fingers,
The moon and the stars, which Thou hast established;
What is man, that Thou art mindful of him?
And the son of man, that Thou thinkest of him?
Yet Thou hast made him but little lower than the angels,
And hast crowned him with glory and honour."
—PSALM 8

The psalmist recognized that the answer to the question *What is man?* would in large measure determine his attitude toward God, toward his society, and even toward himself. And so, with a supreme affirmation of faith, he answered the question not by declaring that man is a golem or a robot, but by the conviction that man is but little lower than the angels.

That is the answer of the psalmist, but what is our answer to the question? Is it the answer of Jean-Paul Sartre, the high priest of the Existentialists, who says, "Man is the incommensurable idiot of the universe"?

Is it the answer of Bertrand Russell that man, with his knowledge of good and evil, is but a helpless atom?

Is it the answer of H. L. Mencken that man is a sick fly, taking a dizzy ride on a gigantic flywheel?

Is it the answer of the late Justice Oliver Wendell Holmes, who said: "I think that the sacredness of human life is a purely municipal ideal of no validity. I see no reason for attributing to man a significance different in kind from that which belongs to a baboon or a grain of sand."

If man is the incommensurable idiot of the universe, then let him squirm and struggle in the strait-jacket of his own misery. He belongs in it.

If man, with his knowledge of good and evil, is but a helpless atom —a cosmic orphan in a parentless universe—let him dangle there without freedom of will to act, to love, to create a moral society, for then there is no morality, there is no purpose! There are only the winds of chance that drive him and blow him through a meaningless mockery of time.

If man is a sick fly, then crush him as you would any other such filthy disease-carrying insect.

If we believe that man is nothing more than the sum total of chemistry and materialism, then it's easy to look at an infant and refer to it as "a screaming, squalling mass of angry protoplasm." If we believe that our greatest need is the honesty to face the fact that we are what we are—nothing but animals—then why shouldn't man look upon himself and his species with cynicism and contempt? "What is man?" is not simply an academic question. Our attitude toward man will in large measure determine our attitude toward ourselves. If we think of man as selfish, corrupt, primitive, ferocious, evil, and depraved, then we must think of ourselves in the same way, and we have no choice but to despise and hate ourselves as despicable components of a depraved humanity.

Man Is Evil

One of the most ignorant and vicious doctrines promulgated by respectable religion is the primitive doctrine of original sin. The passage in Genesis 3.1-24 describing the "fall of Adam" from divine grace has exercised an indescribable influence upon so-called religious thought. This doctrine holds that the sinfulness of Adam imposed a chain reaction of sinfulness upon all his descendants. As a result of the fall of Adam, all of his direct and indirect progeny have been plummeted into the abyss of evil, tainted with a mobile sinfulness that has by hereditary transmission rendered all human beings depraved. Paul used this as the basis of his theology which reflects the conviction that "by one man sin entered into the world. . . . By one man's disobedience many were made sinners" (Romans 5.12, 19). This was a logical extension of the narrative in Genesis asserting that it was through Adam's fall that all women suffer in childbirth and all men must work for a living by the sweat of their brows. Both Jewish and Christian religious thought have been influenced and exploited by what is now regarded as a myth and a discredited superstition.

If we are to use biblical myths as the criteria for theology, accepting superstition for fact, are we not likewise compelled to adjust the laws of astronomy to the myth that Joshua made the sun stand still, and the principles of astronautics to the myth that Elijah ascended unto heaven in a fiery chariot? It is just as ridiculous to predicate the depravity of man upon the myth that Adam sinned and that consequently all men are sinful.

A couplet from the New England Primer taught:

"In Adam's fall
We sinned all."

Are we to believe in a God who would permit the human race to be contaminated with sin throughout all the ensuing generations because of the sin of one individual? Is it possible to reconcile the doctrine of original sin reported in Genesis with the doctrine of individual responsibility taught by Ezekiel? Is it rational to believe that man is inherently sinful because of the disobedience of Adam—especially in view of the contention that the story of the first man as recounted in Genesis is a myth? To consider the fall of Adam as a symbolic representation of man's alienation from God is logically tenable. To accept the antediluvian fantasy of a serpent speaking to woman, or even to consider the theory of some psychoanalysts that the serpent is a phallic symbol beguiling Eve to tempt man, who in turn disobeys God by eating of the fruit of the tree of the knowledge of good and evil and thus contaminates all future generations, transcends the credulity of even the most childish adherent of kindergarten religion.

Moreover, if man is regarded as evil, the thinking religionist has the further problem of reconciling this concept with the belief that man was and is created in the image of God. It follows that the belief in the depravity of man demands the corresponding conclusion that God is evil, sinful, and depraved—a conclusion that no rational being can possibly accept. To do so is to make a demon of man and a devil of God.

The belief in the depravity of man precludes the possibility of the imitation of God. This was pointed out as early as the seventeenth century by Pascal, who was perplexed by the problem of how religion "bids man recognize that he is vile, even abominable; and bids him desire to be like God." Who would want to imitate the attributes of a God whose most majestic creation is polluted with sinfulness? If I were compelled by conviction or by theology to believe in the inherent depravity of man, I would likewise be compelled to hold God in contempt and yield to a misanthropic disgust that would leave no room for religion in my life.

Respectable religion still clings tenaciously to the belief in the inborn, unlearned sinfulness of man. John Calvin strengthened this conviction of the depravity of man by his religious preachments and writings. The theologians Emil Brunner, Karl Barth, and Soren Kierkegaard in our own time base their philosophy of life upon the inherent weakness and evil of man. The playwrights Eugene O'Neill and Tennessee Williams construct the plot of their plays on the basic sinfulness of man battling against environmental forces that shape his destiny and coerce him into tragic consequences. Poets and writers such as Jean-Paul Sartre, Albert Camus, T. S. Eliot, and Simone Weil equate life with misery and man with futility. Contemporary literature further spells out and designates the unhappy fate of the "lonely man" of David Riesman, "the hollow man" of

T. S. Eliot, "the last angry man" of Paul Eliot Green, "the organizational man" of William Whyte, "the irrational man" of William Barrett, and "the sexual man" of Kinsey. Man, "trapped in the tenement of the flesh," journeys from "death to death." What is man? Lonely, hollow, angry, enslaved, and irrational man is robotized, electronized, compartmentalized, conditioned, predestined, postdestined, controlled, and exploited—a puppet machine, robot, golem, automaton. This is what not to believe about man.

If man is evil, the world of men is evil, life is evil, the Creator of life is the Supreme Evil, and the statement of Genesis 1.31, "And God saw everything that He had made, and, behold, it was very good" is a masterpiece of biblical deceit. If we agree with Schopenhauer that "life is a bed of red-hot coals with a cool spot here and there," then it was a fiendish demon and not a loving God who placed man upon the earth to suffer through the torment of physical pain and spiritual frustration. If we believe with David Riesman that "to be born is to be mortgaged—to live is to be crippled," then man wastes his years incurring an increasing indebtedness for the dubious privilege of living, and hobbles, stumbles, and drags himself through a divinely ordained hell on earth with the surcease of death as his only hope. Clarence Darrow, the famous criminal lawyer, once began a lecture with these words: "Intellectually I am satisfied that life is a serious burden, which no thinking human person would wantonly inflict on someone else." The belief that man is evil leads unerringly to the conviction that life is not only evil but Godless. Those who maintain such an attitude toward man, if consistent, should encourage suicide, condone murder, sanction war, and hold the cessation of life as the greatest good.

Mature religion is not to be held accountable for such beliefs foisted upon the mind of man. Kindergarten religion may give theological credence to original sin, but a rational, mature, and adult faith must predicate its theology upon original virtue that derives its essence from the divine image within man.

The Body Is Corrupt

Co-existent with the belief in the depravity of man is the patently juvenile dualism that regards the body as evil and the soul as good.

Such a system of religious thought contends that the flesh is in constant combat with the soul, tempting man to sin, seducing him into the satisfaction of his material appetites. The purity of the soul is dependent upon the subservience of the body to the rigorous demands of the soul. The doctrine of the corrupt nature of the flesh would seem to validate the contention of Epictetus that "man is a little soul carrying around a corpse." This potentially putrescent corpse is vile, corrupt, and evil by its very nature. Consequently, it must be subdued, humiliated, dominated, controlled and ultimately destroyed in order to liberate the soul from the shackles of the flesh, so that it may emerge pure, undefiled and eternally free.

Such a deprecation of the body regards the appetites of the body as inferior, unworthy, and ignoble. The hunger for food is a necessary evil to be tolerated but rendered secondary to the hunger of the soul. Sex is a dirty word that is to be unmentionable even in the context of religious mythology. Thus, the sexual implications of the fall of man are to be politely ignored. One may recognize the existence of the sex drive, but reluctantly and sadly, for it is an admission of a bodily need —a physical appetite to be regulated and expressed solely for the perpetuation of the human race. Marriage, too, is a concession to the demands of the lustful flesh, and a means of preventing the kind of illicit sex relationship that consigns man to damnation. In the words of Paul, "it is better to marry than to burn." Continued virginity, chastity, and continence are the coveted characteristics of piety, requisites for the life of holiness and Godliness. From such an infantile point of view, God has given man appetites that are, if not evil, certainly to be viewed as suspicious correlatives of that which is base, unworthy, and animal-like.

If man is to be thought of solely as an animal, not a thinking animal, and not a religious animal, but just an animal, then the cynical Cowley was correct when he said that "Man is too near all kinds of beasts: a fawning dog, a roaring lion, a thieving fox, a robbing wolf, a dissembling crocodile, a treacherous decoy and a rapacious vulture." Such an attitude toward man ignores and repudiates the sanctity of the human personality created in the image of God. It robs man of his divine potential and relegates him to the status of a predatory beast prowling through the jungles of history in search of victims to claw and devour.

Bertrand Russell, in *Human Society in Ethics and Politics*, considers the possibility of the self-destruction of mankind, declaring, "When all is said and done, it would be a pity if mankind turned out to be no more dignified than an ape playing with a box of matches in a petroleum dump."

The nature of man, even viewed by his own species, Homo sapiens, is anything but holy and commendable. From Genesis to the final Revelation "the imagination of man's heart is evil from his youth." He is disobedient, shameful, murderous, lustful, envious, and vengeful. We are led to the inescapable conclusion that to be human is a mark of weakness, guilt, shame, and inferiority. The low estate of man is summed up by Seneca in his *Questiones Naturales*: "Oh how contemptible a thing is man unless he can raise himself above humanity."

From the view of kindergarten religion:

> "How art thou fallen from heaven,
> O day-star, son of the morning!
> How art thou cut down to the ground,
> That didst cast lots over the nations!
> And thou saidst in thy heart:
> 'I will ascend into heaven,
> Above the stars of God
> Will I exalt my throne;
> And I will sit upon the mount of meeting,
> In the uttermost parts of the north;
> I will ascend above the heights of the clouds;
> I will be like the Most High.'
> Yet thou shalt be brought down to the nether-world,
> To the uttermost parts of the pit."
>
> —ISAIAH 14.12-15

Man Is Not Divisible

The kindergarten attitude toward man supports infantile concepts of the racial and religious superiority and supremacy of classes of men in society. It avers that God has designed races of men as inferior and superior, that some human beings are born to servility by reason of blood, and that other human beings are born to privilege and favor because of pigmentation.

Anthropologists seek to classify man by establishing indices that distinguish one racial group from another. Equipped with calipers, metric tapes, and goniometers, they measure the human body for definitive data on the shape of the skull, nasal index, pelvic breadth, and bizygomatic diameter to ascertain the distinguishing characteristics of the Mongoloid, Negroid, and Caucasoid divisions. The intent of such anthropological research is not to substantiate spurious racial claims of superiority. Quite to the contrary, the evidence indicates the need for a reappraisal of prejudicial categories of the superior and inferior man, and suggests that the mature faith should regard man in terms of his membership in the human race and the family of man rather than in terms of a specific racial identity that consigns him to the category of Mongoloid, Negroid, or Caucasoid divisions.

Contrary to the childishness that perpetuates the fantasy of superior and inferior groups of men, a passage from the Talmud declares that "man was originally created as a solitary individual for the sake of peace among men, that no man might ever have cause to claim to another: 'My ancestor was greater than yours.'" The first man, according to rabbinic legend, was created from the dust that gathered from the four corners of the earth, so that no one people should say, "The first man was created from the dust of our country."

In the second century, Rabbi Akiba, son of Joseph, was asked about the greatest principle of Judaism. He said it was the commandment in Leviticus, "Thou shalt love thy neighbor as thyself." When God said "neighbor" He did not specify the neighbor's religion, nationality, or the pigmentation of his skin.

His friend Rabbi Simeon, son of Azzai, disagreed. He said that the greatest verse is from Genesis: "This is the book of the generations of man. In the day that God created man, in the likeness of God made He him." God's word is meant for all people, not for one religion alone, one race alone, or one nation. All men share the sacred image of God.

When Paul stood at the summit of Mars' hill and declared that God "hath made of one blood all nations of men for to dwell on all the face of the earth" (Acts 17.26), he was articulating the Christian concept of the indivisibility of men and nations.

Kindergarten religion regards man as a dual being, with a clear demarcation between body and soul, the spiritual and the material, and the supposition of mutual antagonism and continuous conflict. The mature faith accentuates man's search for wholeness and integrity. It sees in the root meaning of religion, *religare*, "to bind together again," the definitive purpose of life. It looks to religion to bind men together again, to heal his moral schizophrenia, and to enable the individual to make the outer and the inner man whole and one. The chasm between man's inner aspirations and his outer acts must be narrowed and bridged if he is to achieve the glory of his humanness.

The Holiness of Being Human

There is not only wholeness, but there is holiness in being human. Kindergarten religion insists: that which is divine is holy and sacred. That which is human is weak, profane, and debased. The mature faith seeks the essential unity of man and God through the divinity that is inherent within man and yet transcends man. The mature faith does not hold that the fallibility, the finitude of man negates his divine nature. Quite to the contrary, the very humanness of man testifies to his uniqueness as the only creature on earth who approaches the divine by being human. Martin Buber expressed this when he wrote: "He [man] can approach Him through becoming human. To become human is what man has been created for."

Rabbinic Judaism recognized this in the homily that tells of the time when Moses complained to God against the children of Israel, castigating them as stubborn, stiff-necked, and rebellious. Whereupon God chastised Moses gently, saying: "I have created man as a flesh-and-blood human being, and not an angel. Therefore, do not expect men to be angels. Rather teach them to be truly human." The rabbis beheld wonder and glory in the ability of man to aspire to communion with Divinity. Since man was created in the image of God, to be fully and completely human meant the exalted effort of man to approximate and imitate moral attributes of God.

To maintain contempt for that which is human is to disparage man, and thereby hold in contempt the Divinity within him. For too long have we made the term "human" a synonym for weakness. The mature faith must endeavor to equate the term "human" with holiness, compassion, beauty, truth, love, and the quest for the knowledge of God.

We need the mature faith to assure us of the worth of being human. The concept of man as a puppet manipulated by a divine Puppeteer, a dangling marionette jerked about by a supreme Will is not only infantile; it is also inimical to the dignity and divinity, humanness and holiness of man. It shrinks his moral stature as a child of God, deprives him of the right of ethical choice, obviates his freedom of will, and negates the possibility of fulfilling his sacred destiny of building God's kingdom on earth.

6

What Not to Believe About the Bible

In religion
What damned error but some sober brow
Will bless it and approve it with a text,
Hiding the grossness with fair ornaments?
—Shakespeare, *The Merchant
of Venice, III, ii*

Handle with Care

The late Professor William Lyon Phelps of Yale once remarked that the Bible "ought to have written on the cover: Highly Explosive— Handle with care. It is the book which by the dynamite of its message has lifted empires off their hinges and turned the course of human events. It has put down the mighty from their seats and hath exalted them of low degree."[1]

The admonition of Dr. Phelps should be heeded by all those who quote the Bible as the authoritative source of religious arguments. The Bible has been used and misused to motivate the most exalted aspirations of mankind, and yet to validate the most prejudiced, debased, ignorant, and bloodthirsty inclinations of man.

The subject of the teaching of religion in the public schools in one of the most controversial of contemporary society. The opponents and the proponents are equally vigorous in their arguments and demands. Solutions range from the outright teaching of sectarian religion in the schools, through Release and Dismissal Time, a Common Core, and the teaching of spiritual and moral values, to the religion of democracy. This hotly contested subject has an explosive potential of danger, divisiveness, and contention that might well destroy our public-school system, and demolish the traditional American principle of the separation of Church and State.

Dr. Phelps was not being an alarmist when he urged that we handle the Bible with care. Inflammable and combustible, arguments about the Bible can set man against his fellow man, and destroy the very principles of morality and the objectives of harmony, peace, and cooperation that are regarded as the desirable effects sought by the study and teaching of Holy Scripture.

The Bible has been exploited and perverted, twisted and tortured to support war and peace, capital punishment and opposition to capital punishment, birth control and lack of birth control, capitalism, socialism, democracy, monarchy, child labor, prohibition and antiprohibition, slavery and antislavery, segregation and integration, poverty, religious prejudice, racial discrimination, vaccination, the resistance to education, art, science, and every other controversial subject that has been debated by man.

Dr. Everett Tilson in *Segregation and the Bible* offers a searching analysis of the scriptural evidence that is adduced to favor both integration and segregation, and indicates that both the supporters of integration and segregation utilize Holy Scripture as the divine source and authority for their views.

[1] Quotation from *Magazine Digest*, November, 1945.

In the *Liberator*, February 5, 1831, the abolitionist William Lloyd Garrison records a dialogue:

" 'Well, sir, I can prove from the Bible that slavery is right.'

" 'Ah!' replied I, 'that is a precious book—the rule of conduct. I have always supposed that its spirit was directly opposed to everything in the shape of fraud and oppression. However, sir, I should be glad to hear your text.'

"He somewhat hesitatingly muttered out—'Ham—Noah's curse, you know.'

" 'O, sir, you build on a very slender foundation. Granting even—what remains to be proved—that the Africans are the descendants of Ham, Noah's curse was a prediction of future servitude, and not an injunction to oppress. Pray, sir, is it a careful desire to fulfill the Scriptures, or to make money, that induces you to hold your fellow-men in bondage?' "

It is interesting to note that in 1957, three years after the decision of the Supreme Court to integrate Negroes in the public schools, a minister in Nashville, Tennessee, declared: "The Bible teaches that God wants the Negroes to be inferior. God was the first segregationist."

Because of the almost universal reverence for the Bible, it has been invested with a sanctity that makes critical evaluation a dangerous endeavor and rational examination a hazardous effort. Regarded as the irrefutable word of God, a divine revelation of the will of God, Holy Scriptures have been the untouchable taboo literature, a sacred fetish that must be kept undefiled by doubt and uncorrupted by the questioning mind.

In the Body of Liberties, adopted in 1641 by the Puritans, blasphemy and the worship of any but the true God appear in the catalogue of capital crimes. According to Henry W. Lawrence, by an act of 1646, "whoever denied that any book of the Bible was the infallible Word of God might be whipped forty lashes and fined fifty pounds; on the second offense, he was to be put to death or banished."[2]

In 1654 James Ussher, Archbishop of Armagh, declared that the creation took place at 9:00 A.M. on October 26th in the year 4004 B.C., basing his claim on a careful study of the Scriptures. For more

[2] Henry W. Lawrence, *The Not-Quite Puritans.*

than a century this date was regarded as valid. Anyone who suggested an earlier date was considered a heretic.

In our own day a man may not be fined, banished, or put to death for denying that any book of the Bible is the infallible Word of God, but he will suffer the loss of prestige, the fall from conformity, and risk the social and economic penalty of being castigated as a radical, freethinker, and atheist. Even worse than being condemned as a heretic, he will be contaminated with the most unpardonable taint of all, namely, the malady of maladjustment.

When we refer to the Bible, precisely what do we mean, the King James Version, the Holy Scripture of the Jews, the Douai edition of the Catholics, the Greek Septuagint, the Latin Vulgate, or the new Revised Standard Version authorized by the National Council of Churches?

The Bible Is Not to Be Worshiped

The Bible—actually a collection of books—has been translated into 1,068 languages. It is the most widely purchased and yet the most unread, the most misunderstood, and the most venerated of all sacred literature. Because of reverence for the Bible as the word of God, it has frequently become a substitute for God, a literary idol equated with Divinity.

In our judiciary system, a witness is sworn in by placing a hand on the Bible and being adjured to tell the truth, the whole truth, and nothing but the truth. It is as if the Bible has become personified as God, and as if by telling a lie when in physical contact with the Bible one incurs the threat that punishment will be meted out by God. Bibles are placed in hotel rooms, motels, schools, and homes as a reminder of the ubiquitous presence of the Deity.

The Bible is to be respected and revered as the repository of divine truth, but it is never to be equated with God or worshiped as a surrogate for the divine.

The Bible Was Not Written at One Time and One Place

Those who are termed "fundamentalists" claim that the Bible was revealed by God at one time and in one place, and is to be taken literally and accepted in its entirety as the authoritative divine will of God. Another group, termed "modernists," claim that the Bible is the record of man's quest for the understanding of the will of God. Modernists regard it as a collection of books, transmitted orally and ultimately committed to writing over a period of a thousand years, that reveals not only divine truth but also the history, myths, folklore, law, ethics, religious institutions, and aspirations of the Jewish people and the Christian faith.

For many years the divine authorship of the Pentateuch at one time and one place was accepted as unassailable dogma. By Talmudic times, however (500 c.e.), the rabbinic scholars had indicated the belief that portions of the Bible were not of divine origin, that some parts of the Bible antedated Moses, that Joshua and Samuel were not the sole authors of the books that bear their names, and that the books of Isaiah and Jeremiah contain parts not composed by the prophets. The sages conjectured on the question of how Moses could write about his own death. Two theories were advanced: first, that God gave Moses foreknowledge of his death, and second, that Joshua completed the book of Deuteronomy and described the death of Moses.

Prior to the canonization of Scripture there were rabbinic debates as to whether the Song of Songs and Ecclesiastes should be included. Because of the supposed authorship of Solomon, it was finally determined that these books should be included in the canon.

In the tenth century a Jewish sage, Hivi Al-Balkhi, attempted to explain the miracles of the Bible in natural terms, and prepared an expurgated text of the Bible from which everything irrational and objectionable was eliminated. Another sage, Moses ibn-Jikatilla, suggested that David had not written all the psalms, concluded that there was a second Isaiah, and hinted that not all the passages of the Pentateuch were of Mosaic origin.

Spinoza was not the first to discover that Joshua is similar to the Torah (five books of Moses) or that Chronicles contradicts Samuel and Kings or that the arrangement of chapters in the book of Jeremiah follows no plan or that Psalms was compiled during the days of the Second Temple.

The man who started higher biblical criticism on its present course was Jean Astruc, the court physician to Louis XIV. A devout Catholic, he was troubled by the many contradictions and duplicate accounts of the Pentateuch. He observed that names for God vary in Scriptures and that the two most frequently encountered were the names Elohim and JHWH. Following this clue, he divided Genesis into two parallel accounts, each complete in itself. One column listed the name of God as Elohim, the other as JHWH. This theory, promulgated in 1753, was received with ridicule or regarded with indifference until the year 1780, when Johannes Gottfried Eichhorn elaborated upon it in his *Introduction to the Old Testament*.

Other biblical scholars, such as Kosters, Kayser, Colenso, Duhm, Kuenen, and Wellhausen, reassessed the historical value of the Pentateuch and the earlier Prophets and asserted a firm belief in the evolutionary development of the cultural and religious institutions of Israel. Their studies resulted in the division and subdivision of the biblical sources[3] into J^1 J^2 J^3 E^1 E^2 E^3 p^1 p^2 p^3 D^1 D^2; and while much of higher biblical criticism has been exaggerated, there is no doubt that the thesis has been conclusively demonstrated that the Bible is made up of various documents *written compositely over an extended period of time*, corrected, amended, changed to reflect the religious and political views of the multiple authorship, but all the while indicating the progressive and revolutionary account of the law, mythology, ethics, history, and religious aspirations of the Jewish people, and later, as the New Testament was appended, those of the Christian faith.

Knowing that the original text of the Bible was written without vowels, and that it wasn't until the massoretes[4] remedied what was an apparently difficult and painful effort to read the text, that vowels were added. Editors, scribes, and redactors all had a share in the revised texts, which were written on parchment scrolls.

Stanley Rypins, in *The Book of Thirty Centuries*,[5] indicates to us how the text of the opening verses of Genesis would appear if written in English:

[3] Jawistic, Elohistic, and Deuteronomic codes.
[4] Massoretes, derived from the Hebrew root word "to hand down," the men who preserved the traditional Bible text, and provided the vowels for the exact meaning of the Hebrew vocabulary.
[5] New York, The Macmillan Company, 1951, p. 31.

```
INTHEBEGINNINGGODC
REATEDTHEHEAVENAND
THEEARTHNOWTHEEART
HWASWITHOUTFORMAND
VOIDANDDARKNESSUPO
NTHEFACEOFTHEDEEP
```

Written without vowels, as in the Hebrew text, the same verses would appear in this still stranger form:

```
NTHBGNNNGGDCRT
DTHHVNNDTHRTH
NWTHRTHWSWTHT
FRMNDVDNDDRKN
SSPNTHFCFTHDP
```

With such explanations of how the text of the Bible came to be, we are in a position to understand why there are different interpretations and versions of the same word. We can readily discern the possibility of error and confusion. What is more important, however, even one who is not a biblical scholar recognizes that there are different writers expressing different points of view, using terms that were characteristic of their age, and thus indicating to us that the Bible was not written at one time or in one place, but rather over an extended period of time by many editors, correctors, and scribes.

Recent archaeological discoveries are bringing new light to the obscurity of biblical passages. Instead of being an enemy of religion, science is on the contrary finding evidence to demonstrate the truth of portions of the Bible. Certain passages and stories are myths, others fables. There are facts and fictions, history and folklore, exalted morality and ignorant superstition, law and taboo, ethics and culture—all reflecting man's tortuous journey through the ages, his struggle to grow spiritually from kindergarten religion to a mature faith—but always seeking, questing to bring man to God and God to man. This leads to the conclusion that not every word in the Bible is to be accepted as literally and historically true, no more so than every word of a young child, although uttered sincerely and innocently, may be regarded as accurate or based on fact.

Every Word of the Bible Is Not the Revealed Will of God

If we accept the fundamentalist point of view and regard the entire Bible to be the revealed word of God, then we are confronted with inconsistencies, superstitions, and outmoded theological concepts that may not be rationally reconciled or spiritually harmonized with a mature faith or an adult conception of God. For example, to believe literally in the Bible as the source of inerrant divine truth, one must believe that:

The world was created in six days.
Eve was created out of Adam's rib.
Cain married a woman who had not been created.
Methuselah lived 969 years.
The sun stood still for Joshua.
The witch of Endor brought up the spirit of Samuel from the grave.
Elijah ascended in a heavenly chariot.
Moses brought forth water from a rock.
Jonah was swallowed by a whale, and lived.
Daniel was not attacked by voraciously hungry lions.
The ass of Balaam spoke to his master.

The scholars who have devoted a lifetime to biblical study are convinced that these are fables, legends, and myths. These were the stories taught at the dawn of history when imaginative and sensitive men tried to explain how the world was created, why women suffer in childbirth, why men have to work for their livelihood, and why people speak different languages. Just as an imaginative storyteller will create fantasies and embellish wondrous stories to give color and interest to the narrative, so did early man use his growing intelligence to recount fascinating tales of heroes and the events that happened in their lives. The value and glory of these accounts is not in their absorbing narrative, but rather in the yearning of man to probe the mysteries of the universe, to ponder the eternal "why," and to bring morality and God into a primitive world of brutality, ignorance, and pagan superstition.

It is incorrect to say that the whole of the Bible is the word of the living God, just as it is incorrect to assume that the mere reading of a page of the Bible will guarantee spiritual inspiration and religious conviction. How do the following passages from the Bible contribute to the strength of faith, or enhance the beauty of holiness?

"These are the generations of Shem. Shem was a hundred years old, and begot Arpachshad two years after the flood. And Shem lived after he begot Arpachshad five hundred years, and begot sons and daughters.

"And Arpachshad lived five and thirty years, and begot Shelah. . . . And Shelah lived thirty years, and begot Eber. . . . And Eber lived four and thirty years, and begot Peleg. . . . And Peleg lived thirty years, and begot Reu. . . . And Reu lived two and thirty years, and begot Serug" (Genesis 11. 10-19).

As a chronological genealogy it has interest, but is it inspiring, elevating, and the revealed Word of God? How will the above passage of "begots" afford inspiration to the dejected spirit and how will the following commandment sustain those in need of religious strength?

"These ye may eat of all that are in the waters: Whatsoever hath fins and scales may ye eat; and whatever hath not fins and scales ye shall not eat; it is unclean unto you" (Deuteronomy 14. 9-10).

Will the above passage feed those who are hungry for the Word of the living God?

A man is compelled by his vow to sacrifice his own daughter. Is this the revealed will of God, or a story from a primitive, ignorant, and infantile period of biblical history?

"And Jephthah vowed a vow unto the Lord, and said: 'If Thou wilt indeed deliver the children of Ammon into my hand, then it shall be, that whatsoever cometh forth of the doors of my house to meet me, when I return in peace from the children of Ammon, it shall be the Lord's, and I will offer it up as a burnt-offering'" (Judges 11. 30-31).

This *is* in the Bible, but what religious lesson may be derived from this specific passage that will enable a person to sanctify life with holiness and religious fervor?

A minister urged a distraught woman who was emotionally disturbed to read the Bible. She asked, "What part of the Bible?" He said, "Open the Bible anywhere, and there are inspiration and help for you." What if she, in trustful obedience, turned to the 15th chapter of Leviticus, verses 19-20: "And if a woman have an issue, and her issue in her flesh be blood, she shall be in her impurity seven days; and whosoever toucheth her shall be unclean until the even. And everything that she lieth upon in her impurity shall be unclean. And whosoever toucheth her bed shall wash his clothes, and bathe himself in water, and be unclean until the even." Will such a passage help her to gain a mature religious faith?

One should read the Bible selectively and with discriminate judgment. The Bible is not a cure-all for the spiritual ailments of mankind. There are portions of it that are incomparably beautiful and inspiring beyond anything to be found elsewhere in literature. To read the Bible without guidance, however, is frequently unrewarding and occasionally dangerous.

Many a thinking youth has turned away from religion and God because of the assumption that every word of the Bible is the literal word and will of God. To read the 31st chapter of Numbers as a manifestation of the will of God is to equate God with cruelty, vengeance, and barbaric blood lust. No matter what is recorded in the Bible, is he to believe that "the Lord spoke unto Moses, saying: 'Avenge the children of Israel of the Midianites.' . . . And they warred against Midian, as the Lord commanded Moses; and they slew every male." Is he to believe that Moses was speaking in the name of God when he commanded: "Now therefore kill every male among the little ones, and kill every woman that hath known man by lying with him. But all the women children that have not known man by lying with him, keep alive for yourselves"? This is what primitive man believed about the will of God. God was made to conform to the social, cultural, and military patterns and stereotypes of man's milieu. But this is the will of man, and not the divine revelation of God.

Were I to believe that God commanded the destruction of His children as indicated in the 31st chapter of the Book of Numbers, I would reject and despise God as I would any other bloodthirsty savage. I would devote my life to erasing the name of God from the vocabulary of man. Where is the God of mercy, compassion, and infinite love taught by Judaism and Christianity? Where are the religious inspiration and the spiritual exaltation that the fundamentalists claim may be found by simply reading the Bible? To agree with the fundamentalist doctrine that every word of the Bible is the direct revelation of the will of God is to agree that God commanded the merciless destruction of the Midianites as detailed in the 31st chapter of Numbers, and established the pattern for genocide and mass extermination.

The fundamentalist approach is a sincere but futile and infantile effort to justify the divine authority of Holy Scripture as irrefutable and unalterable. In essence, it is religious blasphemy and a scathing indictment of a God of Love. Such an approach detracts from the strength of religious faith, and condones ignorance, superstition, and misunderstanding. It yields to theological dogma in a manner whereby verses are twisted and tortured out of context to substantiate ecclesiastical doctrine. How laborious has been the effort to explain in religious terminology that which was never meant to be accepted as the word of God but which was originally set forth as mythical, allegorical, moralistic, and homiletical literature!

If a secularist were to declare that man is neither more nor less than any other animal, he would be excoriated as a freethinker, atheist, blasphemer, and negator of Scripture. And yet, such a statement is to be found in Scripture itself, in the 3rd chapter of the Book of Ecclesiastes. The gentle cynic (regarded traditionally as Solomon) states: "I said in my heart: 'It is because of the sons of men, that God may sift them, and that they may see that they themselves are but as beasts.' For that which befalleth the sons of men befalleth beasts; even one thing befalleth them; as the one dieth, so dieth the other; yea, they have all one breath; so that man hath no pre-eminence above a beast; for all is vanity. All go unto one place; all are of the dust, and all return to the dust. Who knoweth the spirit of man whether it goeth upward, and the spirit of the beast whether it goeth downward to the earth?" (18-21)

If we are to regard the Book of Ecclesiastes as divinely revealed, the immutable word of God, then we must equate man with any other animal. The Book of Daniel gives assurance of resurrection and everlasting life. Yet the Book of Ecclesiastes contends that there is no more immortality for man than there is for the beast of the field. Such contrast reveals the danger of regarding every word of the Bible as literally true. The evidence strongly favors the claims that Holy Scripture is a cumulative account of man's progressive advance from an infantile religion to a more mature faith.

Not all the personalities of the Bible are worthy of emulation. That these names are recorded is hardly a passport to worth or nobility. Cain kills his brother. The daughters of Lot commit incest with their father. Jacob dissembles and cheats. David lusts after Bathsheba and perpetrates one of the most vicious murders in biblical history. Saul attempts to kill his son-in-law. Jephthah sacrifices his daughter. Peter denies Jesus. Thomas was a doubter. How then can the reading of such accounts of villainous actions enrich the soul? By what strange reasoning can one conclude that every word of the Bible is literally true?

It is difficult to believe that God would reveal that the world was created in six days and thus communicate as divine truth what geology, anthropology, and cosmography with indisputable evidence attest to be a scientific error. Zoologists would find it difficult to give credence to a speaking serpent or a talking ass. The ten plagues may be explained historically and even scientifically, but it is difficult to reconcile a God of Love with a deity who would destroy the first-born of the Egyptians to demonstrate His power and expedite the exodus of the children of Israel. The dividing of the Red Sea may have a perfectly feasible explanation, but the real miracle is a slave rabble and undisciplined mob advancing from servitude to the heights of Sinai. The miracle of the bush that burned but was not consumed fades in importance before the miracle of organic power in a leaf, the development of the human embryo in the womb of the mother, and the redemptive power of a human tear.

The mere reading of the Bible in itself does not convey a mystic power or enable the reader to choose the good life. There is no magic in the Bible that may be converted into a source of power, prosperity, and success. To believe in the Bible is a poor substitute for belief in the living God. Actually, it is ridiculous to make the statement: "I believe in the Bible." Do we believe in the Bible or do we believe in God? What does this mean—to believe in the Bible? That it exists? That it is the Bible? That it is, in totality, the revealed word of God? That everything in the Bible is' true? Is it enough to believe in the Bible without believing in its moral truths and ethical precepts? Is it enough to believe in the moral truths and ethical precepts revealed through the Bible without applying them to life, without using them, living by them? A rabbinical student said to his teacher, "My teacher, I have gone through the Bible twenty times."

"That is gratifying to know, my son," replied the teacher. "You have gone through the Bible twenty times, but how many times has the Bible gone through you?"

To know the Bible is important. To believe in the moral laws of God revealed in selected portions of Holy Scripture is important. It is even more important to live by these moral laws, and permit the radiance of God reflected through the Bible to bring light into darkness, truth where there is error, understanding where there is prejudice, and love where there is hate. The reading or study of the Bible must never be a substitute for religious action.

One need not be a biblical scholar to conclude that the Bible is the greatest and the holiest religious document ever bequeathed to man. But at the same time one does not need the advanced knowledge of higher criticism or archaeological discovery to realize that there are discrepancies, inconsistencies, scientific error, and primitive thought revealed in the collection of sacred books we call the Bible.

A rational, modernist approach to the Bible need not detract from religious faith, nor must it necessarily eliminate divine truth from Scripture. Quite to the contrary, a mature understanding of the Bible contributes to an awareness of the divine content of Scripture and enhances the appreciation of the Bible not only because it is so indescribably divine, but also because, in part, it is so magnificently human.

The intent of the critical study of the Bible is not to engage in iconoclastic demolition of that which is sacred. The ultimate objective is to remove the dross and the gloss, to evaluate in historical perspective, to point up the eternal message of living faith revealed through the Bible, by. first distinguishing between the transitory and the eternal, history and myth, the true and the false. We should know what not to believe about the Bible before proceeding to an examination of the abiding contribution of Scripture to a mature and meaningful religious faith. There should be also a cogent awareness of how that which is divine has been debased by those who would make of the Bible a fetish, a sacred talisman, a magical formula, without understanding it or living by its teachings.

7

What Not to Believe About Immortality

Through me you pass into the city of woe;
Through me you pass into eternal pain. . . .
All hope abandon, ye who enter here.
—DANTE, *Divine Comedy*, Canto III

The Hope of Eternal Life

Nowhere does respectable religion appear more infantile than in the kindergarten concept of immortality that suggests an ambivalent God oscillating between divine wrath and love as He punishes His erring children with the tortures of hell and rewards His obedient children with the bliss of heaven.

From the dawn of human thought to the present day, countless millions have clung tenaciously to the hope of eternal life beyond the grave. Because of this hope, born out of the "will to live," they have been theologically seduced by the alluring promise of a heavenly bliss beyond all human understanding. Because of this hope they have been terrorized by the ominous threat of eternal hell and damnation. Like a shiny new toy, the promise of heaven has been held before man as an inducement for being good. The consequences of disobedience, the wages of sin are meted out by a divine bogyman as a deferred payment in an afterlife of eternal punishment in hell. Such childlike eagerness for reward and the infantile dread of punishment have been exploited by medicine men, shamans, religious functionaries, and ecclesiastical bodies for the purpose of securing absolute commitment and unquestioning obedience.

The Doctrine of Resurrection

Closely identified with the hope of eternal life is the doctrine of resurrection. Sir James Frazer, in *The Golden Bough*, offers conclusive evidence that the primitive belief in resurrection is associated with the birth and death of the gods in the recurring seasonal cycle of the year. He writes of Attis, Osiris, Dionysus, and other pagan deities who died only to be resurrected and reborn in relationship to the inexorable transition from autumn to winter and winter to spring.

"In the resurrection of Osiris," writes Frazer, "the Egyptians saw the pledge of a life everlasting for themselves beyond the grave. They believed that every man would live eternally in the other world if only his surviving friends did for his body what the gods had done for the body of Osiris. . . . The thousands of inscribed and pictured tombs that have been opened in the valley of the Nile prove that the mystery of the resurrection was performed for the benefit of every dead Egyptian; as Osiris died and rose again from the dead, so all men hoped to arise like him from death to life eternal."[1] From the death and resurrection of their great god the Egyptians drew not only their support and sustenance in this life but also their hope of life eternal beyond the grave.

Frazer also points out the association of the Corn Goddess at Eleusis with the mystery of death and the hope of a blissful immortality. "The reasoning that satisfied Saint Paul and has brought comfort to untold thousands of sorrowing Christians, standing by the deathbed or the open grave of their loved ones, was good enough to pass muster with the ancient pagans, when they too bowed their heads under the burden of grief, and with the taper of life burning low in the socket, looked forward into the darkness of the unknown. Therefore we do no indignity to the myth of Demeter and Persephone —one of the few myths in which the sunshine and clarity of the Greek genius are crossed by the shadow and mystery of death—when we trace its origin to some of the most familiar, yet eternally affecting aspects of nature, to the melancholy gloom and decay of autumn and to the freshness, the brightness, and the verdure of spring."[2]

Although Hebrew Scripture does not emphasize the doctrine of resurrection, rabbinic Judaism accepted this doctrine as a fundamental of the Jewish faith, teaching that anyone who denies resurrection excludes himself from the category of Judaism. The Sadducees denied resurrection, but the Pharisees affirmed their belief in the resurrection as a fundamental dogma. In the extracanonical Apocalypses,

[1] New York, The Macmillan Company, 1922, p. 367.
[2] Ibid., p. 398.

the author of the Slavonic Book of Enoch believed in a resurrection of spirits without a body, asserting that the righteous are clothed in the glory of God.

The idea of resurrection is indicated in the verse from Isaiah 26.19: "Thy dead shall live; my dead bodies shall arise." The vision of the prophet Ezekiel concerning the dry bones indicates that the idea of resurrection was familiar to the Jewish people. Orthodox Jews to this day repeat the benediction in daily prayer praising God who "revivest the dead." Reform Judaism, unwilling to accept either the concept of a netherworld or the resurrection of the dead, has changed the wording of the prayer to praise God "who has implanted within us immortal life."

The Jewish hope in the resurrection of the dead at the time of the coming of the Messiah provided the basis for the Christian belief in the resurrection of Jesus. The New Testament asserts that Jesus came forth from the tomb, was resurrected on the third day, revealed himself and ascended into heaven. At the time of the second coming of Jesus, "the dead in Christ shall rise first," and believers will be resurrected to life eternal.

The belief in resurrection for the saved is not something that comes to us from the past. It is an integral requisite of fundamentalist Christian doctrine today. Only those who accept Jesus as the Christ will be resurrected; all others will be doomed to eternal punishment and suffering in hell.

Immortality

In the Hebrew Scripture, eternal life was first ascribed exclusively to God and to celestial beings who "take also of the tree of life, and eat, and live for ever" (Genesis 3.22). By being driven out of the Garden of Eden man was deprived of the opportunity of eating the food of immortality.

According to Scripture man's original destiny was to live forever. The divinely elected, like Enoch and Elijah, ascended to heaven alive. This was a presentiment of a cherished hope for the time when God would destroy death forever.

For centuries the Jewish people believed with the Babylonians and the Phoenicians that the dead continue to exist in the shadowy nether world called Sheol,[3] a world of silence and oblivion. The wicked are destined for Sheol, but the souls of the righteous go directly to God. The threats and promises of retribution, however, apply to this world, and do not suggest judgment in the world to come. Biblical thought is consistent with the exclamation of King Hezekiah: "For the nether world cannot praise Thee; death cannot celebrate Thee. The living, the living, he shall praise Thee, as I do this day" (Isaiah 14. 15-19; Ezekiel 32. 21-30).

The belief in the immortality of the soul entered into Jewish thought from Hellenistic philosophy, principally the teachings of Plato. Plato in turn was influenced by the Orphic and Eleusinian mysteries which are made up of Babylonian and Egyptian views depicting Minos and Rhadamanthus as rulers of Hades.

The Hebrew Scriptures abound in contradictions about the existence of life after death. Isaiah, Ezekiel, Daniel, and many of the Psalmists affirm the belief in immortality, while Ecclesiastes insists that there is no hope for eternal life. Rabbinic Judaism, particularly Talmud Judaism, insists upon the belief in eternal life as a fundamental of Judaism.

Christian theology is categorical in its conviction of eternal life; but, as in the matter of resurrection, so is eternal life contingent upon salvation through Jesus, the Christ.

What do you have to do to be saved and inherit eternal life? This is the question that is basic to the fundamental doctrine of salvation. It has been declared that, according to the teaching of Paul, "There is neither Jew nor Greek, there is neither bond nor free, there is neither male nor female: for ye are all one in Christ Jesus. And if ye be Christ's, then are ye Abraham's seed, and heirs according to the promise" (Galatians 3. 28-29). While this appears to teach the universalism of God's love, in reality it doesn't, because of the explicit condition Paul imposes, namely, "if ye be Christ's." Paul's universalism applies to professing Christians only, and of them only to those who profess correctly, that is, in harmony with Paul's ideas. All other men are damned. To put the statement in Jesus' own words, "He that believeth not is condemned already" (John 3.18).

[3] Sheol—underneath the earth, the point of greatest distance from heaven. The idea of Sheol is also found in Assyro-Babylonian descriptions of the state of the dead found in the myths concerning Ishtar's descent into Hades.

The position of Roman Catholicism is similar because of its doctrine, "Extra ecclesiam nulla salus" (Outside the Church there is no salvation). This is an exclusiveness that belies the universalism of God's love. It suggests that a man must believe according to a specified Church doctrine in order to be saved.

The Most Important Question of Life

The following tract was distributed by the Berean Gospel Distributors, Inc., Indianapolis, Indiana:

"My friend: I am asking you the most important question of life. Your joy or your sorrow for all ETERNITY depends upon it. The question is: Are you saved? It is not if you are a member of some church, but, Are you SAVED? It is not how good you are, but ARE YOU SAVED? No one can enjoy the blessings of God or go to heaven without being saved. . . .

"There is NO CHANCE to be saved unless you come to realize you are a SINNER.

"Because you are a sinner, you are CONDEMNED TO DIE.

"This means separation from God, in HELL, FOREVER."

A Jewish Evangelism Clinic in Nashville, organized to "save the 3,000 lost Jewish Souls" of the city, included in its program instruction for Jewish Home Visitations. Although kindly motivated, in effect the salesmen of salvation were asking Jews to forsake the religion of their fathers and become traitors to their faith. The implication of such a visit is that the Jewish faith is not only antiquated, meaningless, and false, but that it is dangerous because, in maintaining his faith, a Jew subjects himself to the certainty of eternal punishment in hell. The implication of such conversion efforts to the effect that there is only one truth, one way, one Church, and one formula for salvation is patently juvenile, and is antithetical to the realization of a mature, rational, and liberal faith.

While one may be impressed with the zeal of those who attempt to convert and save the unbelievers, it is difficult, nonetheless, to understand how they can be so presumptuous and theologically arrogant in their dogmatic convictions, knowing that so many of the supposedly saved are far from living up to the teachings of Jesus. Should not the zealous members of this fundamentalist denomination be devoting their efforts to strengthening their own brethren in the teachings of their Savior, instead of canvassing for Jewish converts? Do they think they are so pure, so perfect, so saintly that they can afford the time and the effort to turn from saving those of their own faith to convert the lost Jews? Aren't Christians lost who fail to live up to the preachments and precepts of their own faith? What a mockery of religion to save others when Negroes of that same denomination are not permitted to worship with their fellow Christians!

At a time when racial prejudice is distorting the minds and hearts of countless thousands of their own denomination; at a time when high schools, churches, and synagogues are being dynamited; at a time when eighty ministers of Little Rock, Arkansas, many of whom were members of this same fundamentalist denomination, were declaring publically: "We believe that integration is contrary to the will of God. Our beliefs are not based on prejudice or bias, but on sound Bible interpretation, while integration is based on the *false* theory of the 'universal Fatherhood of God and the universal brotherhood of man'"—at such a time isn't it the most blatant arrogance for those of this fundamentalist denomination to turn away from the ignorance, the bigotry, and the prejudice in their own ranks to save the three thousand lost Jewish souls of Nashville from eternal damnation?

It is shocking to learn that a group of ministers will deny the Fatherhood of God and the brotherhood of man, but it is even more disturbing to recognize that in the twentieth century the concept of damnation and hell is promulgated by respectable and responsible religious denominations seeking to save those who do not share their beliefs.

God Damn You to Hell

The above is not only a colloquial curse, it is also a manifestation of a theological doctrine that makes God a divine Judge who relegates the wicked to suffering in hell.

Jonathan Edwards insisted: "The damned shall be tormented in the presence of the glorified saints. . . . The view of the misery of the damned will double the ardor of the love and gratitude of the saints in heaven."

Perhaps when he finished his sermon, the congregation sang Isaac Watts' hymn:

> "What bliss will fill the ransomed souls,
> When they in glory dwell,
> To see the sinner as he rolls,
> In quenchless flames of hell."

Dante Alighieri's *Divine Comedy*, which was originally entitled "Commedia," describes a journey through hell, up the mountain of purgatory, and through the revolving heavens into the presence of God. Although Dante's description of hell has been literally embodied in Church doctrine it is a graphic example of what not to believe about immortality.

Accompanied by Virgil, his guide, Dante passes through the gates of hell to witness the wretchedness of souls who passed their time in apathy and indifference, "sorely stung by wasps and hornets, which bedewed their cheeks with blood mixed with tears, dropp'd to their feet, and by disgustful worms was gather'd there." He sees the souls of those who lived virtuously but are being punished for lack of baptism. The suffering of the sinful surpass adequate description as carnal sinners are tossed about ceaselessly in the dark air by the furious winds. Gluttons lying in the mire are under a continual and heavy storm of hail, snow, and discolored water, with Cerberus barking over them with his threefold throat and rending them piecemeal. Heretics are punished in tombs burning with intense fire. Those who have committed violence against their neighbors are tormented in a river of blood. Suicides are changed into trees adorned with harpies chased and torn by black female mastiffs. Those who have sinned against God, nature, and art are tormented by flakes of fire eternally showering down upon them. Seducers are scourged by demons; speculators are plunged into boiling pitch. Dragons breathing fire pursue blasphemers. Gossips and heretics have their limbs maimed or divided in different ways.

Dante proceeds from hell to purgatory to paradise where he beholds bliss, ecstasy, and the eternal light. He ascends unto the seventh heaven as he utilizes his poetry for polemics against Catholicism, papacy, and clergy. In the ninth heaven he beholds the nine choirs of angels, which gives him an opportunity to condemn theologians and preachers who substitute their convictions for the pure word of the Gospel. At last he beholds Ruth (ancestress of the Messiah), Rachel, Sarah, Judith, and Rebecca who dwell with Christ and the Virgin Mary, and as mortal man he is privileged to behold the mystery of the trinity and the union of man with God.

Dante in a Gray Flannel Suit

It is difficult to believe that a rational human being living in the twentieth century would give credence to this medieval miasma redolent with the sulphuric fumes emanating from such an ignorant, bedeviled, obscene concept of hell. This is not an anachronistic survival of an ancient, discredited doctrine; but, as a tract that was recently sent to my desk reveals, this concept of hell is preserved and perpetuated in contemporary theology. As we compare the following with the writings of Dante, we can understand why so many intelligent, thinking people are turning their minds and hearts away from kindergarten religion.

"You may say 'I do not believe in Hell' but my friend, two minutes in Hell amid the weeping, wailing and gnashing of teeth, will change your mind. When you realize then, as every one in Hell realizes today, that THE BIBLE IS THE WORD OF GOD; that you are a sinner, that Christ died for you, and that you could have been saved had you believed and accepted Him as your personal Savior, you will cry aloud in agony, as you weep and wail and gnash your teeth. 'Fool that I was, TOO LATE, TOO LATE.' There are no unbelievers in Hell, but they believed—TOO LATE. There is no escape—they would give all they ever had to again have YOUR opportunity to believe—but it is TOO LATE. You may say you do not believe all this, but the mere fact that you do not believe it does not alter the facts. THE BIBLE IS TRUE. WHO ARE THOU THAT REPLIEST AGAINST GOD? The Bible describes the place of future punishment for sinners and unbelievers to be: 'A lake of fire' (Rev. 20:10-15)—'A place of torment' (Luke 16:22-24)—'A place where lost souls never die and the fire is not quenched' (Mark 9:43-48)—'A place of weeping, wailing and gnashing of teeth' (Matt. 25:30) (Matt. 8:12) (Matt. 24:51)—'A place where sinners drink of the wine of God's wrath' (Rev. 14:10)—'A place where the smoke of their torment ascendeth up forever and ever' (Rev. 14:11). The responsibility of spending eternity in the LAKE OF FIRE AND BRIMSTONE is yours and YOURS ALONE. GOD LOVES YOU—CHRIST DIED FOR YOU. OH, WON'T YOU BELIEVE IT, AND ACCEPT HIM TODAY AS YOUR SAVIOR?

"Do not let anyone deceive you that you can be saved and go to heaven in any other way than the Bible teaches. There are many deceptions and false religions in the world today. Joining some church, trying to be good by your own good works, good morals, OR ANY OTHER BELIEF will not save us.

"After you are saved, then follow your Lord in water baptism, attend regularly some good, spiritual, fundamental church of your choice; enjoying the worship of God and the fellowship of Christian people of like faith."

The author of such a tract—sincerity, conviction, and good intentions notwithstanding—substantiates the statement of Diderot: "Lost at nightfall in a forest, I have but a feeble light to guide me. A stranger happens along. 'Blow out your candle,' he says, 'and you will see your way better.' That stranger is a theologian." Diderot's strictures against theologians suggest a false generalization. In this particular instance, however, a stranger to mature religion asks us to blow out the candle of reason in order to find our way through the dark forest of ignorance in quest of the living God.

Having extinguished the light of reason, the stranger would have us accept, not a God, but a supernatural monster who would commit man to suffering in hell because of his misdeeds. Moreover, he would not behold the Christian Christ in the perspective of love, but would gaze upon him as the son of God who calmly accepts the anguish of men, women, and children duly and officially relegated to hell. Where is the Jesus who forgave sins and sinners? Where is the Jesus who said, "Father, forgive them; for they know not what they do"? Such a tract is not only a blasphemy of God, a rape of reason, and an affront to liberal theology, but an insult to the sanctity of the Christian faith.

How is it possible to reconcile the concept of a heavenly Father, a God of compassion and love with the doctrine of eternal suffering in hell? Are we to believe that God damns a man to everlasting torment because he does not accept a creed formulated by ecclesiastical fiat? If we are, then who is to blame those who reject such a concept of immortality as irrational, infantile, and barbaric, and summarily repudiate religion?

Only the most extreme and fanatical fundamentalist can honestly subscribe to a theology of torment and agony for the damned. Undoubtedly some will interpret this symbolically to denote a hell on earth for those who disobey the moral commandments of God. Others may agnostically concede the possibility that there may be punishment for sins in the mystery of the world to come, but hold the torments of hell described by Dante and promulgated by the neo-Dantean writers of our day as literary effusions of an imaginative and possibly psychotic mind, rather than the revealed will of a compassionate and loving God.

The concept of hell has no place in a liberal, mature religious faith. It is inconsistent with reason, and constitutes an unspeakable blasphemy against God. A heavenly Father who damns is not worthy of the love of His children. To exploit God as a theological bogyman to frighten the ignorant and the naïve is inimical to the belief in a God of love. How I wish that we could expunge the word "fear" from the vocabulary of religion! "Fear" is a mistranslation of the Hebrew word "yiroh," which means "reverence." Man should revere God, not fear Him. The goal of the religiously mature is to be God-loving and God-revering rather than God-fearing.

A young Christian woman of college age was sent to me for counseling. She was convinced that she was doomed to hell because she had committed an act of immorality. She believed that she was irrevocably doomed to eternal damnation. A psychiatrist had attempted to help her, but recognizing that her problem was basically theological, he sent her to me for religious therapy. The young woman had refused to eat and was gradually starving herself. She refused to discuss her problem beyond the categorical and oft-repeated statement, "I have sinned and must suffer in hell throughout all eternity." All efforts to draw her out to the point where she would benefit from emotional catharsis failed. The counselor's assurance that God is love was met with stony silence. She shrugged away Heine's statement that "it's God's business to forgive." Finally, the question, "Have you told your father about this?" seemed to motivate a response. She said that she had told her father the whole story.

"How did he react?" asked the counselor.

"He was upset, shocked, and grief-stricken," she replied.

"But did he ever forgive you?" the counselor persisted.

She said: "Yes, my father loves me, and he forgave me; but God will never, never forgive me for what I have done."

"Suppose your father had it within his power to make you suffer for your sin, not for a day or a week or a year, but through all eternity. Would he do it?" I asked.

Exasperated, the girl retorted forcefully: "I told you, my father loves me. I'm his child. What father would want his child to suffer?" She paused, struck with a new insight. "Could this mean," she asked, "that since God is my heavenly Father, He will forgive me too?"

Gradually, she came to realize that if a father of flesh and blood, bound by mortal limitations, could forgive his child, a heavenly Father of love and compassion could also forgive His erring child, and receive her repentance, no matter how grievous the sin or how gross or immoral the act. While this young woman had heretofore referred to God as a heavenly Father, in reality she thought of Him as a vengeful, adamant, stern, and unforgiving executioner and Grand Inquisitor of the most horrendous torture chamber ever conceived by man.

Even though this young woman was twenty years of age, she had not grown up beyond the kindergarten religion she had accepted as a child. In time she recognized that it is impossible to reconcile the mature belief in a God of love with the juvenile concept of hell and damnation. There are many people who are like her—trapped in a snare of religious infantilism, their days haunted by inchoate terror, and their nights filled with phantoms of fear.

The fear of hell is not only juvenile; it is also irrational. If we contend that "dust returns to dust and the soul to God who gave it," then we must conclude that the body does not persist in an afterlife. If there is no body, how is it possible for spirit, the nonmaterial essence of Divinity, to experience physical pain and torment? There can be no sensation of physical pain without the stimulation of ganglia and nerve endings. Dante's conception of hell may be fascinating literature, but it is manifestly irrational theology—unless we are willing to concede that the body descends into hell replete with a functioning nervous system.

The Bliss of Heaven

By the same token, and by force of the same argument, if a body does not persist into hell to experience pain, a body does not persist into heaven to experience pleasure. In order to experience the physical bliss of mortal appetite and sensual delight, there must be the erogenous zones correlated with anatomical structure and nerve response.

In a questionnaire of children of kindergarten age, distributed by the writer, the query, "What do you think heaven is like?" elicited the following answers: Sitting on a cloud playing with angels. Having as much candy as I want to eat. Not having to go to sleep at night. Listening to television all day long. Having all the toys I want. Flying through the clouds with wings. Playing a harp. No taking of baths. Being rocked to sleep by beautiful fairies. Seeing my Grandmother who is in heaven. Eating cake, ice cream, and pie, and never being forced to eat what I don't like. Wading through ponds without shoes. Never being sick. Angels carrying me on their soft wings.

The same questionnaire given to a group of adults produced the following answers: Seeing my mother and father again. Not having to work. Flying through the clouds with wings. Not having physical pain, but experiencing eternal bliss. No worries. Being fed delicious food. Doing what I want to without interference. An eternal sleep without dreams. The question is silly because nobody knows. Just being with God. A life without sinfulness. I don't know because I haven't thought much about the next life. Being a single man again. Sitting near the throne of God.

The responses of the children of kindergarten age and of those classified as chronological adults differ but little. Both emphasize the absence of pain and the blissfulness of sensory appetite. Regardless of age grouping there is a clear indication of a lack of maturity in the concept of the afterlife. The "pie in the sky bye and bye" belief in heaven indicates a childishness and a religious infantilism that has been perpetuated beyond reason.

Both concepts, punishment in hell and reward in heaven, reveal the need for theological enlightenment. The prevalence of the kindergarten doctrine of immortality not only suggests, but cries out for a revolutionary rethinking of unchallenged dogmas, a critical reevaluation of theological beliefs, and a radical excision of ignorance, bigotry, irrational blasphemy, magic and superstition from respectable religion, in order to pioneer into new spiritual frontiers and advance toward the realization of a mature and rational faith.

II

Toward a Radical Faith

《 》

8

The Requisites for Religious Maturity

Religion does ill if it clings to old interpretations of human life simply because it has built these into revered institutions and practices.—H. A. OVERSTREET

The Semantics of Religion

Book I of this volume attempted a reverent demolition of antiquated, respectable, and juvenile concepts of religion in order to permit the building of a rational faith that will help us to bring God into our lives and into our world. Book II has as its purpose a positive exposition of the theological beliefs and religious practices that will help us to progress toward a more mature faith.

Undoubtedly, some readers have been annoyed and others outraged by chapters of this book that seem to indicate a blasphemous disrespect for respectable religion. Cherished theological beliefs, as beloved childhood fantasies, are not subjected to evaluation without resulting in a painful reaction of resistance and hostility. This suggests a consideration of the semantics of religion—our emotional reactions to religious terms and concepts to which we have been favorably or unfavorably conditioned.

Two men may argue and quarrel over religion without pausing to define what they mean by the term "religion." Men may sacrifice for religion, devote their lives to religion, withdraw from the world for religion, and even die for religion without ever thinking through clearly and rationally what the term really means. So intense are our reactions to the word "religion" that we fight "holy wars," enter upon "bloody crusades," foment hate, intensify rivalry, and despise our fellow man in the name of the very religion that sets forth peace, love, self-abnegation, charity, mercy, and brotherhood as its definitive goals.

The very terminology of religion evokes conflicting and disparate reactions in different people, depending upon their background, church affiliation, and theological convictions. The word "Jesus" may call forth thoughts of love, holiness, gentleness, mercy, and holiness to a devout Christian. The same word may evoke fearful thoughts of terror, violence, hatred, prejudice, and danger to the East European Jew whose home has been burned and whose family has been massacred by religious fanatics goaded to violence at the Easter season by the recitation of the story of the crucifixion of the Christian Savior with full blame directed to the Jews. "Immaculate conception" doesn't mean the same thing to a Protestant that it means to a Catholic. The word "Allah" may leave those of the Western world without apparent reaction. The same word may inspire the Moslem to heights of reverence. "Torah" is a precious word to a Jew, and evokes love, reverence, and a warm feeling of identification with the Jewish people. The same word leaves a Protestant, Catholic, and Moslem emotionally untouched.

Obviously, the religious terms that we use so frequently and familiarly do not mean the same thing to all people. Ask any group of people to set forth what they mean by "God," "religion," "holiness," "reverence," "revelation," "original sin," "baptism," "salvation," and "faith," and we shall receive a multiplicity of reactions, definitions, and meanings—and yet we argue, debate, and quarrel over these terms with the assumption that they mean the same thing to all people.

A requisite of religious maturity is the ability to assess and evaluate what we mean by the terms we use without permitting our subjective feelings to prejudge, or allowing them to impede the quest for the knowledge of God and our search for religious truth.

What Do We Mean by Religion?

On September 15, 1682, Cotton Mather addressed a letter to "Ye aged and beloved John Higginson." In this letter he informs Mr. Higginson: "There bee now at sea a shippe called ye Welcome, which has aboard an hundred or more of ye heretics and malignants called Quakers, with W. Penne, who is ye Chief Scampe at ye hedde of them. Ye General Court has accordinggely given secret orders to Master Malachi Huxett of ye brig Porposse, to waylaye ye said

Welcome slylie as near ye coast of Codde as may be and make captive ye said Penne and his ungodlie crew so that ye Lord may be glorified and not mocked on ye soil of this new countrie with ye heathen worshipe of these people. Much spoyle can be made by selling ye whole lotte to Barbadoes, where slaves fetch goode prices in rumme and sugar and we shall not only do ye Lord great service by punishing ye wicked but we shall make great gayne for his ministers and people. . . . Yours in ye bowels of Christ, Cotton Mather."[1]

Will you call this religion?

The theology of Jonathan Edwards, a dedicated and devout man of God, inspired him to declare: "The sight of hell torments will exalt the happiness of the saints forever. It will not only make them more sensible of the greatness and freeness of the grace of God in their happiness, but it will really make their happiness the greater, as it will make them more sensible of their own happiness; it will give them a more lively relish of it." This is what Jonathan Edwards meant by religion.

The Bishop of Trèves, Peter Binsfield, ordered the death of some 6,500 people. Nicholas Remy, Inquisitor of Lorraine, caused nearly 900 witches and sorcerers to be burned to death within fifteen years (1575-1590). He was a very conscientious man, and toward the end of his life he had a guilty feeling because he had spared a few children. "Is it right to spare baby vipers?" he asked.

The greatest blasphemy against religion is not the critical evaluation of its tenets, institutions, and beliefs, but the perversion and denial of its eternal message of love, mercy, and human sanctification. Let there be a thousand voices from heaven attesting to the divine sanction given to Moses' command to destroy the women and children of an enemy tribe, I will not believe this is religion or the will of God. Let there be a thousand voices from the academies of learning and the halls of science attesting to the falsehood of Deuteronomy 24.14, "Thou shalt not oppress a hired servant that is poor and needy, whether he be of thy brethren, or of thy strangers that are in thy land within thy gates," and I will believe this to be a requisite of religion.

Men have sanctioned war, ignorance, prejudice, witchcraft, sorcery,

[1] Thomas James Holmes, *Cotton Mather, A Bibliography of His Works* (Cambridge, Harvard University Press 1940), Vol. III, pp. 1299-1300. Although attributed to Cotton Mather, there is some doubt that he wrote the above letter.

divisiveness, poverty, injustice in the name of religion. Religious functionaries have countenanced inquisitions, councils of heresy, political chicanery, excommunication, and torture chambers for the unbeliever in the name of God. Pomponazzi was rejected from the church. Bruno was burned at the stake after years of imprisonment. Galileo, imprisoned by the Inquisition for daring to suggest that the earth moves around the sun, stubbornly insisted under his breath, "And yet it moves," even as he recanted.

Although there are over a thousand definitions of religion, a single definition cannot adequately set forth the total meaning, the ethical nuances, and the many-splendored connotations of that which must be experienced and practiced rather than defined.

The dictionary terms religion "Any system of faith or worship." Theodore Reik, the psychiatrist, believes that "religion is a source of pathogenic repressions and a great therapeutic step would be the abolition of religion." Alfred North Whitehead, the mathematician-philosopher, defines religion as "what man does with his solitariness." It has also been called "the cooperative quest for the good life," "the dynamics of social ethics," and "the consciousness of the sacred." Some have asserted that the simplest and most adequate definition is a part in the word itself, in that *religio* in Latin means "to bind." Thus religion will be a binding to a system of beliefs, or an identification with values. George Bernard Shaw succinctly designates religion as "that which binds men to one another, and irreligion is that which sunders." William James defined religion as "the feelings, acts and experiences of individual men in their solitude, so far as they apprehend themselves to stand in relation to whatever they may consider divine."

It is patently absurd to compact religion into a single definition when the devotees of religion differ so radically in their practices and beliefs. The fetish worship of the aborigines is not the same as the fundamentalist religion of Billy Graham. The Buddhist monk singing praises to Brahma, the divine Guru, is hardly to be compared with the High Church pageantry of Catholicism or the philosophical lecture of a Unitarian minister. Yet all of these are subsumed under the same term, religion.

The muezzin of the Mohammedan faith looks to the next world where the pious "eat and drink with good digestion, reclining on couches in rows, wed to large-eyed maids"—a concept of an afterlife hardly acceptable to puritans. Religion is generally and ubiquitously applied to the Sikhs, Jains, Taoists, Lamaistic Buddhists, Shakers, Dukhobors, Calvinists, Hottentots, Southern Baptists, Yemenite Jews, Jehovah's Witnesses, the devotees of T. S. Eliot and Ezra Pound, the disciples of the "I am" movement, the Greek Orthodox Church, the Ethical Culture Movement, Pantheism, Roman Catholicism, Christian Science, Reform Judaism, Seventh-day Adventists, and Druids, with each associating radically different practices with the same word, each bringing earnest convictions and sacred confusion to the same concept.

With this in mind it is manifestly incorrect to consider religion to be homogeneously constant or definable. Just as there is a difference between the vengeful volcanic God of the Kenite priest and the God of love envisaged by Hosea; just as there is a profound difference between the crassly selfish prayer of Jacob contracting with the Deity for personal protection and material security, and the psalmist's exalted plea, "Create in me a clean heart, O God"; so is there a difference between kindergarten, low, primitive, immature religion and high, elevated, prophetic, and mature religion.

Lower and Higher Religion

According to Professor T. M. Greene, "A religion can be said to be low or primitive in proportion as its beliefs are superstitious, its ritualistic practices magical, its basic orientation egocentric and anthropocentric rather than theocentric, its social precepts directed to conventional correctness rather than to inner spiritual righteousness, and its prevailing attitude arbitrarily authoritarian and dogmatic."

Mature or higher religion requires humility, tolerance, love, freedom, enlightenment, and morality. Its ritual has the purpose of educing from within men the divine potential for holiness, beauty, truth, and justice. Mature religion seeks to bind man to a belief in God that challenges him to become whole, to relate himself to his fellow man, his society, and the world in which he lives in order to sanctify life with holiness.

Mature religion distinguishes between religion and the institutions and the forms of religion, regarding institutions and forms, not as ends in themselves, but as the means to the achievement and the realization of ethical and moral objectives. Mature religion demarcates between the institutions that purport to represent God and speak *for* God, and the values that are inherently Godly. It is concerned primarily with the forms and the ritual that speak of and symbolize God, only to the extent that they symbolize the ideas and the ideals that enable men to experience God.

In the quest for God and the mature faith, we must make a distinction between the institutions and forms that presumably speak for and represent God, and the values and the teachings that we believe to be Godly and divinely ordained.

Not everything that is called religion is necessarily religious. Not every church building, whether a synagogue, mosque, church, or cathedral, serves the true purpose of religion, even though it be so consecrated.

Mature religion must be concerned with the elevation of man and is not limited to the elevation of man-made religious institutions. It rises above and beyond physical structures, and looks to the sacred purpose of the church, the synagogue, and the cathedral.

A parable from Jewish lore tells of Moses descending from Mount Sinai with the tablets of the law in his hands. When he approached the camp, thinking at first that he heard the noise of war, and beheld the children of Israel dancing around the golden calf, breaking the commandments, then the tablets fell from his hands and shattered into fragments on the ground below.

The rabbis, pondering this, asked, Was Moses right to drop the Ten Commandments even though he had provocation? After all, were they not the holy words of God? And they answered: When Moses descended from the mountaintop and saw the children breaking the commandments, then the letters, as it were, took flight and left the Ten Commandments and all that remained was stone, so heavy that the stone dropped from the hands of Moses. They proceeded to elaborate on this by rabbinical exegesis, teaching that when an institution that we call religious loses its true purpose and meaning and repudiates the basic teachings of the religious faith, then all that is left is a cold, heavy structure bereft of sanctity, holiness, and God, and that such a structure will in time be destroyed and shattered by its own indifference to the principles it espouses.

The purpose of higher or mature religion is to hold Church and Synagogue to the pursuit and implementation of the intrinsic moral ideals that relate to the sanctity of man and the holiness of life. It must protect organized religion from the tyranny of the trivial, the cult of conformity, the supremacy of ceremonial form over ethical principle, and the sacrifice of radical social action for sanctioned respectability.

Not every individual who is formally identified with respectable religion is necessarily religious. Conversely, not every individual who is formally castigated as irreligious is devoid of that which constitutes the attributes of higher religion. Abraham Lincoln belonged to no church, nor was he ever identified with institutional religion. Are we to say that he was not a religious man? Torquemada, the fifteenth century inquisitor who consigned thousands of so-called heretics and unbelievers to the fires of the auto-da-fé in Spain, regarded himself and was regarded as a devoutly religious man. A convicted murderer who claims to have "got religion" and who goes to his execution after repeating prayers with the prison chaplain assumes the status of a humble penitent. Was Galileo less religious when he stubbornly refused to recant his scientific convictions and was condemned as a heretic? Karl Marx, who devoted his life to the exploited masses, but whose followers perverted his teachings into a bloody communism, is called an enemy of religion. Friedrich Nietzsche, who permits Zarathustra to speak for him and declare "God is dead," was accorded the respectability of a bitter but religious prophet.

What do all of our labels, ritual, ecclesiastical divisiveness, and denominational differences mean to God? Does it make a great deal of difference to God whether His children worship Him in a church, synagogue, mosque, shrine, foxhole, or in the privacy of a room or in the solitude of the heart? Does it matter to God whether His children pray to Him in Hebrew, Greek, Latin, English, or Arabic? What difference does it make to God whether men find Him through the Bible, the Upanishads, Koran, the Tripitaka of the Buddhists, the Agmas of the Jains, the Granth Sahib of the Sikhs, the Tao Te Ching of the Chinese, or the Avesta of the Persians? What does it matter to God the names by which men call Him, the style and manner and mode of the ritual through which they seek Him, as long as they seek Him through the holy ideal of brotherhood, manifest their love for Him by service to His children, and rise above denominations to translate their faith into the language of morality that speaks with accents of Divinity, insisting that regardless of his color or his denominational label, or his religious faith, each individual must be cherished with tender solicitude and nurtured with loving kindness because man is a precious child of God, but little lower than the angels.

The Criteria of the Mature Faith

One of the more discerning psychologists who has evaluated the concept of religious maturity is G. W. Allport. He states that rigid and compulsive dogmatism, holier-than-thou intolerance, insatiable need for reassurance, obsessive ritualism, fear of unpardonable sin, and regressive dependence are immature religious attributes. In *The Individual and His Religion*[2] he lists the following requisites for religious maturity:

a. The maturely religious individual has insight into himself. He is self-critical.

b. The mature religion has a motivational force of its own. Religion is a goal to be sought for its own sake.

c. The mature religion imposes moral consequences. It inspires, influences, and motivates the behavior of the individual. The sincerity and intensity of his religious belief is attested to by his outward acts.

d. The mature religion is comprehensive. It relates all the facets of life not only to man, but to the Creator of man, who is outside man's immediate experience.

e. The mature religionist sees the relationship of experience to God, and looks upon life as an integrated pattern that demonstrates the relationship of its parts to one another.

f. The criterion of mature religion is the dynamism that makes man a persistent searcher after light and truth, with the recognition that the quest is a continuous and eternal one.

H. N. Wieman[3] and Erich Fromm have also attempted to establish criteria for measuring religious growth and maturity. Wieman

[2] New York, The Macmillan Company, 1950, p. 57.

[3] *Normative Psychology of Religion* (New York, Thomas Y. Crowell Company, 1935), p. 272.

lists six norms: (1) *worthfulness* of the objective of religious loyalty, (2) *completeness* of the loyalty, (3) *efficiency* in reaching the objective, (4) *sensitivity* in the selection of values, (5) *progression* of loyalties permitting higher aims to supersede, and (6) *social effectiveness* of the loyalty in activating and influencing society.

Erich Fromm distinguishes between authoritarian and humanistic religion. Authoritarian religion is derived from other people and tyrannizes over the impulses of the individual. Humanistic religion emerges from the creative forces within the individual himself, although it may never become entirely independent of social forces. To Erich Fromm, humanistic religion represents the fruition of religious maturity.

The criteria of religious maturity set forth by Allport, Wieman, and Fromm are cogently valid. It is essential, however, that we consider four other requisites of the mature faith. In order to achieve maturity, religion must be radical, rational, this-worldly and prophetic.

Religion Must Be Radical

The concept of religion as the chief contributor to "cultural lag" and the guardian of conservatism must be eradicated to permit the emergence of a mature religion that is essentially radical.

Many of us react with hostility to such terms as "radical," "revolutionary," and "progressive" because of a thought-controlled era that engendered a fear of communism, left-wingers, and fellow travelers. If we consider these terms without reference to the present mood and climate of reactionary political thought, we discover that they suggest valid and worthy concepts. The word "radical" means to get to the root of. Isn't this the purpose of mature religion, to get to the root of evil, bigotry, and ignorance in order to remove that which is obnoxious, unjust, and undesirable from society? Isn't it the objective of mature religion to seek the sources, the roots of love, reverence, holiness, mercy, and truth? Religion must get to the core of those factors that degrade man, that impede his progress, and that separate him from his God.

Maeterlinck in *Our Social Duty* summed up the difficulty that confronts the creative nonconformist when he wrote: "At every crossway on the road that leads to the future, each progressive spirit is opposed by a thousand men appointed to guard the past."

In every generation the religious iconoclast, the social reformer, the dreamer of radical dreams must contend with the mockery of the devotees of organized religion who sneer: Behold the dreamer of dreams. Let us rise up and slay him! Discourage him! Vilify him! Condemn him! Kill his dreams! Murder his ideas! They are dangerous to the established Church.

The great teachers of religion were radicals, rebels, and revolutionaries dedicated to spiritual progress. They too were castigated as "progressives." They were condemned as "troublers" and "disturbers of the peace." Abraham smashed at the idolatry and paganism of his age—and was despised as a radical. The children of Israel murmured against Moses even as he dedicated himself to the cause of freedom and the moral law. Elijah, Amos, Jeremiah, and Isaiah were castigated as radicals who departed from the conservative cult of the sacrificial system and, speaking in the name of God, demanded justice, fought for truth, and proclaimed the moral values required by a moral God. They were spat upon, ridiculed, mocked, imprisoned, and tortured because of their divine discontent and their sacred radicalism. Jesus followed in the prophetic tradition, and was despised as a revolutionary who insisted that man must get to the root of God's teachings. His objective was not to perpetuate cultural lag or conserve the values of established, popular, respectable religion. His was a radical religion for revolutionaries of the spirit, men and women who wanted to progress in the direction of God. And so, the dishonored list could continue to include Martin Luther, Savonarola, Wycliffe, John Huss, George Fox, John Wesley, Thomas Jefferson, Jan Masaryk, Voltaire, Emile Zola, and Mahatma Gandhi—all radicals, revolutionaries, and progressives.

The famous heresies of Church history bear witness to the resistance to respectable religion throughout the centuries. Even in our own nation there is considerable evidence to validate the fact that radicalism permeated the religious thinking of the pioneers and founders of our nation. The liberal religious views of Thomas Jefferson would be anathema to a large segment of our religious population in the United States today.[4] When Yale University was young, members

---

[4] Norman Cousins' *In God We Trust* discusses the religious views of the Founding Fathers in meticulous and fascinating detail.

of the Yale faculty, among them President Ezra Stiles himself, expressed views that would outrage respectable religion of twentieth century America. Leading members of the Harvard-trained clergy were Universalists and frequently Unitarians. Ralph Waldo Emerson, who influenced generations of thinking Americans, was an avowed Unitarian.

Even the Puritans rarely used the word "Trinity," although Trinity College, Cambridge, was the alma mater of the founders of Harvard. Moreover, the Puritans ignored such fundamental concepts as the divinity of Christ and rarely used the words "virgin birth" or Virgin Mary. The Puritans discarded, along with the saints, the entire system of Church holy days, including Christmas, Easter, and Pentecost.

Higher or mature religion summons mankind to return to the moral fervor and the rebellious spirit that characterized the prophets and leaders of the religions of the world. Such religious radicalism demands a bold and critical examination of the religious institutions, ritual, and concepts that are extolled, respected, and revered as sacred, untouchable and beyond mortal evaluation. The weak and the cowardly will shout "blasphemy." The conservative-minded will resist such efforts as sacrilegious. The high priests of respectable religion will denounce, mock, scorn, and excoriate those who dare to profane and enter the forbidden and hallowed holy of holies by their progressive religious thought and action. Despite the most formidable opposition and resistance, however, the followers of mature religion must persist, advance, pioneer into new and unexplored frontiers of faith. Such religious radicals as rebels in a godly cause will continue to devote their energies to the moral and ethical progress of man.

Religion Must Be Rational

The mature faith accepts the summons of God enunciated through Isaiah: "Come now, and let us reason together, saith the Lord" (Isaiah 1.18). That which reason declares to be false, untenable, and superstitious must be summarily rejected as antithetical to religion. While faith goes beyond reason to the unknown and unknowable, the mature faith cannot accept that which contradicts reason in the realm of the known and the knowable.

We can agree with Sydney J. Harris, who said: "The atheist who seriously studies religion in order to attack it is closer to the spirit of God than the bovine believer who supports religion because it is comfortable, respectable, and offers consolation without thought. If God's greatest gift to man is reason, then refusing to exercise reason is the greatest impiety."

To advocate a complete naturalism, however, is to eliminate the supernatural phenomenon of God. This would reduce religion to humanistic ethics devoid of divine sanction and divine authority. The mature faith accepts the proved claim of naturalism, but also holds to the belief in the supernaturalism of God, a God that is in the world and yet transcends it. The mature faith contemplates God as the supernatural Mystery of Mysteries, revealed in the glory and majesty of the natural universe, but it cannot accept miracles that transgress and ignore the laws of nature.

Since Pope Pius IX it has been a dogma binding upon all Catholics that not only Jesus but the Virgin herself was immaculately conceived. Pope Pius XII added the dogma of the Assumption of the Virgin: "We pronounce, declare and define to be a dogma revealed by God, that the Immaculate Mother of God, Mary, ever virgin, when the course of her life on earth was finished was taken up body and soul into heaven."

In November, 1955, the Vatican stated that it is true that Pope Pius XII had a vision of Jesus Christ during his illness of the previous winter. This occurred on December 2, 1954, when he was reciting the prayer "Anima Christi" (Soul of Christ). It was from that moment, said the weekly illustrated Oggi magazine, that the pope began to improve in such a sudden manner that many people considered it a miracle.

Frederico Cardinal Tedeschini, archpriest of St. Peter's basilica, three years prior to the vision told a throng at the Portuguese shrine of Fátima that the pope four times during the holy year of 1950 had "seen the life of the sun under the hand of the Virgin Mary" and that the sun "had transmitted mute but eloquent messages to the vicar of Christ."

The mature faith must reject all such dogma, apparitions, and mystical visions as irrational and incredible. Moreover, any belief, religious institution, or rite that does violence to reason must be categorized as a cherished but untenable accretion of kindergarten religion.

To invoke the name of the Deity for superstition, supernatural visions, magical incantations, and theurgic formulas is to bear false witness to the intellectual love of a God of Supreme Intelligence.

Any Church doctrine, dogma, or tenets of belief that are contradicted by reason, science, and empiric knowledge must be denied as contrary to fact. Mature religion and science are allies, complementing each other, and must never be mutually opposed. A mature religion accepts the truths and laws of science that relate to the physical universe, and refuses to give credence to religious teachings or biblical stories that are at variance with established, verified scientific truth and that indicate an incredible deviation from the laws of nature.

Dr. Donald H. Andrews[5] declares that "one hundred years ago, science, men thought, was opposed to religion. Today science, through this new atomic vision, is affirming religion. The dominant power of the universe is not the shattering physical power of the atom. It is that power which lies beyond the material atom in the unseen world of the music of the spirit, the power of love. It is this power, and this alone, which can guard us and guide us as we move forward into the awesome new world of atomics and automation, rockets and space."

Religious thinkers are becoming more and more convinced that the scientific method must be applied to the problems of religion. This does not mean that religious truth must be validated in the laboratory, but it does mean that religion must be essentially rational, knowledgeable, and dynamic if it is to have an impact upon modern civilization.

The mature faith looks upon religion as a dynamic and evolving process. It recognizes that religion goes through a selfish, grasping, ignorant infancy, grows through a groping, stumbling, wonderful, wondering, credulous, eager childhood, advances unevenly to an unstable, immature, superstitious, inconsistent, exasperating, and yet promising adolescence with heartening intimations of a glorious potential of an enlightened, rational, unselfish, sensitive, and ennobling maturity. In consonance with this dynamism, mature religion will recognize that the various stages of religious growth will bring forth institutions and beliefs that are not in harmony with

[5] "A Faith for the Space Age," *Rotarian*, August, 1958.

reason. In the infancy of religion magic will have primacy over ethics, the supernatural over the natural, theurgy over theology, and ritual will be used to propitiate the spirits, deities, and gods. Miracles, wonders, and incredible folk stories will attest to "chosenness" and the unique role of those identified with the faith. The sacred literature will be divinely revealed, and the religious heroes divinely born. Childhood religion will fantasize religious institutions and concepts to blend the rational with the irrational, the natural and the supernatural. Greater emphasis will be placed upon reward and punishment both in this life and in the world to come. Despite the juvenile attitude toward religion, there will be portents and presentiments of the dawning of maturity in concepts, ritual, and religious institutions.

Mature religion will distinguish between the particularism of folkways, mores, and the universal in thought and moral practice. It will behold the Bible as the cumulative experience of a people in quest of God—a sacred literature containing myths, legends, history, fact, law, and eternal verities, recording not only the divine revelation of God to man, but the divine quest of man for God. As a consequence, the discoveries of archaeology and the findings of biblical science will be used to distinguish the historical from the legendary, the rational from the irrational, and the true from the false. The concept of an afterlife will be divorced from superstition and the crudities of primitive thought, and will place its emphasis upon the immortality of the soul rather than upon the immortality of the body. Mature religion will behold man as the universal child of the universal God and will reject the discriminating criteria of pigmentation, economic status in life, social position, national origin, or adherence to a specific faith or creed.

The following story from the rabbinic tradition graphically illustrates the belief that man should not repudiate reason and rely upon miracles to attest to the presence and the power of God. During a discussion on a difficult point of law, Rabbi Eleazer brought up all possible objections, but the other scholars would not agree with him. Finally he said, "If the rule is as I teach it, let this carob tree give a sign." The carob tree moved back two hundred cubits. But the sages said, "A carob tree proves nothing." So he said, "If the rule is as I teach it, let the water in this channel give a sign." And the water in the channel flowed upward instead of downward. But the sages said to him, "The waters of the channel prove nothing." Then he said, "If the law is as I teach it, let the walls of the school decide." And the walls of the schoo' leaned over as to fall. And Rabbi Joshua chastised the walls, saying, "When the pupils of the sages dispute a point of law, what business is that of yours?" Therefore, out of respect for Rabbi Joshua the walls did not tumble; but out of respect for Rabbi Eleazer they did not stand up straight again, but leaned over. Then a divine voice was heard: "What is the matter with you? Why do you importune Rabbi Eleazer? The rule has always been what he teaches it to be." But Rabbi Joshua, rising to his feet, exclaimed: "It is not in heaven!" (Deuteronomy 31.12)

What did he mean by these words? He meant that the Torah (the law) is no longer in heaven; it was given to us from Mount Sinai, once for all time, and we need no longer pay heed to a divine voice, for in the Torah given at Sinai it is written, "The opinion of the majority shall prevail."

The prophet Elijah appeared to Rabbi Nathan, who asked him, "What was God doing at that moment?" That is, when Rabbi Joshua denied the value of miracles. And the prophet replied: "God was laughing and saying: 'My children have conquered Me, My children have conquered Me.'"

There is no irreverence suggested by the statements of either Rabbi Eleazer or Rabbi Joshua. The story is not to be taken literally. It is a whimsical homily on the subject of miracles, and attests to the rabbinic conviction that voices and visions, mysteries and apparent miracles that contravene the moral law or the physical laws of God may be ignored.

A mature faith does not look for supernatural miracles to solve the problems of this world. Rather does it see miracles in the phenomena of nature, a blade of grass, the miracle of a tear, the orderly functioning of the universe in all its cosmic precision, the wonder of the human body, the sublime glory of love, and the insistent clamor within man to obey the still, small voice of conscience to respond to the needs of his fellow man.

The mature religion will recognize the futility of knowing God completely. God will be regarded as spiritual, incorporeal, without body, form, or the property of matter. With reverence and humility, it will take cognizance of a divine mystery, but seek to identify the belief in God with man's moral and ethical imitation of divine attributes. The mature faith will behold the presence of God in every aspect of life, adhering to the belief in continuous revelation rather than in the static revelation of God's will in one place or at one time. The mature religion is a religion of hope. It predicates hope for the future on the belief in an intelligent, moral, and purposeful God who has fashioned a divine destiny for man in an orderly, meaningful, and providential universe. Rejecting the concept of the depravity of man, the adherents of the mature faith will endeavor to exalt man in his efforts to build God's kingdom. Their belief in the future derives not from naïve yearning for social betterment, but from a fervent and rational conviction that an intelligent God is also a moral God who has ordained a moral purpose for man.

Emphasizing deed rather than creed, the mature religion is an action religion with an orientation in this world, dedicated to the effort to sanctify life with holiness, ennoble the status of man, and create a society of justice, compassion, brotherhood, and peace.

Religion Must Be This-Worldly

Hermann Cohen, the philosopher, taught that "mythology and paganism are concerned primarily with the question: 'What is my fate?' In religion, man asks: 'What is my role? What is my duty? What is my task? How can I fulfill God's will on earth?'"

The dichotomy between religion and life is widened by those who insist that the Church and the Synagogue must deal with the supernatural rather than with the natural, with the ideal rather than with the real, with the next world rather than with this world. This would seem to validate the thinking of those who contend that the real sin of religion is that it projects an illusory concept of life and thus removes religion from the problems of reality. This was the principal point of the teaching of Feuerbach, and was further embellished by Karl Marx in his oft-quoted phrase that "religion is the opium of the people."

Those who believe in the ideals of religion but insist that organized religion is a deterrent to the attainment of those ideals would agree with Tolstoi who wrote: "There is not only nothing in common between the churches as churches and Christianity, except the name, but they are based on principles which are opposed to each other.

There is on the one side pride, violence, self-righteousness, immobility and death; on the other side humility, repentance, subjection, movement, and life."

Mature religion must bridge the dichotomy between religion and life, and identify faith with the effort to foster humility, repentance, ethical action, and militant morality to this world and this life.

Mature religion will resist the effort to make religion otherworldly, to defer the solution of the problems, injustices, and inequities of our society to another world to be effected by supernatural means.

Recently, a woman expressed her opinion to me that it is futile to deal with the problems of the world. "Man was never meant to solve his own problems," she said. "We must wait until the next world where everything will be resolved with divine justice."

Such a point of view must be opposed by the mature faith, as it consecrates itself to a sublime this-worldliness, inspires its adherents to a love for social justice, and the determination to fashion the good society on earth. The mature faith is social and collective as well as individual and personal.

Julian Huxley in *Religion Without Revelation*[6] asserts: "Religion should definitely be a relation of the personality as a whole to the rest of the universe, one into which reverence enters, and one in which the search for the ultimate satisfactions of discovering and knowing truth, experiencing and expressing beauty, and ensuring the good in righteous action, all have the freest possible play."

It must inspire the individual to go beyond himself to an identity with a spiritual whole, to see himself as part of a religiously oriented totality that seeks the fulfillment of a divine plan, to build the society of God on earth. Thus, the mature religion must be this-worldly, rather than otherworldly, concerned with the problems of *this* world, committed to the here and now. Even as man confronts the realities of the present, the mature faith must motivate him to look beyond the present to the imminent religious possibilities and the ethical ideals to be attained in the future. By the future, he means that which is to be in this world, and not a hazy, nebulous, inchoate, amorphous paradise that will gratify his senses, give him rest from his moral obligations, and relieve him of the moral duties imposed by the radicalism of the mature faith.

[6] New York, Harper, new and revised ed., 1957, p. 197.

The solution of the evils of our society will not be accomplished without faith. It is a faith, however, that is defined by Sherwood Eddy as a commitment to action. "Faith," he says, "is not trying to believe something regardless of the evidence. Faith is daring to do something regardless of the consequences."

Religion Must Be Prophetic

The mature religion is equated with a prophetic faith. Prophetic religion will not identify faith with believing. It will identify faith with doing, and insist upon the application of prophetic ideals to the realities of life. In the past, faith has been identified with theology. Prophetic religion demands more than the verbalization of ethical and moral ideals. It insists upon the active implementation of those ideals into the structure of reality. In the future, faith must be identified with social action, the concretization of the theological belief that a God of justice, mercy, and truth demands a divine imitation from those who worship Him.

Prophetic religion holds that salvation is not attained by acceptance of dogmas, but by love of God that fulfills itself in action.

Karl B. Justus in his *What's Wrong With Religion?* correctly states that "the job of religion is not just the salvation of individual souls, but the salvation of society. God help the religionist who thinks of moral wrong only in the sense of immorality and fleshly sin. Too often religion has raised a stentorian voice against these things, but has remained silent about conditions that helped make them possible.[7] The purpose of mature religion is to make man sublimely human by removing the causes and conditions that accentuate bestiality and predatory evil.

Walter Rauschenbusch in *A Gospel for the Social Awakening* calls upon the Christian Church to "make over an antiquated and immoral economic system; to get rid of laws, customs, maxims, and philosophies inherited from an evil despotic past; to create just and brotherly relations between great groups and classes of society, thus to lay a social foundation upon which modern men individually can live and work in a fashion that will not outrage all the better elements in them."[8]

[7] New York, Duell, Sloan and Pearce, Inc., 1946, p. 43.
[8] New York, Association Press, 1950, p. 154.

Rauschenbusch calls for the "Social Awakening" in this world, and not in the world to come. Again and again he emphasizes that "the purpose of all that Jesus said and did and hoped to do was always the social redemption of the entire life of the human race on earth." To him, the social gospel required radicalism, rebellion, progressivism, and faith—a faith that enables man to behold the kingdom of God as a fellowship of righteousness, that seeks the abolition of industrial slavery, and the disappearance of slums from civilization.

Perhaps it is in this area of this-worldliness that the mature or prophetic religion will incur the greatest resentment and agitate hostility, opposition, and bitter enmity. Even the most conservative devotees of popular and respectable religion are content to speak about social justice as an abstract, ethical concept. This is deemed as a sanctioned requisite of the conservative faith. The insistent and irritating demands of the mature faith to concretize, implement, and activate social justice in this world will generate the most acrimonious refusals, and precipitate the most vehement resistance. It is much more comforting to take refuge in theological creeds than to endanger security and disrupt the social calm by means of ethical deeds. "How often the church has had a high blood count of creeds and an anemia of deeds," declares the Reverend Martin Luther King, Jr. In a recent publication[9] he quotes from Dean Liston Pope of Yale Divinity School, who rightly states, in *The Kingdom Beyond Caste:* "The church is the most segregated major institution in American society. It has lagged behind the Supreme Court as the conscience of the nation on question of race, and it has fallen far behind trade unions, factories, schools, department stores, athletic gatherings and most other major areas of human association, as far as the achievement of integration in its own life is concerned."[10]

The same strictures may be applied to the Synagogue, which in all too many instances has repudiated the prophetic heritage of Judaism by a timid, cowardly silence on moral issues. Quoting from an ethical religion, preaching on social ethics, the Synagogue has been all too silent on controversial questions of racial equality, economic exploitation, corruption in government, and the ills and inequities that plague our society, corrupt our social institutions, and belie man's most sensitive and spiritual aspirations in behalf of the good society.

[9] *Stride Toward Freedom* (New York, Harper, 1958), p. 207.
[10] New York, Friendship Press, 1957, p. 105.

The prophetic faith and the institutions identified with the prophetic faith must restore the prophetic spirit to religion by advocating a bold and vigorous radicalism that will get to the root of social evils. It must proceed to eradicate injustice and resolutely oppose any form of discrimination and prejudice against man. It will require its disciples to be men and women of action, as well as men and women of belief. Such religious action will derive from a sacred anger, a divine discontent with injustice, bigotry, ignorance, poverty, intolerance, and war. It will be nurtured by a compassionate regard for every living thing, and will be sustained by the universal love not only for God, but for the dignity and the sanctity of man, created in the divine image.

The chapters that follow will attempt to apply the criteria of the mature, radical, rational, and prophetic faith to the concepts of God, man, the Bible, contemporary religious aspirations, prayer, immortality, race relations, social action, and the building of the future.

9

The Divine Mystery

Shall I ask you whether God is a magician, and of a nature to appear insidiously now in one shape, and now in another—sometimes himself changing and passing into many forms, sometimes deceiving us with the semblance of such transformations; or is he one and the same immutably fixed in his own proper image?

—PLATO, *The Republic*, Book II

What Do We Mean by God?

Dr. Alfred North Whitehead, one of the greatest thinkers of our era, insists that "the only really important question before us today is this: What do you mean by God?" Because that question is so difficult to answer, we would rather evade the intellectual demands and the emotional torment of wrestling with it, and seek complacent refuge in talking about God, professing a belief in God, participating in rites and prayers that enable us to worship God—but never enter the arena of religious struggle to force ourselves to emerge with an answer. The mature faith demands that we think through our belief about God, come to grips with the divine, and, like Jacob, wrestle through the long night of doubt, groping for religious clarity, writhing through the blackness of soul struggle, until the dawn of truth enables us to emerge, humbled but triumphant, with the blessing of faith.

To abandon the simple, understandable, anthropomorphic, kindergarten God of our childhood is to subject ourselves to the growing pains that herald the approach of religious maturity. To wrestle and struggle toward a mature, adult conception of God is to invite the consequences of perplexity, frustration, confusion, humiliation, and intellectual anguish. The blessing is not without cost. Jacob was triumphant, but limped upon his thigh. Mature man in search of a mature conception of God must expect to be wearied and strengthened, purified and debased, exulted and depressed, glorified and dejected, confident and chastened. He will never be the same again.

What do we mean by God? Is God a man, a spirit, a philosophic verbalization of a cosmic force, a metaphysical abstraction, a mode of thought, a moral postulate, the indwelling divinity of nature, the transcendent being remote from the affairs of men? Is God the power that makes for good, the heavenly Father, the divine Judge, the Creator of the universe? Is God one, two, or three, or even an infinite multiplicity of beings coordinated into one integrated Being? Is God a supramyth born out of the yearning of man for a divine Superman to protect, sustain, and guide him? Is God a He, She, or It? Is God a divine Jinni who answers our wishes, a heavenly Hatchet Man who cuts us down for our sins, a kind and gentle Uncle who rewards us for our obedience, a brilliant Mathematician and immortal Engineer who planned and shaped the universe, or is God a malevolent Demon who permits suffering, compounds misery, and exploits the weakness of earth creatures for the gratification of His own Superego? What do we mean by God? These are questions that perplex us as we seek to understand the meaning of Divinity in the perspective of the mature faith.

We begin by applying the criteria of the mature faith, by a radical effort to get to the root and source of Divinity, by utilizing our rational faculties for the understanding of God, and by a prophetic effort to bring God into our world.

The Approach of Humility

The most radical approach to the meaning of God is not to eliminate God and beg the eternal questions relating to God, but to begin with the assumption that *a human being may not and can not ever know God completely*, because the finite cannot comprehend the infinite, nor can the known ever understand the unknowable.

It is well that humility should characterize our quest for the understanding of Divinity and that we should place limits on the possibility of ever attaining absolute knowledge of God. How far from the truth was the philosopher who said, "Were I to know God, I would be God"! Isn't it the height of arrogance for anyone bound by the limits of mortality and finitude to presume to understand the essence of God and to assert with overwhelming certainty a definition, an exposition, or a concrete description of God with positive and absolute knowledge? Can mortal man understand immortal spirit? Is it not beyond the comprehension of man to understand that which exceeds his knowledge? We should be shamed from arrogance by the sincerity of the Psalmist who asked: "Where can I find Thee? How can I know Thee?" A question that Zophar properly asked of his friend Job is, "Canst thou by searching find out God?" The vision of God is denied to us as it was denied to the eyes of Moses. "Man shall not see me and live." But we are enabled to witness the effects of God in our life and in our world, and catch fleeting glimpses of Divinity by the divine promise, "I will make all My goodness pass before thee."

Dr. Kaufman Kohler, in *Jewish Theology*,[1] relates an Oriental fable about a sage who had been meditating vainly for days and

[1] New York, The Macmillan Company, 1918, p. 72.

weeks on the question, "What is God?" One day, walking along the seashore, he saw some children, busying themselves by digging holes in the sand, and pouring into them water from the sea. "What are you doing there?" he asked them.

They replied, "We want to empty the sea of its water."

With a smile he exclaimed, "Oh, you little fools," but suddenly his smile vanished in serious thought. "Am I not as foolish as these children?" he asked himself. "A sea is measurable and finite, but how can I, with my small brain, hope to grasp the immeasurable, infinite nature of God?"

We, who are quick to admit our ignorance about the technical construction of the radio or television, rush avidly into a technical and detailed description of God. We, who cannot fathom the mystery of the atom, with arrogant certainty attempt to explain and describe the mystery of God, the Creator of the atom.

There is no greater presumption than for finite man to arrogate unto himself the ability to understand the nature of infinite God. Maimonides, the great medieval philosopher, said that he could never know what God is, but that he might deduce what God isn't, by reason. As a result, he attempted to define the nature of God in terms of negative attributes. He said that God isn't a body and that God isn't limited in time and space. It was too much for even the gigantic intellect of a Maimonides to venture a positive analysis of the nature of God.

A radical excision of everything we have believed about a physical God is required to enable us to heal ourselves of the irrational concept of a God who speaks with human resonance, who appears in human form, who sees with eyes, hears with ears, and is a divine superman in physique and function.

The Bible attests that in the great theophany on Sinai, no physical form was apparent, but only an invisible presence. "The Lord spoke to you out of the midst of the fire; ye heard the voice of words, but ye saw no form; only a voice. And He declared unto you His covenant, which He commanded you to perform. . . . Take ye therefore good heed unto yourselves—for ye saw no manner of form on the day that the Lord spoke unto you in Horeb out of the midst of the fire" (Deuteronomy 4.12ff.). This was a warning lest the children of

Israel make for themselves a graven image, or make deities of the sun, the moon, and the stars, "and worship them and serve them."

The writer in Deuteronomy was radical, but not radical enough. He conceded that God has no physical form, but he could not permit himself to believe that God could speak without articulating words. "Ye saw no form; only a voice." Radical religion insists that just as God doesn't have a body, so God doesn't have a voice, nor does He speak to us with the resonance of human speech.

What then is the nature of God, and how may we define Him? God is undefinable. When Moses asked God, "Whom shall I say sent me to lead the children of Israel from captivity to freedom?" the authors of Scripture were sensitive enough to believe that God refused to define Himself by saying, *Ehyeh asher Ehyeh*, "I will be what I will be." Tell them "I will be what I will be" sent you.

The rabbis pondered the exegetical meaning of "God of Abraham, God of Isaac, and God of Jacob," asking why God was repeated each time. Wouldn't it be enough to say: "God of Abraham, Isaac, and Jacob"? No, answered the sages. God is repeated each time to teach us that the God of Abraham was not defined and regarded as the God of Isaac, and the God of Isaac was not defined in the same way as the God of Jacob. Each generation must remember that God is the *En sof*, the Being without limit, infinite and mysterious. They admonished their pupils not to compare God to man, remembering the verse taught by the prophet Isaiah: "My thoughts are not your thoughts, and My ways are not your ways, saith the Lord."

The Union Prayerbook of Reform Judaism offers a beautiful prayer that begins: "O God, Thou art hidden from the eyes of all the living and art beyond the comprehension of all creatures." Man's arrogance crumbles into abject humility as he struggles to find and know God, until at last he concedes that God is a mystery, a Power, a Being, a Force, a Something, a Reality that has not been or cannot be explained, hence a sacred Reality, a sacred Mystery, beyond human comprehension.

When man accepts this, he can understand what Albert Einstein meant when he wrote: "The most beautiful thing we can experience is the mysterious. It is the source of all true art and science. He to whom this emotion is a stranger, who can no longer pause to wonder and stand rapt in awe, is as good as dead; his mind and eyes are closed. To know that which is impenetrable to us really exists, manifesting itself as the highest wisdom and the most radiant beauty which our dull faculties can comprehend only in their most primitive forms—this knowledge, this feeling, is at the center of true religiousness. In this sense, I belong in the ranks of devoutly religious men."[2]

Albert Einstein, the radical scientist, who revolutionized man's conception of the universe; Albert Einstein, the rationalist who subjected the knowable to empiric examination, permitted himself to rest on the bosom of a mystery too great for the human mind to fully comprehend.

With the philosopher Hume we ask those who would fathom the mystery of God and the universe, "By what right do we take this little agitation of the brain, which we call 'thought,' as the clue to all this?" By what right do we, finite mortals, arrogate to ourselves the ability to comprehend the infinite mystery we call God? How pitiful are the efforts of those who would prove God's existence as one would prove a mathematical formula! How blasphemous is the belief that God reveals Himself completely to psalmist or prophet or seer, through Bible, Scripture, or sacred literature—and that the infinity of God and the mystery of God have been compassed, bound, limited, and circumscribed completely within the mind of a man or the pages of a book, sacred and holy though they may be! Man is, by the blessing of God's image, permitted to catch glimpses of Divinity. A book records the glimpses of God's revelation to man—but who is to say that this or that alone is the absolute, total, and undeniable revelation of God's word and God's will?

If God is unsearchable, why should we seek Him? If God is a mystery too wondrous for the human mind to comprehend, how can we know Him? Longing to behold a God we cannot see with our eyes; sensitizing our souls to a Voice we cannot hear with our ears; struggling to comprehend a God we cannot understand, how can we behold God and make Him a reality in our lives?

[2] "What I Believe," *Forum Magazine*, October, 1930.

The Revelation of God

Although we cannot, with certain knowledge, understand God completely, we still yearn to find Him and know Him. Although we cannot offer absolute proof of the existence of God, there is no feasible explanation of an orderly universe without divine Intelligence, First Cause, and a divine Creator. God cannot be proved like a mathematical equation. However, when we consider the physical universe in its mystery and order, the belief in a divine Creator is inescapable.

The opening words of the Bible still offer the most cogent explanation of Creation: "In the beginning God." The theory of evolution may take us back to the one-cell protozoa and amoeba. The theories of physics today may take us back into positive and negative electrons, protons, neutrons, and atoms, from which the one cell derived; but when the scientists and the physicists are asked, "How did the neutrons, the electrons, and the atoms come into being?" they too must return to the answer contained in Genesis, "In the beginning God." The human mind cannot possibly conceive of a creation without a Creator, and although we may not understand how God created the universe, we cannot conclude other than that God, however named or however described, was the Creator of the universe. Whether the earth is the product of an exploded meteor or whether it is a cooled remnant of what was once a burning particle hurled from the sun, the question must still be answered, "Who created the sun?" or "Who created that from which the sun evolved?" Ultimately and irrevocably, we must go back to the thesis, "In the beginning God," and say with the psalmist, "How manifold are Thy works, O Lord! in wisdom hast Thou made them all" (Psalm 104.24).

A. Cressy Morrison, former president of the New York Academy of Sciences, in his book *Man Does Not Stand Alone*, says:

"Behold . . . an almost invisible drop of protoplasm, transparent, jelly-like, capable of motion, drawing energy from the sun. . . . This single cell, this transparent mistlike droplet, holds within itself the germ of life, and has the power to distribute this life to every living thing, great and small. . . . The powers of this droplet of protoplasm and its contents were and are greater than the vegetation that clothes the earth in green, greater than all the animals that breathe the breath of life, for all life came from it and without it no living thing would have been or could be. . . . Nature did not create life; fire-blistered rocks and a saltless sea did not meet the necessary requirements. Who, then, has put it here?"[3]

We long to behold God. This scientist sees the revelation of God in a drop of protoplasm; others see God in the process of coagulation, a magic network that prevents us from bleeding to death when cut or wounded; in the order of the universe; in the sense of wonder that the earth is the proper distance from the sun, that the slant of the earth provides the seasons, that oxygen is released, and that there is a chemistry that operates in the tiniest leaf. Is our sense of wonder anesthetized so that we are prevented from thrilling to the revelation of God in the human fetus, nurtured by and growing in the mother's body? Can we experience no sense of God's indwelling presence in the thought that the infinitesimal genes and the microscopic chromosomes transmit characteristics from one generation to another?

The philosopher Kant saw God in *"der gesternte Himmel über mir und in das Sittengesetz in mir."* He beheld the divine in the starry sky above and in the moral law within.

It was in this spirit of reverence that Abraham Lincoln said: "I can see how it might be possible for a man to look down upon the earth and be an atheist. But I cannot conceive how a man could look up into heaven and say there is no God."

There are miracles in faith, and there is magic in nature. The psalmists did not need the proof of supernatural miracles to give them a rapturous faith in God. They beheld the earth transformed from one season to another at the touch of Nature's magic wand. They beheld the wonder of the heavens as the moon and the stars moved through the skies in a celestial procession of wonder.

When the psalmist looked at the sun, moon, and stars, he felt himself in the presence of a mystery so awesome that he could only bow in reverence before the indescribable holiness of God.

In recent times, Dr. Max T. Krohn experienced this sense of awe and mystery when he saw a photograph taken through the 200-inch telescope at Palomar—a picture of a star so far away that its light had taken billions of trillions of light years to reach that sensitized photographic plate, even though the light traveled at the phenomenal speed of 186,324 miles a second. It is difficult for the human mind

[3] Westwood, N.J., Fleming H. Revell, rev. ed., 1944, pp. 35, 38-39.

to comprehend such speed, or understand the incalculable vastness of eternal time and space.

It is this sense of wonder and awe before the mystery of God that leaves us breathless, inarticulate and humble. All we can do is to proclaim with the psalmist:

> "The heavens declare the glory of God,
> And the firmament showeth His handiwork."
> —PSALM 19.2

If we must have miracles, then let it be the miracle of God's creative power in the heavens above, and on the earth beneath, and in the heart and mind of man. If we must have magic, then let it be the magic of a God

> "Who stretchest out the heavens like a curtain;
>
> . . . . ' . . . .
>
> Who makest the clouds Thy chariot,
> Who walkest upon the wings of the wind;
> Who makest winds Thy messengers,
> The flaming fire Thy ministers."
> —PSALM 104.2-4

Job said, "I had heard of Thee by the hearing of the ear, but now mine eyes seeth Thee." If God is not physical, how can we witness manifestations of divinity? Moses saw God in a burning bush. Elizabeth Barrett Browning, in her *Aurora Leigh*, asserts:

> "Earth's crammed with heaven,
> And every common bush afire with God;
> And only he who sees takes off his shoes;
> The rest sit round it and pluck blackberries."

Richard Halliburton relates the time he climbed to the top of the Matterhorn with a friend. When they reached the summit, the view was awe-inspiring and majestic in splendor. His friend was silent for a moment. Halliburton waited to hear what spiritual thoughts were inspired by the mountaintop. At last the friend spoke. He said, "I have always wanted to spit a mile, so here goes." Some see beauty and magnificence of God in every leaf; others see nothing but a piece of greenery. Richard Halliburton beheld God on a mountaintop. His friend saw only the possibility of fulfilling an impulse to spit a mile.

In *A Reporter in Search of God*,[4] Howard Whitman relates the story of a Brahman priest in India who was sitting at the side of a water-lily pond one evening watching the sun inch lower in the western sky. An American missionary approached him and took a seat beside him at the edge of the pond. The missionary talked about his religion, its doctrines, its theology, its philosophy and liturgy.

The Brahman priest listened. Thinking him unconvinced, the missionary began again. He marshaled propositions and syllogisms, cited authority, interpreted history.

Still the Brahman priest listened.

The missionary stood up impatiently. He began to explain God in terms of his own religion. He told of the miracles God had performed. He told of God's works and power.

Now it was the Brahman priest who stood up.

He simply pointed to a night-blooming lily unfolding its petals, revealing the breath-taking pageant of color within it.

"Brahma," he said, and walked away.

The Existence of God

How does God manifest Himself in the universe? How do we know that there is a God? Man has wrestled with these two questions since the dawn of human thought, without clear, unequivocal and universally accepted answers. Hebrew Scriptures attempt to explain how God reveals Himself to man, but nowhere is there any effort to prove the existence of God. It is only the fool who says, "There is no God." The authors of Hebrew Scriptures defined, explained, and illustrated the nature and the attributes of God, but they no more questioned the existence of God than they questioned the existence of man or life itself.

Arguments and proofs abound in later religious and philosophical literature to validate the belief in the existence of God. Aristotle offers the "argument from motion," insisting that since the universe

[4] New York, Doubleday & Company, 1953, pp. 234-235. By permission.

is constantly in motion there must be a Force, a Power that caused and perpetuates this motion. There is the "cosmological proof" that there can be no creation in nature without a creator, that an effect must have a cause, and that since the world could not have come into existence spontaneously by itself without a first cause—that first cause is called God. The "ontological proof" asserts that the existence of God derives from the idea of God, and that the idea of God could not be produced by anything finite, and hence must be caused by the infinite God. The "teleological argument" is based on the order of the universe, a universe that presupposes meaning and purpose. In like manner, "proofs" for the existence of God are adduced ad infinitum. The moralist proves the existence of God by the existence of morality. The scientific-minded attempt to give empirical evidence for the existence of God, citing the Second Law of Thermodynamics, the conservation of energy, and the complete absurdity of creation without first cause. The philosophers debated, argued, and proposed logical proofs for the existence of God. Kant concedes that God is the Creator, a postulate of moral reason, but makes man the center of the universe. Descartes taught that God created everything, even contradictions. Fichte transferred the "absolute" to man who is viewed as the absolute Ego, and claims that Divinity is the absolute moral ideal. What we call God is the infinite goal toward which we are ever striving.

This volume is based on the conviction that we can no more "prove" the existence of God than we can "prove" that God doesn't exist. The purpose of mature religion, therefore, is not to help man prove that God exists; it is not to know about God, but to experience God, and be ethically motivated by God. It is futile to attempt to define or describe God. The God who is "the ineffable," "the indescribable," "the divine mystery," the "I will be what I will be," is beyond definition and description.

Paul Tillich in his *Systematic Theology*[5] projects God beyond the narrow limitations of the word "existence." He writes: "God does not exist. He is being-itself beyond essence and existence. Therefore, to argue that God exists, is to deny Him." This is more than most ordinary mortals can comprehend—a God who exists enough to have "being" without existence.

[5] Chicago, University of Chicago Press, 1951, I, 205.

More understandable is the statement of Emil Brunner that "revelation, as the Christian faith understands it, is indeed by its very nature, something that lies beyond all rational arguments; the arguments which it certainly claims in the support does not lie in the sphere of rational knowledge, but in the sphere of that divine truth which can be attained only through divine self-communication, and not through human research of any kind."[6]

This, too, suggests that we cannot know God, but that we can experience God in a human-divine dialogue, a communication between man and God, and God and man.

Paul Tillich has stated that " 'Personal God' does not mean that God is *a* person. It means that God is the ground of everything personal and that he carries within himself the ontological power of personality. He is not a person but he is not less than personal. It should not be forgotten that classical theology employed the term *persona* for the trinitarian hypostases but not for God himself. God became 'a person' only in the nineteenth century, in connection with the Kantian separation of nature ruled by physical law from personality ruled by moral law."[7]

Rejecting the impersonal God of the philosophers, Blaise Pascal imputes moral attributes to God, stating: "But the God of Abraham, the God of Isaac, the God of Jacob, the God of Christians, is a God of love and of comfort, a God who fills the souls and hearts of those whom He possesses, a God who makes them conscious of their inward wretchedness, and His infinite mercy, who unites Himself to their inmost soul, who fills it with humility and joy, with confidence and love, who renders them incapable of any other end than Himself."[8]

The "existentialists," whether Brunner, Kierkegaard, or Martin Buber, attempt to solve the problem of reconciling the transcendence and the immanence of God by means of an existential "I and Thou" relationship. Recognizing the futility of measuring the infinite by finite means, yielding to the apparently irreconcilable conflict between demonstrating God by scientific means and believing in God by the urgency of faith, they insist that the only valid knowledge of God

[6] *Revelation and Reason* (Philadelphia, Westminster Press, 1946), pp. 205-206, copyright 1946 by W. L. Jenkins.
[7] *Op. cit.*, p. 245.
[8] *Thoughts*, ed. by Thomas S. Kepler (Cleveland, World Publishing Company, 1955), p. 24.

is that which is obtained by the personal, mystical, subjective experiencing of God in an intimate encounter with the divine. In essence they contend that if God is to be experienced, then the divine must be more than a "transcendent It"; it must be rendered accessible to man as the "immanent Thou" personally affecting and relating to the life and behavior of man.

Whether we accept or reject the "existential hypotheses" propounded by these theologians, we must still wrestle with the question of how to conceive of God as the "divine mystery," transcendently beyond the affairs of men, and the personal God who is indwelling, the moral God who covenants with man to fulfill divine purpose and to strive for the moral perfection of the individual and the society in which he lives.

The Moral Attributes of God

The prophets of Israel and the gospels of the New Testament helped man advance to the threshold of religious maturity. Hypersensitive to the presence of God, they beheld the divine in man's ethical relationship with his fellow man. Amos believed in God as the authority for justice, proclaiming *Coe omar Adonoi*: "Thus saith the Lord: Let justice roll as the waters and righteousness as a mighty stream." Micah set forth the requirements of God: "To do justly, to love mercy and to walk humbly with Thy God." Hosea beheld God as love. Jonah proclaimed a God of forgiveness. Elijah, Nathan, Jeremiah, Isaiah, Malachi, and Habakkuk, spokesmen of God, proclaimed the moral requisites for the worship of the moral God. Jesus followed his prophetic predecessors by insisting upon compassion, meekness, self-sacrifice, love, righteousness, and peace as the requirements of his heavenly Father. The sages of the Talmud, in a beautiful homily, imagine God praying to Himself, saying: "May it be acceptable before Me. May it be My will that My compassion may overcome Mine anger, and that it may prevail over My justice when My children appeal to Me, that I may deal with My children in mercy and in forgiveness."

Man evolved in his religious thinking from infantile concepts of spirits, demons, and gods to the belief in monotheism, one God of the universe. In time, he advanced beyond monotheism to ethical monotheism, predicated on the *imitatio dei*, the mortal imitation of the divine attributes of God. "Ye shall be holy; for I the Lord your God am holy" (Leviticus 19.2) became the scriptural basis for ethical monotheism, and allowed man to refine his God-concept beyond sacrifices, ritual, and ceremonial rites, to the belief in an ethical God whose relationship to man imposes upon man a commitment to moral values and ethical behavior.

The belief in the moral God is emotionally and religiously satisfying. It establishes a divine authority for ethics, morality, and all the values that we deem desirable, noble, and sublime. It seems to absolve us from the tortuous necessity of probing and exploring into the unknown and the mysterious. A loving Father is understandable. A God who hates injustice and cruelty is comprehendible. We are now using the language of man and imputing ethical attributes to God. However, the belief in the moral God poses difficult and perplexing problems.

The discerning reader may properly ask: "If it is immature to project physical qualities to God, isn't it equally immature to project spiritual qualities to God? If it is juvenile to impute to God such morally undesirable attributes as vengeance, anger, and hatred, isn't it just as illogical and childish to impute to God such morally desirable concepts and attributes as love, compassion, justice, and forgiveness? I can understand the concept of a divine Mystery, that God *exists*, that God is the unknown and the unknowable, that God is eternal Consciousness that knows Itself, that knows us, and the universe—but a Consciousness we can never know. If, however, God is unknowable, then how can we know that He is good, just, merciful, and loving? What happens then to the belief in the moral God, and ethical monotheism? Moreover, is there such a thing as absolute justice, absolute truth, absolute mercy? Are the truths and moral concepts contained in the Bible the word of man or the word of God? How is it possible to reconcile God's absolute attribute of justice with God's absolute attribute of mercy?"

Philosophers and theologians have attempted to answer these questions by the ontological argument that the very concepts of morality, justice, mercy, and love could not have come into existence without a God whose attributes are morality, justice, mercy, and love. This is not completely satisfying because it may be argued that

God is immoral, unjust, vengeful, and hateful because these concepts could not have come into existence without a God whose attributes are immorality, injustice, vengefulness, and hateful cruelty. One may not contest the yearning for the belief in a moral God, but the ontological argument is not convincing. One may understand why Paul Elmer More in *The Sceptical Approach to Religion*[9] supports the ontological argument so passionately when he writes: "You ask me to believe that nature planted in me, and not in me alone, but in all men, [moral] desires which I must eradicate as pure deceptions, that I am the victim of a cosmic jest only the more cruel if unintended, that the ultimate fact of existence is a malignant mockery." He believes that a world without morality is a cosmic jest, and that God is not capable of the malignant mockery of creating a world without moral purpose. We can sympathize with Dr. More, but as yet there is no convincing proof from the ontological argument to substantiate the belief in the moral God who is concerned with a moral universe.

There is another perplexing problem suggested by the concept of the moral God and the belief in ethical monotheism. This is the problem the theologians call "theodicy," the effort to reconcile the existence of suffering, pain, and evil with the divine attributes of God's love, justice, and compassion.

We cannot accept David Hume's suggestion that evil may be due to the fact that this is an imperfect world created by a bungling God. Nor can we accept the answer of an unquestioning and incredibly naïve faith.

Again the answers of the philosophers and theologians border on rationalization, theological casuistry, and feeble argumentation. Some claim that suffering is good and that it manifests the onset of illness. Others insist that suffering is meant to purify, strengthen, and refine in the crucible of pain. Still others aver that suffering is God's will imposed as a means of allowing man to make expiation and atonement for his sins. That these arguments are unconvincing is attested in *The Unsilent Generation*,[10] written by a professor at Princeton University, Otto Butz. He quotes the statements of Princeton students as they comment on the problems of religion. The first student to give his views writes:

[9] Princeton University Press, 1934, pp. 24-25.
[10] New York, Holt, Rinehart and Winston, Inc., 1958, p. 25.

"And where, I've sometimes been asked, does God fit into this scheme of mine? The truth is that religion has become a very touchy subject with me. When I look at the world around me, I find it difficult to conceive of an omnipotent, all-good, fatherlike deity. Such a deity wouldn't permit pain and suffering that exists. It seems to me that deity can be all-good and fatherlike only if he is infinite. But if he is really infinite, he must be very sadistic to allow the things he does. The argument that God tortures us to test our faith is so much bull to me, because if he's truly infinite, he *knows* how we will react. He doesn't need to test the faith of tiny infants in India by letting them starve to death! I prefer to believe in no god at all rather than in this kind of a god. . . . I figure I can be indifferent to an indifferent god."

This student is in good company as he articulates his perplexity and ponders the problem of theodicy. It has tortured the mind of man since Job questioned God about the suffering of the righteous, when his friends advanced the orthodox view that suffering is a punishment meted out for sins.

Mature religion must consider the problem of establishing some basis for belief in the morality of God, and must struggle with the problem of theodicy even if it means limiting divine omnipotence and omniscience. Both problems will be probed more fully in the following chapter that analyzes the nature of man, but we cannot avoid or escape the problems in relationship to a mature faith in a mature God which is the theme of this chapter.

God Is Both Moral and Amoral

We cannot *know* that God is a moral God any more than we can *know* that He exists. We *believe* without rational and demonstrable proof that an intelligent God has the power to reveal to sensitive men and women intimations of values we call moral. In a sense, this makes God moral. We believe, because we have to believe, that an intelligent God is a purposeful God and that man was not permitted to evolve and refine his sensitivities to morality in order to satisfy a divine caprice.

The belief in a moral God is also substantiated by the belief in the moral potential of man. However morality may be defined, man's yearning for moral perfection is both learned and unlearned, inherent and taught, spontaneous and conditioned. His morals may be influenced and even determined by the mores of the society in which he lives, but there *is* morality, which as man matures is directed, beyond himself and his needs, to a consideration of others through unselfishness, helpfulness, justice, mercy, and love.

In essence, however, mature religion does not have to look to God as the authority for morality. It looks to man as the *agent* of morality. Mature religion contends that there is no absolute but God—the absolute Divinity. Therefore, what we call goodness, truth, justice, love, and mercy are relative terms rather than absolute concepts. Since nothing really exists outside God, that which we call evil, as well as that which we call good, is part of the absolute Divinity. God is, using man-made terminology, both moral and amoral—an absolute Divinity that fills the world, that *is* the world, and yet transcends it. The goodness of the world makes God good. The evil in the world would seem to make God evil.

To be consistently rational and convincingly logical, it must be submitted that God is not the authority for morality in the world any more than he is the authority for immorality. It is man who has projected moral attributes to God, and created God in his moral image. It is man, by his conception of God, that makes Him moral. Reason alone asserts that the essence of God is amoral—not to be assessed as good or evil, just or unjust—God is. His essence is beyond all values or ethical or unethical attributes imputed to Him. Reason without faith does not permit the belief in the ethics and morality of God.

Such a conception of an amoral God whose morality is a projection of man's yearning for a moral authority may be regarded as heretical. Respectable religion will undoubtedly condemn it as a contemptuous, irreverent, and damnable blasphemy against a religious belief in God. Such a belief, however, is more rationally tenable and adds more to the moral stature of God than the estimate of a moral God who by ethical default sanctions the misery and suffering and evil that torment His children. And yet, does this belief in an amoral God detract more or less from the essential "goodness" of God than the theological pretensions of respectable religion that offers God as the source and the agent of human suffering, of innocent men and women blown into cosmic dust by the will of God, of children who starve by the will of God, of young mothers and fathers who die of cancer and heart disease by the will of God? If this is the will of God, such a God deserves our hatred and contempt for He is cast in the role of a God who can remove suffering, pain, and evil, but does not.

If, however, God is bound by His own laws, limited in omnipotence, then God has no direct relationship to human suffering, misery, or evil, which are man-willed and created and not God-willed and created.

Faith, however, declares that God *is* moral in that He has endowed man with the potential for morality. God *is* moral in that He has granted man freedom of will—which glorifies him and exalts him above all other creatures. Without freedom of will, there can be no morality or immorality. With freedom of will, man has the choice to wage war or pursue peace. This same freedom permits man to perform destructive acts or noble deeds. An amoral God is not responsible for the evil, suffering, or misery of humanity. It is immoral man that is the causative factor, and not the amoral God. It is in the order of nature that to live is to die. The human body is subjected to stress, to imperfections, to illness, deterioration, and ultimately death. This is the heritage of mortality. We cannot have pleasure without the alternative of pain. We cannot have life without the alternative of death. We cannot have morality without the alternative of immorality. Man has the freedom to affirm God, but that same freedom gives him the right to deny God if he so wishes.

Professor Peter A. Bertocci, in his *An Introduction to the Philosophy of Religion*,[11] logically points out that "we simply cannot have water which will quench thirst and yet not drown people, fire which will warm homes and not scorch flesh, minds which are sensitive but not capable of becoming insane." A controlled existence may appear to offer greater security, but it places a limitation on man's freedom, and in so doing eliminates morality. The alternative to freedom is determinism—a world in which God ordains every act of man and thus deprives man of his greatest blessing: freedom of will. The amoral God grants man freedom·of will, but in so doing He removes Himself as a divine Agent of man's suffering, frustration, sickness, wars, poverty, injustice, and evil.

Man's freedom is limited, as God's freedom is limited by His own laws and His own essence. Man has freedom of will to choose good or evil, love or hate, justice or injustice. God has no such freedom of

[11] New York, Prentice-Hall, 1951, p. 414.

will. He is limited and bound by His nature as absolute, infinite Deity. God transcends morality. God exists. God is. God is the eternal, divine Mystery too overwhelming to be grasped by the feeble, finite intellect of man. It takes greater reverence to worship such an infinite, unknowable God, than the predictable, understandable superman deity of respectable religion.

Logic and reason may adduce cogent arguments in the attempt to prove that there is no God, or demonstrate rationally that God is amoral—and yet the very nature of God as divine Mystery transcends the intellectual conclusions of syllogistic reasoning. The absolute knowledge of God is beyond the comprehension of man. He can only estimate and conjecture as to the nature and essence of God. What man thinks of God and what God actually is may not be the same. Reason takes man to the threshold of the infinite, and then transfers the quest for the knowledge of God to the faith that enables him to advance into the unknown.

Philosophers, metaphysicians, theologians, logicians, and scholars may question the morality of God, and debate the possibility of ethical attributes, and yet how is it possible to account for moral revelation, the ethical insights of the prophets, psalmists, and sages, the potential of man for compassion, justice, and holiness, and the progressive development of humanity from the laws of the jungle to the laws of Sinai, without the belief in a moral God who demands the imitation of moral attributes?

Science is predicated upon reason, and seeks demonstrable proof for its hypotheses. The mature faith is predicated upon reason, but it is no longer a faith if it relies upon reason alone, and insists upon demonstrable scientific proof for the existence and the morality of God. The complexity, the seeming contradictions, the tormenting inconsistencies, the finite limitations of man's quest for the divine do not permit absolute and certain knowledge of the insoluble Mystery we call God.

The Indwelling God

Where is God? How can we find God, to fill our hearts with meaning, and to help us sanctify life with holiness? Where is God? That is the same question the disciples of a rabbi in ancient times asked their teacher. He turned to them and repeated the question "Where is God?" And then he answered: "Wherever man lets God in."

To remove God from the world, however, is to strike at the very essence of religion. To make God amoral is to expunge the divine authority for human morality. Man cannot be inspired to worship a moral postulate, a cosmic force, or even a divine Mystery that is devoid of personality, purpose, relatedness, or relevance to the life of the individual or the moral perfectibility of the society in which he lives.

If there is no absolute but God, the absolute divinity, and if nothing exists outside God, then not only is man a part of God, but God is a part of man. Just as God is immanent in the world and yet transcends the world, so God is moral even though He may transcend morality. Not only is He in the heavens above, but God is in the earth beneath. Not only does God exist—He exists in the world and is inherent in the soul of man.

The author of Psalm 139 was awed by the transcendence of God, and yet he sensed the ubiquitous presence of Divinity in every aspect of life. Recognizing the futility of ever comprehending the complete meaning of the divine Mystery, he could concede: "Such knowledge is too wonderful for me;/Too high, I cannot attain unto it," and yet he knew that the omnipresent God had a direct, personal relationship to him. His inability to define God or comprehend the essence of Divinity did not prevent him from exclaiming:

"Whither shall I go from Thy spirit?
Or whither shall I flee from Thy presence?
If I ascend up into heaven, Thou art there;
If I make my bed in the netherworld, behold, Thou art there.
If I take the wings of the morning,
And dwell in the uttermost parts of the sea;
Even there would Thy hand lead me,
And Thy right hand would hold me."
                                        —Psalm 139.7-10

The transcendence of God did not contradict the immanence of God. The omnipresent God was accessible, personal, indwelling, a source of help and inspiration, a God who leads him, a God whose right hand holds him, a God who was and is "nigh unto all who call upon Him; to all who call upon Him in truth."

Mature religion has reason as a criterion, but mature religion cannot divorce reason from faith. Mature religion would agree with Matthew Arnold in describing God as the "Power, not ourselves, that makes for righteousness." It concurs with A. Eustace Haydon in the belief that "faith in God is the daring confidence of man that the universe in its deepest meaning does allow and give support to our human hopes and ideals." A mature, radical faith, therefore, must seek to arouse and awaken the indwelling Divinity that is the sacred endowment of man. Such inherent Divinity must be intimately personal as well as objectively impersonal, a God who is "farther than the farthermost star, and yet is as close to us as breathing," a God who is not only the God of the philosophers, not only the God of Abraham, Isaac, and Jacob, not only the God of Jesus, Paul, and John, but *my* God, the God who is the ever-present source of help in time of trouble. This is what the Chassidic rabbi meant when he said that he could point his finger anywhere toward the heaven or earth and say with Moses and the children of Israel: "This is *my* God, and I will glorify Him; My father's God, and I will exalt Him" Exodus 15.2); and what Job meant when he said (42.5): "I had heard of Thee by the hearing of the ear; But now mine eye seeth Thee."

Man needs the assurance of the immanence of God to sustain himself against the terror of infinity, a fear that was graphically expressed by Pascal, who wrote: "When I consider the brief span of my life, swallowed up in eternity past and to come, the little space that I occupy, lost in the immensity of space of which I know nothing and which knows nothing of me—I am terrified." The man who believes in the nearness of God obviates the terror induced by the immensities of time and space. He has the faith that God spans the chasm between the finite and the infinite, and by his identification with God he finds an important place in the universe. He is related to God, and therefore is related to infinity.

Man is not capable of knowing God completely, but he can know something about God, and that "something" is his glimpse of Divinity. Man cannot find God completely, but in searching he directs his life to values and ideals that are holy. Through searching he sensitizes his vision to behold God's presence in every aspect of life, in the universe of restless energy and growth, in the creative power that pulsates through the millenniums, in the beauty of a sunset, the miracle of a new-born child, the emotional chemistry of a tear, and in the surpassing wonder and moral grandeur of a human being who cannot see God but beholds the divine as He fulfills His promise: "I will make all My goodness pass before thee" (Exodus 33.19).

The poet saw God when he said, "Where mercy, love, and pity dwell, I see God dwelling, too." Walt Whitman did not behold God in mystic visions, but, "In the faces of men and women, I see God, and in my own face in the glass."

A mother and father told me they saw and heard God when their child, afflicted with bulbar polio, said through her partially paralyzed throat, "Mother, Daddy, now I can swallow my own spit!"

We don't have to search for God in the cosmic universe alone. Some see God everywhere, in every bush that is aflame with Divinity. Others see nothing in this world but "blackberries." The mature religionist looks upon the totality of life, upon the world and his innermost being, and says with Jacob: "Surely, the Lord is in this place; and I knew it not" (Genesis 28.16).

Once we concede that God is immanent, resident in our world, commanding and demanding, revealing moral truths, compelling the implementation of ethical precepts, then each individual must agree with Martin Buber that God is "Thou" rather than "It," and that man must enter into a human-divine dialogue that enables the "I" to communicate with the "Thou." This confrontation, this divine encounter has as its purpose the sanctification of the individual to meet the moral imperative, the challenge to perfect himself and his society through his personal relationship with God.

To believe in God is not enough. We must believe that God lives, lives in the cosmos, lives in the world, lives in our society, and lives within man. If we contend with Nietzsche's madman: "God is dead. God will remain dead! And we killed Him!" then the authority for moral behavior is no longer religious. If we believe that God lives, then that belief must commit us to moral action, and impose upon us the heavy responsibility of meeting God's ethical requirements.

This is the teaching of the Chassidic rabbis who tell of what happened over a hundred years ago in the town of Berditchev. The saintly rabbi of the community, Levi Yitzhak, summoned the people to meet him in the town square to hear an announcement of vital significance. The shopkeeper grumbled as he closed his store. The housewife complained as she left her domestic chores. The discontent grew into a storm of protest. Nonetheless, out of respect for their teacher, the people gathered in the town square to await the important announcement. At last the rabbi made his way through the crowd to take his place before them. When they were silent, he said: "I have asked you to close your shops and leave your homes to come here, because I have news of great importance which cannot be delayed for even another hour. And this is my announcement: *I wish to announce—that there is a God in the world!*"

The people departed, chastened and humbled. They knew exactly what the rabbi meant. They talked about God. They professed their belief in God. They prayed to God—but they acted as if God were dead. Their deeds belied their belief in the existence of God. They permitted the God within to remain unawakened. Rabbi Levi Yitzhak offered no philosophical evaluation of the nature or the attributes of God. He simply announced that there is a God in the world. His people understood. Do we?

10

But Little Lower Than the Angels

God sleeps in the stone, breathes in the plant, moves in the animals, and wakes to consciousness in man.
 —JONATHAN BRIERLY, in *Studies of the Soul*, Chapter I

The Divine Within Man

One of the ugliest blasphemies ever perpetrated against the human race is the unspeakable doctrine of the depravity of man. To believe that an infant is born in sin, polluted by the mythical disobedience of the mythical Adam and Eve, contaminated by the sexual experience of some genetically remote biblical ancestors, destined for purgatory without the redemptive water of baptism, is rationally untenable, theologically inconsistent, and religiously insulting.

Mature religion is based, not on the depravity of man, but on the divinity of man—a conclusion that derives from the conviction that man is created in the spiritual image of God, endowed with an immortal soul, a questioning mind, the freedom of will to make moral decisions, and a sacred potential for holiness.

Professor Ashley Montagu, in *On Being Human*, asserts that "there is not a shred of evidence that man is born with 'hostile' or 'evil' impulses which must be watched and disciplined. Discipline of basic impulses is, indeed, necessary, but it is the discipline of love, *not* frustration, which they require."[1]

Though man is rooted in nature, he transcends nature. Faith avows that mortal man, a child of dust, transient and temporal, bound to the earth that finally claims his body, is endowed with an immortal soul that enables him to fuse his being into eternal life. Classified as an animal, he is a rational animal, but even more, he is an animal with a soul. Tempted by material appetites, he disciplines and refines his desires, subjugating them to his moral will. Inextricably bound to his Creator, he exercises an independence of mind, will and behavior that enables him to deny or affirm the Power that created him. Influenced by heredity and environment, he is gifted with the freedom to elevate himself above them. Man, the human mystery, limited by his mortality and yet exalted by his immortality, is the only animal that is privileged to grope for a glimpse, a partial understanding, of the divine Mystery he calls God. Man, described by the author of Psalm 8 as "but little lower than the angels," is the only animal that has the ability to wake to consciousness the Divinity within.

If man is a robot, a thing, a mass occupying space, stuff—if man is an automaton conditioned by his environment, determined by his genes, and compelled by his libido—if man is nothing but a composite of the elements on a chemical valence chart—if man is only a thing, a creeping, crawling conglomeration of molecules—why not

[1] New York, Abelard-Schuman Limited, 1950, p. 45.

rain down bombs upon him? What difference does it make if heaped-up corpses rot at Maidenek, Bergen-Belsen, and Dachau? Of what significance is it if the fats of human bodies are converted into soap? These are only things, stuff, animate matter. Turn back in time to the 1940's in Nazi Europe, and look. There in a concentration camp is a mother crooning a lullaby to a bar of soap—all that remained of what might have been once a precious child. There is a man talking to a piece of soap—all that remained of what might have once been a beloved wife.

When man is regarded as a thing, stuff, chemistry without a soul—what difference does it make if human fats are converted into soap and human skin is stitched into lampshades? But if man is created in the image of God, a precious and priceless child of God, then we have a responsibility to help him, elevate and serve him—not only because God made him but also because God made him but little lower than the angels.

If we believe that man is nothing more than the sum total of chemistry and materialism, then it's easy to look at an infant and refer to it as "a squalling mass of angry protoplasm." If we believe with a modern writer that our greatest need is the honesty to face the fact that we are what we are—nothing but animals—then we cannot blame man for looking at himself with cynicism and contempt.

Our attitude toward man will in large measure determine our attitude toward ourselves, our society, and our world. If we think of man as being selfish, corrupt, primitive and ferocious as a depraved animal, then we have to think of ourselves in the same way, and we are compelled to despise and hate ourselves. If, on the other hand, we think of man struggling and groping to emerge from the jungle of bestiality, endowed with a divine potential for goodness, beauty, truth and holiness, guided and motivated by the spiritual image of God within, then we can begin to find a new respect for man and for ourselves. Moreover, if man is created in the image of God, if man is a sacred personality, if man is but little lower than the angels, then we have a responsibility to man, to serve him, to help him, to elevate him—not as a thing, a robot, or a statistic, but as a precious and priceless child of God.

This, then, imposes an obligation and presents a formidable challenge to those who not only believe in the divinity of God but who also believe in the divinity of man created in the image of God.

We may not like to face it, but if the assertion that man is created in the image of God is more than a facile phrase on our lips; if we answer the question *What is Man?* by affirming that *Man is but little lower than the angels*, then try as we will to run away, to escape into the idyllic garden of indifference, a Voice will seek us out and will find us asking, *Where art Thou?* If we ignore the Voice and try to run away from it, a compelling and realistic faith must grasp us, seize us, and shake us, demanding to know: "What are you going to do about those who are dying of hunger, pleading for a crust of bread, little children whose emaciated, vermin-ridden bodies are too weak even to reach for food? Aren't they also *my* children?

"What are you going to do about those who cry out of the depths, who drink of their own tears, and who eat the bread of affliction? Aren't they also created in the image of God?

"What are you going to do about the oppressed and the enslaved who yearn for freedom, who plead for liberation, who struggle to emancipate themselves from the yoke of tyranny, hoping and praying that they may not have to live out their years in the shadow of fear? Aren't they also but little lower than the angels?"

Space exploration has its scientific rationale. Yet, when we consider the huge sums being spent on interplanetary exploration with the need of funds to conquer the dread diseases that afflict man, when countless numbers of men, women, and children are dying of starvation, the priority given to the conquest of outer space appears to be morally indefensible and criminally negligent.

Yes, we say we believe in the Fatherhood of God and in the brotherhood of man; we say we believe in the sanctity of the human personality; but it isn't enough to say it or to believe it. Our words, our beliefs, and our faith must goad us, torment us, motivate us to respect that image, to worship God by service to man, not only because man may be weak or oppressed or suffering, not only because man is human but also because he is divine—and but little lower than the angels.

A remarkable document has been discovered in the ruins of the Warsaw ghetto by the Jewish Joint Distribution Committee. It gives the report of a scientific study of starvation undertaken in the ghetto by a group of Jewish physicians and their families who were slowly, purposely, and systematically starved to death by their Nazi jailors. The work began in February, 1942. These twenty-two Jewish doctors knew that they and their families were going to starve, so instead of crying and protesting, shrieking at their fate, they resolved to contribute to scientific knowledge and provide a study of the effects of starvation on the human mind and body. They had no instruments, and so they made their own to accumulate data and precise observations of the effects of starvation on children. These were their own starving children they studied. With precise scientific terminology, they showed the mental changes and attitudes of adults subjected to starvation. These were their own wives and dear ones they were observing.

With detailed care, they recorded the pathological changes, the sluggishness, the indifference, the retardation of reflexes accompanying starvation. Even after their wives and children had starved to death and had been carted away to the furnaces to be burned or to have the fat that remained in their bodies converted into soap, their scientific study continued—on themselves. They handed the manuscript one to the other even as doctor after doctor was led off to the extermination center, until the last survivor was forced to bury the manuscript in the ruins of the ghetto, hoping and praying that someday it would be discovered. Each physician who contributed to this study was exterminated, but this amazing, remarkable document does more than contribute to medical and scientific knowledge. It is a testament to the phenomenal courage, the stubbornness, and the faith of these men who believed that despite all the horror and the terror and the killing, man would yet elevate himself to a moral future of decency, justice, and love.

Couldn't these scientists have answered the question *What is man?* by a bitter and cynical answer: "Man is a beast, a fearful denizen of the jungle, a tiger with a swastika, a demon, a devil with a *Sieg heil* on his lips?" Couldn't they have said: "*Why bother with a world that has gone mad? Why contribute to a civilization that is starving us as a prelude to death? Why shouldn't we give up and yield to defeat?"* But they refused to yield; they refused to give up. Even in the miserable rat-infested horror of the Warsaw ghetto, they determined to contribute to the future of mankind. A golem would not have done so. A robot would not have done so. Mark II, an idiot of the universe, a helpless atom, a sick fly, a grain of sand would not have done so, because they weren't created in the image of God. We should think of these ghetto physicians, of Albert Schweitzer serving as a medical missionary in Africa, of all the men and women who have suffered and sacrificed and died serving humanity, when we ask *What is man?*; then we will be able to concur with the psalmist, who said, "Man is but little lower than the angels."

If our civilization is to survive, we must accept the Divinity in man as a reality, and mobilize our resources to serve and elevate man as a sacred child of God.

A Talmudic parable relates the story of a rabbi, Joshua Ben Levi, who took a trip to Rome in the second century of the Christian Era. He was thrilled by the magnificent buildings and edifices that he saw. He looked upon the beautiful statues that were covered with costly tapestry to protect them from the cold of winter and the heat of summer, and while he was admiring the magnificence of the Roman civilization, a man tugged at his sleeve, and he turned to behold a beggar in rags, cold, hungry, emaciated, pleading with him for a coin in order to buy a crust of bread. He looked at the magnificent buildings so carefully protected with tapestry, and he looked at the man in rags, and he said: "Here is a building of stone—cold, lifeless—and yet it is protected and watched over; and here is man, created in the very image of God—man, but little lower than the angels—man who has within him the spark of Divinity, clothed in tattered rags. A civilization that places more emphasis upon buildings and upon things than upon human values and human beings cannot survive!"

Confronted by the threat of a philosophy of calculated, ruthless materialism, terrified by the imminence of atomic annihilation and radioactive death, man must find a way to fulfill the potential of Divinity we call his soul. In a world that is destructible, he must identify himself with the indestructible. The futility of predicating his hopes upon finite matter must motivate him to renewed faith in the infinite spirit that summons man to be holy.

Ye Shall Be Holy

The divine image within man is his inherent potential for holiness. It is through holiness that man awakens the God within. It is through holiness that man achieves a moral relationship with God and his fellow man.

Contrary to the prevailing supposition, holiness is not a vague, nebulous, pietistic, mystical state of being that enables a man to withdraw from the world and limit himself to prayer, ritual, and a mystic communion with God. The state of holiness is unalterably related to man's ethical behavior. It is his active concern with and participation in the effort to promote human relations by man's humanity to man.

The command to be holy has its source in the nineteenth chapter of Leviticus, beginning with the second verse: "Ye shall be holy; for I the Lord your God am holy." It is significant to note that here the requisites of holiness are: respect for parents, the observance of the Sabbath, consideration for the poor and the afflicted, honesty, justice, equality, truth, sexual purity, assistance to those being attacked or oppressed, and abstinence from vengeance. The list of moral requirements for holiness culminates in the commandment "Thou shalt love thy neighbor as thyself." It is by the observance of these moral precepts that man achieves holiness. He does not isolate himself from society and the problems of life, but expresses his potential of Divinity by his ethical behavior toward his fellow man.

This appears to be at variance with the stereotype of holiness so commonly held by respectable religion, where the holy man is seen to retreat from the affairs of life. In self-imposed isolation he bypasses the problems of society to contemplate and meditate. His countenance is stern, his demeanor is serious, and he is totally lacking in a sense of humor. In short, to be holy is to be a self-righteous prig.

Such holiness is easier to achieve than the holiness required by mature religion. In very practical terms, holiness requires the giving of our earnings to the poor, the afflicted, and the oppressed. It means the application of justice and compassion in our everyday dealings with our fellow man. It means purity of speech, and regards slander and malicious gossip as moral defilement. Such holiness demands the sanctity of family life, the most sensitive manifestation of love in marriage, and selfless devotion to our children. It demands that we take action against injustice, bigotry, and ignorance even though it may endanger our respectability and security. It imposes the require- ments of humility, lovingkindness, truthfulness, compassion, and the quest for wholeness.

By "wholeness" we mean that which is articulated in the prayer of Socrates at the end of the *Phaedrus:* "Make the outer and the inner man one." This is closely associated with the root meaning of religion, *religare,* which means "to bind together again." This is the basic purpose of mature religion; to make the outer and the inner man one, to make man whole. Such wholeness motivates the individual to bind himself to the totality of mankind, and enables him to look upon humanity as one indivisible unity. No one is complete until he joins himself with the totality of being, until he experiences empathically the joys and sorrows, the hopes and aspirations of his fellow man.

Holiness is demonstrated in man's concern for his fellow man as expressed in social action. The image of God within man is not to be limited to the concept of an immaterial soul that is unrelated to hu- man behavior. It is fruitless and futile to make the theological suppo- sition of a soul the substitute for social action. Man cannot examine the soul and dissect it into component parts. Faith and reason attest to the belief in a soul—that man is more than chemistry—but what do we mean by the soul?

The Concept of the Soul

A great deal of theological baby talk is babbled about the concept of the soul. There are some who envisage the soul as carrying on an independent existence in the next world, endowed with wings, soaring through the heavenly realm, strumming ethereal music on a golden harp. The soul is referred to as a spiritual body that eats, drinks, cogitates, and experiences emotional joy and sorrow. The rabbis in the Talmud argued endlessly about the point of time in which the human embryo becomes endowed with a soul. Rabbi Judah said, "At the moment of formation." His Roman friend Antoninus said, "At the moment of conception." Some sages contend that the soul in the womb was taught the entire Torah and at the moment of birth an angel tapped the infant on the head and made him forget all of his learning. This is similar to the Platonic doctrine that the learning process is the recall of that which was once known.

Does the soul exist, or is it a fictitious projection of man's yearning for preeminence over the beast? The gentle cynic Ecclesiastes insisted that "that which befalleth the sons of men befalleth beasts . . . they have all one breath; so that man hath no pre-eminence above a beast; for all is vanity. All go unto one place; all are of the dust, and all return to dust. Who knoweth the spirit of man whether it goeth upward, and the spirit of the beast whether it goeth downward to the earth?" (3.19-21)

Man's preeminence over the beast is not limited to a soul. His superiority over the beast is in his ability to communicate by speech, in his pursuit of values, in the freedom to choose between good and evil, in his capacity for moral decision. Man may be an animal, but he is a metaphysical animal as well as a thinking, a questioning, and a God-seeking animal.

Kurt Reinhardt states "that being, called 'man,' who asks philosophical questions, wants first of all to know what he is and where he stands. And why is he so anxiously and vitally concerned with his own existence? Simply because by his very nature he is a questioning being, a philosophical creature. The irrational animal, on the other hand is essentially unphilosophical; it does not question the meaning of its existence, nor the meaning of its surrounding world. It merely accepts both and uses them to the best of its ability. But man is that peculiar kind of being which perpetually questions and wonders and doubts."[2]

The soul, however, is not to be equated with the rational faculty or with the intellectual process. This would mean that one who is congenitally, or as the result of illness, lacking in the ability to reason is devoid of a soul. It would further imply that the more rational the individual, the more he is exercising the power of the soul. Such a concept of the soul divorced from a relationship with God, ethics, and holiness may be philosophically acceptable, but it is religiously untenable.

The commonly accepted concepted belief is that the soul is the

[2] *The Existential Revolt* (Milwaukee, Bruce Publishing Company, 1952).

immaterial, noncorporeal essence wholly other than physical. It is the psyche of the human being, which is his exclusively; it is *Geist*, spirit, breath, the immortal part of his composition infused by God. The theologian believes that the soul is the spirit of God within man, ethereal, undefinable, and unknowable. He contends that the soul is the spiritual image of God, but does not clarify or expound upon what he means. Those who are inclined toward the scientific method reluctantly concede the possibility of the soul as being energy which remains resident and constant in the cosmos. In this sense they grant the possibility that the energy we call "soul" may become one with divine energy which is equated with God.

Aside from personal considerations of vanity, ego, and the fear of contemplating the extinction of one's own personality, metaphysical deliberations about the nature of the soul serve no vital religious purpose. However we may argue, or whatever we may believe, it is not too essential to ethical religion whether the soul continues an independent existence, with intelligence, emotional reactions, and a life of its own after death, or whether it becomes absorbed into the World Soul we call God.

Faith compels us to believe that there is a soul and that the soul is indestructible, eternal, and immortal, but faith does not define or explain the nature of the soul. What is important and meaningful is that we correlate the soul with the impetus to seek and implement moral and spiritual values. The belief that man is created in the spiritual image of God should be interpreted to mean that man is endowed with ethical attributes and is committed to an *imitatio dei*, a moral imitation of divine attributes of justice, compassion, and holiness. Mature religion considers the soul as man's inherent potential for wholeness, the divine within that impels him to quest for beauty, justice, truth, and love. The mature faith urges man to equate his soul with his capacity for holiness—which is the God within. Such a belief in the soul inevitably leads to the conviction that the more we serve our fellow man, and the more we manifest qualities that imitate the ethical attributes of God, the more we educe the divine potential which is Divinity within man.

A rabbinic parable tells of the subjects of a king who came before him to declare their loyalty and their love. "What words of praise may we offer you?" they asked. "What gifts may we give thee to demonstrate our love?"

The king replied: "My subjects, I am touched by your devotion, but you need not speak my praise for I understand what is in your hearts. As for your gifts, do I not own the entire kingdom? If you would show your love for me, go forth and serve my children."

Mature religion suggests that we demonstrate our love of God not only through prayers, ritual, and offerings, but by dedicating ourselves to social justice in behalf of God's children.

The Vocabulary of God

There are many motivations for man's effort to achieve brotherhood. The secular materialist seeks brotherhood for the sake of the state. The humanist seeks brotherhood for the sake of man. The religionist seeks brotherhood for the sake of God and the God within man.

The late Rabbi Joshua Loth Liebman, author of *Peace of Mind*, expressed this beautifully when he elaborated on a rabbinic homily to illustrate the teaching that we advance in our quest for God through the brotherhood of man:

"An old rabbi centuries ago asks the question, 'We are told, "Thou shalt love the Lord thy God with all thy heart, with all thy soul and with all thy might." How can we love the Lord our God with all our heart and soul and might when we can never see God, the invisible spirit of the universe?' We can love God best by loving His letters best. Just as a child learns the alphabet one letter at a time and then combines the letters into words and the words into sentences until at last he is able to read a book, so should we regard every human being as but one letter in the alphabet of God. The more letters we come to understand and to treasure, the more we can read the Book of God and love its Author."[3]

In another address, Rabbi Liebman added:

"The question that comes to every human being is this: Are we treasuring or blurring the letters of God? We have succeeded in erasing the letters of God, millions of them, in war. The challenge that

[3] *Psychiatry and Religion*, Joshua Loth Liebman, ed. (Boston, Beacon Press, 1948), p. 38.

comes to our generation is to learn how to treasure the letters of God in the knowledge that every human being, white, red, yellow, black, of every race and every creed, in every corner of the earth, is one equal consonant in the vocabulary of Divinity."

In similar spirit the author of Psalm 8 doesn't say that only those of the white race are but little lower than the angels; he doesn't say that only those of the colored race are but little lower than the angels; he doesn't specify that those of a particular religious faith are but little lower than the angels, *but Man, the universal Man, the child of God*, without a label, without a designation, without any denomination—*Man, the entire human family, is but little lower than the angels*. He didn't isolate Man into neat little groups and say that God is a Father to this one and not that, or that God has endowed this segment with Divinity because of the pigmentation of skin, or because of the mode of religious worship. The psalmist could not make such restrictive claims because he was praying to a universal God and Father whose love for His children rises above all denominations, above all considerations of race or faith—because they are all but little lower than the angels.

If, in the words of the poet: "Somewhere behind space and time, there is only wetter water and slimier slime," then man doesn't have a soul created in the image of God because there is no God, and if there is no God there is no morality, no freedom of will and no soul. But if, transcending space and time there is a universal God of justice, compassion, and love, then we must go forth in search of that God, to find him not only somewhere behind space and time, not only in "the heavens, the work of His fingers, the moon and the stars which He has established," but also in man, the bearer of His image.

As explorers of the soul we must quest for this divine image within us so as to release its sacred potential for holiness, goodness, beauty, and truth.

The belief that "man is but little lower than the angels" leads us to the conclusion that God's kingdom is internal as well as external. It assures us that the kingdom of God lies within us. Human happiness depends more upon the inner spirit than upon the outer circumstances.

The Divinity in man is the holy potential of the human spirit. It is immortal, indestructible essence. Call it what we will: spirit, image, soul, *Geist*, breath, *élan vital* or unknowable "X," it is the God within man. This is the sacred duty of man: to arouse, awaken, and utilize this divine potential for the purpose of achieving wholeness, the sanctification of life, and the building of a just and moral society. Sin may be defined as indifference to this sacred potential, permitting the inherent Godliness to remain dormant and unawakened. Religious aspiration or virtue is the effort to explore, educe, and bring into active being the Divinity within. This is the spiritual glory of man and the ennobling purpose of human existence.

To believe this, to predicate a religious way of life on the belief that man is endowed with holiness, is to believe not only in God but also in man. The acceptance of the doctrine of the divineness of man compels the acceptance of the conviction that man is essentially good. He may be tempted and beguiled by his emotions, his appetites, his passion, and his weakness, but man is holy. To believe this is to reject Kierkegaard's statement, "It is not that man is a sinner because he sins, but man sins because he is a sinner."

To believe this is to be filled with compassion for every human being. It is to seek the strength of faith to understand and not to judge or condemn. To believe in the divineness of man is to believe in the brotherhood of man and dedicate oneself to the cause of social justice. To believe in the divineness of man is to maintain a God-ordained stubborn, uncompromising hope for man, for his future, and for his purpose. Such a belief resists the most dogmatic assertions of the "fundamentalist" that man is evil. It rejects the most persuasive predictions of science that man is doomed to degenerate into a race of degenerates, that carbon 14, a radioactive isotope of common carbon produced by a neutron bombardment of the nitrogen in the air caused by hydrogen bombs will someday make of us a generation of monsters. Those who adhere to the mature faith will insist, not that man is but little lower than carbon 14, but that man is but little lower than the angels, and that the divine heritage bequeathed to man will triumphantly, after time and struggle, "make the outer and the inner man one" in order to create a better life and build a better society.

William Faulkner believed this and accepted this at the time he was awarded the Nobel Prize Award and said: "I decline to accept the end of man. It is easy enough to say that man is immortal simply because he will endure; that when the last dingdong of doom has clanged and faded from the last worthless rock hanging tideless in the last red and dying evening, that even then there will still be one more sound, that of his puny, inexhaustible voice still talking. I refuse to accept this. I believe that man will not merely endure; he will prevail. He is immortal not because he alone among creatures has an inexhaustible voice, but because he has a soul, a spirit capable of compassion and sacrifice and endurance."

The Double Search

Even though we may be convinced of the invincibility of the human spirit, the sustaining purpose of man cannot be understood without contemplating the implications of the double search. These terms were given by the late Rufus M. Jones when he wrote a book with that title. His thesis was that man must be ever in search of God, even as God is ever in search of man.

Similarly, Martin Buber explained it in this way: "God's grace consists precisely in this, that He wants to let Himself be won by man, that He places Himself, so to speak, into man's hands. God wants to come to His world, but He wants to come to it through man. This is the mystery of our existence, the superhuman choice of mankind."[4]

Man needs God, but God also needs man to fulfill a divine purpose. This does not imply irreverence or a pious blasphemy. Without man, God, whose existence is timeless, will persist, but it is man who gives the most sacred meaning to the reality of God. God needs man as a co-partner for the building of His kingdom and the fulfillment of a divine plan.

God is ever in search of man, inquiring of Adam, the prototype of all mankind, *Ayecho*, "Where art thou?" "Thou dost hunt me like a lion," exclaimed Job. All human history reveals God in search of man, asking, "Where art thou?"

Such is the infinite holiness of man, a speck of dust fused with Divinity; a creature of matter whose life span is but a tick of the clock merged with eternal timelessness. Man is not, as we are told in

[4] *The Way of Man* (Chicago, Wilcox & Follett Company, 1951), p. 45.

current existentialist philosophy, miserable and wretched, sinful and worthless refuse to be cast upon a cosmic manure heap. Man is not doomed by his very nature to be evil and guilt-ridden. Man is but little lower than the angels not only because of his eternal soul but also because God needs man for a sublime purpose.

God needs an Antonio Stradivari to make violins, a Michelangelo for a masterpiece of painting, a Louis Pasteur, a Lister, a Fleming, and a Jonas Salk as the instrumentalities for bringing healing to mankind —but God also needs an instrument, a means to bring spiritual healing to mankind. God needs a Moses, an Amos, a Micah, a Jeremiah, a Jesus through whom to channel divine revelation. God needs dedicated men and women of every faith, race, and nationality, dedicated and covenanted to fulfill a divine destiny.

The imperative need of our age is not guided missiles, but guided men and women who will direct their thoughts and their lives on high. It is not the conquest of outer space, but the conquest of inner space that will shape the future. For this we need the strength, power, and inspiration that come from God. For this we must learn to go beyond our own resources, and we must learn to live beyond our means.

Faced with the crisis of cold wars, "dirty" bombs, and the threat of nuclear destruction, the nuclear scientists are appealing to clergymen and educators to take action, to teach, preach, and educate so that we may achieve understanding, good will, and peace. They are not appealing to robots to take action. They aren't asking the test tubes to implement moral ideals and ethical values for the salvation of our world. They aren't asking the molecules and the isotopes to pray for divine guidance and spiritual inspiration. They know that God is not in search of robots, automatons, golems, and machines. They know that mechanical man created in the image of a blueprint cannot serve a divine purpose. They are asking man to pray, to act, to make moral decisions, because man is endowed with a soul. Man is linked to Divinity by his divine nature. Man has the power to communicate with God, to permit himself to be found by God, to enter into a covenant with Divinity. It is prayer that reveals the divine nature of man, and enhances his preeminence over the beast. It is through prayer that man confronts God and God confronts man in the culmination of the double search.

11

Living Beyond Our Means

Prayer is an invitation to God to intervene in our lives, not only through our walking in His ways, but through His entering into our ways.—ABRAHAM HESCHEL in *Man's Quest for God*

The Spiritual Bridge

Prayer is the spiritual bridge that enables man to approach God, and permits God to come near to man. It is the sacred fusion of the infinite with the finite, the summoning of the divine within man to commune with the divine beyond man. Prayer is that which inspires, making the immanent God ever more indwelling. It distinguishes man from the beast, elevates him from the status of an animal to a praying animal, and enables him to bring his potential of holiness into sublime reality. It permits man to go beyond self to an identification with others, to join and become one with humanity and further his quest for wholeness.

Prayer not only expresses a sense of awe and reverence before the divine Mystery, it is the means of making love to God and experiencing the answering response of infinite tenderness and compassion.

Through prayer we direct our thoughts on high and elevate our lives to values that make for holiness. It is through prayer that we articulate our dependence upon a power greater than ourselves, and invite God to intervene in our lives.

One of the popular delusions cherished by mankind is the belief that man is self-sufficient. Mature religion enables us to accept the reality that the objective of human aspiration is to achieve a spiritual dependency upon God. Living beyond our means may be bad economics, but it is good religion. Man does not live entirely by his own resources. We are all mutually dependent not only upon the efforts of our fellow human beings, but also upon God. Prayer is the effort of man to go beyond himself, to obtain spiritual strength, moral guidance, and religious power so that he may live beyond his human resources.

There isn't one of us who cannot learn to tap the spiritual resources available through prayer. Every man can be stronger and more mature if he will determine to live beyond his natural means by utilizing the strength, power, and inspiration that come from God. New strength comes through prayer by which we examine ourselves in the solitude of our souls; the prayer that guides us and directs us to sanctify life with holiness; the prayer that enables us to enter into a communion with Divinity, talk with God, listen to God, and invite God to enter our lives.

Today there are those who find themselves emotionally disturbed and seek the help of competent psychiatrists—and it is proper that they do so. There should be no stigma or disgrace identified with emotional or mental illness. They should be encouraged to seek and receive such help. But there are the so-called normal people who are also emotionally disturbed and who have a greater need for God than a psychiatrist. Do we take the time to talk to God? Do we approach Him with our hopes, our fears, our guilt, and our troubles?

The purpose of psychotherapy is to evoke our innermost feelings, our hunger, our yearning to be whole and complete, and apply sound rules of mental health to those feelings and yearnings. Prayer serves to do all of this, and more. The greatest physicians of the soul have applied these very principles since the dawn of human history—principles that help us to become whole—principles that help us to learn to live with ourselves, our society, and our God.

The psychiatrist may designate "wholeness" as *Gestalt*, "soul" as psyche, "sin" as guilt psychosis, a backward person as "regressive," and a happy man as "a well integrated personality," but his object is primarily the same as that of the minister, rabbi, and priest—to educe the inherent strength for an individual to achieve his greatest potential for living in harmony with himself, his God, and his society.

Once, the pious individual would take his problem to God, and in the outpouring of his soul there was a mental catharsis, an emotional release that purged him of many of his maladjustments and disturbing conflicts. He lived beyond his means by turning to God as a healer, counselor, and spiritual confidant. It was God who served as a divine Psychiatrist and it was divine inspiration that gave man moral insights and provided a source of strength beyond his means.

Unfortunately, today the exaggerated emphasis placed upon psychiatry may lead many into thinking that the psychiatrist is a substitute for God, that the psychiatrist's office supplants the House of God, and that it is only a question of time before the couch replaces the pew.

In *God and Freud* Leonard Gross quotes a dialogue between a woman and her minister:

" 'I hate God,' she began at once.

" 'Tell Him,' said the minister.

" 'How do you talk to Him?'

" 'Talk to Him the way He talks to you,' [the minister] said. . . . So she cursed God. She called God a son of a bitch."[1]

The woman was encouraged by her minister to curse God because his knowledge of modern psychiatric counseling told him this was one way to get at the root of her hatred. The author contends that the minister was thus able to guide her to a more adult view of God.

Job's wife told him, "Curse God and die!" This minister told a woman to curse God so that she could live more maturely. Such psychotherapy may have some beneficial effects, but it is not to be equated with prayer, nor is it a substitute for prayer.

Prayer Without God

Ludwig Feuerbach (1804–1872), in *Das Wesen des Christentums* (The Essence of Christianity), explained religion as man's fallacious effort to project himself as infinite. When man believes that he is communing with God, in actuality he is only communing with himself. God, then, is nothing but a personified wish, and prayer a meaningless experience.

Martin Buber, following the tradition of Hermann Cohen and William James, has helped to make us mindful of the personal relationship that exists between the "I" and the "Thou." God is not to be spoken about, but is the "Thou" to be spoken to and listened to. God is not an "It" absolutely transcendent and impersonal, but the One with whom we communicate in an intimately personal relationship. The more an individual is able to experience the "Thou," the more he becomes a person participating in a divine confrontation.

The French scholar who prayed in the hour of his need, "God, if

[1] New York, McKay, 1959, p. 57.

there is a God, save my soul, if I have a soul," may have been honest and sincere, but such agnosticism does not make for meaningful and reverent worship. A cynic once declared: "Prayer is good as a catharsis. You talk yourself out. In reality, however, prayer is like a telephone conversation with no one on the other end of the line." If prayer is nothing but talking to oneself with no one at the other end of the line, then such a prayer has nothing to do with religion or God. In fact, it is not prayer. Without the belief in God, the individual might just as well take a laxative, or seek his emotional catharsis on a psychiatrist's couch.

To regard God as completely transcendent is to remove the religious basis for prayer. Paul Tillich, the noted theologian, wrestling with the problem of God and human freedom, contends that the personal God of theism is dead and that the demise of such a God is fortunate because the very belief in Him reduces, limits, and ultimately destroys human freedom. To Professor Tillich, God transcends all human life and history. The personal God is a myth that must be destroyed to preserve the possibility of human freedom.

To subscribe to Professor Tillich's belief is to make prayer a telephone conversation with no one on the other end of the line. It is to remove God from human life and history and regard Him as the absentee Landlord of the universe who presides over the cosmos but has no personal relationship to man. Once we agree to this, then we must also agree that there is no immanent God, no religious basis for prayer, and no divine authority for morality, social action, or ethical conduct.

The belief in an immanent God does destroy human freedom if freedom is interpreted to mean that man may do as he pleases: kill, steal, commit adultery, and violate the requisites of the moral law. If, however, freedom is interpreted to mean the ability to make moral decisions, the possibility of choosing between ethical alternatives, the capability of ignoring or activating the divine potential of holiness inherent within man, then the belief in an immanent God enhances freedom of will and moral decision. The belief in a personal God does not compel man to make moral choices. It gives him the freedom to accept or reject, even as it sets forth the standards of morality that are required by God. Man is free, if he so chooses, not to believe in God.

It is only in an extremely logical and casuistic sense that Professor Tillich is correct. The belief in a personal God does influence man's choice of values, and accordingly detracts from an absolute freedom of will. If this so-called limitation contributes to man's choice of morality, truth, justice, mercy, and peace, it is greatly to be desired.

It is because he has freedom of will that man may go beyond himself to commune with God in prayer. Even as he prays he surrenders a portion of his sovereignty to the King of all kings. The very act of prayer suggests that man is not able to live within his own means and must go beyond himself for divine help. Even though prayer manifests his dependence upon God, man exercises his freedom of will to ask God to strengthen and guide him to make moral decisions. According to Professor Abraham Heschel, "Prayer is an invitation to God to intervene in our lives, not only through our walking in His ways, but through His entering into our ways."

The Efficacy of Prayer

Although we may argue, debate, and question the need for prayer, most of us are inclined to agree with William James, who said, "We pray because we cannot help praying." Any prayer that places us in communion with God has religious value, but frequently there is disillusionment with prayer because our requests and petitions are seemingly ignored. From the kindergarten point of view, the efficacy of prayer is judged not by what happens within us, but by what is given to or withheld from us. The content of our prayer and the reasons why we pray significantly indicate the infantilism or the maturity of our religious faith.

Karle Wilson Baker wrote:

> "Courage is armor
> A blind man wears;
> The calloused scars
> Of outlived despairs;
> Courage is Fear
> That has said its prayers."[2]

[2] "Courage," *Masterpieces of Religious Verse*, ed. by James Dalton Morrison (New York, Harper and Brothers, 1948), p. 376.

Man, confronted by a myriad of apprehensions, anxieties, doubts, threats, and dread, needs the courage engendered by fear that has said its prayers. Professor Alfred North Whitehead has stated that it is through the facing of fear and dread that man truly arrives at a religious faith that is founded on the love of God.

Abraham, Isaac, and Jacob, patriarchs, prophets, and sages experienced fear, but through their fear they found the way to God. Moses was afraid, but his fear said its prayers, and then, "Moses drew near unto the thick darkness where God was." Through prayer, man is given the armor of courage and faith to meet the challenge of life. He is given the assurance that he is not alone. God is with him, even in the thick darkness.

Man cannot help praying when he is afraid, confused, despondent, suffering, and bereaved. Talking over a problem with God helps to clarify, illumine, and direct one to make moral decisions. The presence of a Power greater than ourselves gives us comfort and assurance in our fear, suffering, and bereavement. There is the strength of faith that comes from communion with God. In yet another sense, however, prayer enables us to direct our lives to values that are sacred and holy.

"But this is such cold, obtuse, colorless, abstract theological verbiage," says the embittered man. "When I pray, I want action and response. Prayer is all right for the mystic who can commune in metaphysical ecstasy with supreme Reality, but what about the realities of a human being confronted with all the misery, suffering, and perplexity of life? Can a prayer ease the pain of a throbbing toothache? Can prayer heal a liver corroded with cancer? Can prayer help a headache as much as medicine? Can a prayer mend the fragments of a broken heart? You talk about God entering into our lives. Is there any way that God can enter a life that is black with despair, where darkness fills the void where a soul should be? To walk in God's ways! Who knows whether they are really God's ways, divinely revealed commandments, or whether they are man's ideas of what God's commandments should be? How can a man even think of walking in God's ways when he can't even walk out of the doorway of his house because his legs are shaken and withered by Parkinson's disease? Can all the prayers in the world bring back the loving, living touch of a child now moldering and rotting in the grave, companion to worms, cradled in everlasting nothingness? Pray to God, you say, commune with the Most High. I lift up my voice and shout until I'm hoarse. I croak froglike sounds and preface them with a proper 'O Lord.' I say, 'My Heavenly Father, it's Your child speaking. Hear me!' I beg God to enter my life, or just speak to me, and if not with a voice, just whisper, whistle, curse me, damn me—but let me know that He is there, that something is there, that I am not crying and pleading and praying into an empty, unanswering void. I hear nothing. I feel nothing, and am supposed to believe that this inarticulate, inchoate nothingness is an answer. I commune with the Most High. I look up and dust falls in my eyes. There is a spark within me, you say. I breathe upon it with hope. I fan it with wind, will, spirit, and it fades out, winking obscenely as it dies. I bow, genuflect, kneel, prostrate myself, and a painful arthritis reminds me that I am flesh, sick flesh, inflamed joints, rotting bones. Gnarled fingers clasp together in the posture of piety. Breathe upon these fingers, O Lord. Command the diseased bones to kneel that they may praise God with a mighty hallelujah. So God is my co-partner. Thanks, Partner, for nothing!"

Such a man cries out of the depths, and our hearts go out to him in his suffering, but the efficacy of prayer is not to be assessed by the poignancy of his suffering, the bitterness of his spirit, or the appeal to a God of magic to effect miraculous cures by means of prayer. It is understandable that he would feel more assured of the presence of God were he to hear a divine voice or even a heavenly whisper. However, the mature faith does not project a concept of God who articulates sounds. Prayer cannot make us hear even a whisper spoken by God. Prayer will not ease the pain of a throbbing toothache, because prayer is not an equivalent of novocain. Prayer will not cure cancer or arthritis. Prayer is not a resurrecting force that can bring back loved ones from the dead.

A mature faith assures us not only that God *is*, but that God exists, that God is near, available, accessible to man in his need. When Holy Scripture relates that "Moses entered into the thick of darkness where God was," to the Jewish sages this meant that God is present not only in joy and in light, but in suffering and in darkness, in pain, sorrow, and the anguish of the soul.

The nature of prayer enables us to gain the kind of faith described by Josiah Royce when he wrote that faith is the discovery of a Reality that enables one to face anything that can happen to one in the universe.

The following is an example of a mature prayer that does not ask God to perform miracles:

> "O God grant us the serenity to accept
> What cannot be changed;
> The courage to change what can be changed,
> And the wisdom to know one from the other."[3]

The mature prayer does not express the selfish yearning of the heart with petitions for personal favors or material gifts, but seeks to enter into communion with God so that man may find a source of spiritual strength in a Power beyond himself.

The saintly Rabbi Levi Yitzhak of Berditchev,[4] called "The Compassionate," once lifted his voice to God at a time when the Jews were besieged by enemies. Heavy-laden with sorrow, he cried out: "Lord of the universe, I do not beg You to reveal to me the secret of Your ways, for who am I to know them? But show me one thing, show it to me more clearly and more deeply, show me what this, which is happening at this very moment, means to me, what it demands of me, what You, Lord of the world, are telling me by way of it. Dear God, I do not ask You to take away my suffering. I don't even want to know why I suffer; but only this, my God, *Do I suffer for Your sake?*" The magnificence of such a prayer reveals the true and basic meaning of prayer. The rabbi did not ask God to remove his suffering. He did not make of God a divine magician. All he wanted to know was whether his suffering was in accordance with the will of God; whether his pain and his misery were of significance in fulfilling God's divine purpose. It is proper for us to call upon God in the extremity of our grief, and it is fitting to implore God's help when we suffer, but we must not expect God to break the natural laws that He has created, solely because we petition Him to do so.

There are many soul-stirring documents that have come to us out of the suffering of the Jews during the horrible and catastrophic

[3] Reinhold Niebuhr.
[4] A Chassidic teacher who lived in the eighteenth century.

period of European history when Hitler's *Wehrmacht* and the Nazi forces marched through Europe. In a remarkable volume by Zvi Kolitz, called *The Tiger Beneath the Skin*,[5] there is revealed the following inscription, found on the wall of a cellar in Cologne where a number of Jews hid themselves for the entire duration of the war: "I believe in the sun even when it is not shining. I believe in love even when feeling it not. I believe in God even when He is silent." This is surely a most remarkable evidence of faith. This is more than a credo. It is a prayer attesting man's love for God even when God seems to be silent. It is easy enough to have faith in God during periods of happiness, prosperity, and joy, when we are blessed with health and comfort. There is no great merit in loving God when He bestows his divine blessings upon us. The test of faith is during those periods of suffering and pain, when the poison of doubt embitters our hope, when it seems that there is no possibility of personal happiness. To believe in God even when He seems to be silent, to love God when our lives, hopes, and dreams are placed in the crucible of anguish—this is the real test of faith; this is the real measure of the power of prayer.

In the same book Mr. Kolitz relates that in the ruins of the ghetto of Warsaw, among heaps of charred rubbish, there was found packed tightly into a small bottle a testament, written during the ghetto's last hours by a Jew named Yossel Rakover. It is dated "Warsaw, April 28, 1943." A portion of it reads: "My rabbi would frequently tell the story of a Jew who fled from the Spanish Inquisition with his wife and child, striking out in a small boat over the stormy sea until he reached a rocky island. A flash of lightning killed his wife; a storm rose and hurled his son into the sea; then, as lonely as a stone, naked, barefoot, lashed by the storm, terrified by the thunder and lightning, hands turned up to God, the Jew, again setting out on his journey through the wastes of the rocky island, turned to God with the following words: 'God of Israel, I have fled to this place in order to worship You without molestation, to obey Your commandments, and to sanctify Your name. You, however, have done everything to make me stop believing in You. Now, lest it seem to You that You will succeed by these tribulations in driving me from the right path, I notify You, my God and the God of my fathers, that it will not avail

[5] New York, Creative Age Press, 1947, p. 81.

You in the least. You may insult me, You may castigate me, You may take from me all that I cherish and hold dear in the world, You may torture me to death; but I will always love You, and these are my last words to You, my wrathful God: Nothing will avail You in the least. You have done everything to make me renounce You, to make me lose my faith in You; but I die exactly as I have lived, crying, "Eternally praised be the God of the Dead, the God of Vengeance, of Truth, and of Love, Who will soon show His face to the world again, and shake its foundations with His almighty voice. Hear, O Israel, the Lord our God, the Lord is one. Into Thy hands, O Lord, I consign my soul." ' "

Yossel Rakover defied God to make him lose his faith even in the extremity of suffering. Knowing that he was writing his last will and testament, he bequeathed a legacy of faith and an inheritance of indomitable courage not only to his people, but to all mankind. How different is Yossel Rakover's appeal to God from the petty requisitions that we sometimes place upon the desk of Divinity! This man asked no favors of God. He did not ask God to perform a miracle that would convert the last scene of his life from horror and dread into a finale of happiness and triumphant victory. Yossel Rakover died in the ruins of the Warsaw ghetto, stubbornly affirming his faith in God.

The Mature Prayer

Prayer cannot change God, but it can change us. Prayer does not help God; it helps us. The Hebrew word for prayer—*Tefila*—means to judge oneself, to subject oneself to Divinity. It is a spiritual inwardization that enables us to achieve religious insight. Prayer is not begging for something we want; it is experiencing the presence of God in our thoughts and deeds. Prayer brings God down to man and elevates man toward God. It is through prayer that we are spiritually revitalized and strengthened in the effort to lift ourselves above pettiness, selfishness, greed, hatred, and envy to a mood of reverence by which we learn to identify ourselves with moral and spiritual values.

The lines of St. Francis of Assisi demonstrates the reverent magnificence of a mature prayer:

"Lord, make me the channel of Thy peace,
That where there is hatred I may bring love;
That where there is wrong I may bring the spirit of forgiveness;
That where there is discord I may bring harmony;
That where there is error I may bring truth;
That where there is doubt I may bring faith;
That where there is despair I may bring hope;
That where there are shadows I may bring Thy light;
That where there is sadness I may bring joy;
Lord, grant that I may seek rather to comfort than be comforted;
To understand rather than be understood;
To love than be loved;
For it is by giving that one receives,
It is by self-forgetting that one finds,
It is by forgiving that one is forgiven,
It is by dying that one awakens to eternal life."

One who utters such a prayer illumines his soul with light, casts out the darkness of despair, and achieves a selflessness that reflects the radiance of Divinity. The sincere articulation of such a prayer lifts man above material desires and animal passions to spiritual heights of exaltation. It enables one to probe within and explore the potential of holiness that is the inherent image of God.

The mature prayer, then, is not the supplication to a divine magician, but the inwardization that enables us to draw upon a source of divine power to live and mature beyond our means. To pray is to participate in a divine mystery that permits man to commune with ubiquitous God, transcendent and immanent, beyond and within. It is a religious experience that sanctifies our thoughts with holiness and invites God into our lives.

Worship Without Words

A fallacy of kindergarten religion is the belief that prayer is a substitute for moral action. It is important to articulate and give vocal expression to our yearning for God. It is essential to learn to listen, to hear the music of eternity singing through our souls. It is equally necessary, however, to give active and ethical expression to

our love and yearning for God by adherence to His moral commandments, by worship without words, revealing a communion with God
through our deeds.

Once Israel Salanter, a pious rabbi, failed to appear in the synagogue for worship on the holy eve of Atonement. The members of
his congregation went out to search for him and found him in the
barn of a neighbor. What happened to keep him from leading the
congregation in prayer? On the way to the synagogue, he found a
neighbor's calf lost and tangled in the brush. Fearing that he might
hurt the animal, he freed it tenderly and brought it back to its stall.
When he was asked: "How could you do that? Your first duty as a
rabbi is prayer." He answered: "God is called Rachamono, Merciful
One. An act of mercy is a prayer, too."

John Greenleaf Whittier expressed this thought with poetic wisdom when he wrote:

> "O brother man! fold to thy heart thy brother;
> Where pity dwells, the peace of God is there;
> To worship rightly is to love each other.
> Each smile a hymn, each kindly deed a prayer."

This is worship without words, prayer in action. When we witness
a man or woman serving God by serving His children with loving-
kindness and compassionate solicitude, that is worship without words,
that is a prayer that walks and moves and lives. Every time an individual goes forth to do justice, to love mercy, to feed the hungry,
clothe the naked, and bring light into darkness, that is worship without words, a prayer that humbly and reverently walks forth with God.

We usually don't identify prayer with walking, moving forward,
action, because we are so accustomed to thinking of prayer in terms
of words, talk, language, and the verbal outpouring of the sentiments
of the heart, and yet the salvation of the world and our hopes for a
life of justice, truth, brotherhood, and peace depend in large measure
upon our ability to transpose our prayers into action.

Those who seek the mature faith must identify prayer with moral
action. When Pharaoh and his army pursued the Israelites at the
Red Sea, Moses began to cry unto God in urgent prayer for salvation.
God said: "Wherefore criest thou unto Me? Speak unto the children

of Israel, that they may go forward!" Prayer is never a surrogate for moral initiative or ethical responsibility. Mature prayer does not transfer the burden of action to God, but motivates man to direct his faith into avenues of constructive achievement. We listen and talk with God in order to learn how to walk with God and permit God to enter our lives.

To walk with God is to keep His commandments and adhere to His moral laws. An act of justice or mercy that is in accordance with God's will is worship without words. When we implement the ethical and moral commandments of God, we are manifesting our love with an eloquence that transcends the most ornate and prolonged prayer. Our verbal prayers must motivate us to ethical action; otherwise they are incantations and magical formulas, and we differ in little respect from the primitive savage who divorced the gods from morality and mated them to fear, war, and the fertility of the soil.

According to the rabbis, when Moses complained to God that the children of Israel were lacking in belief, God answered, "Let them not believe in Me, as long as they keep My commandments." To say we believe in God isn't enough. To profess our belief in God isn't enough. We demonstrate our belief in God and manifest our love of God by the way we act, by the way we live, by obedience to God's moral commandments, by converting our prayers into action.

It is erroneous to believe that God has an important relationship to what is said, but is not to be seriously considered in relationship to what is done. God is a member of the church or synagogue in good standing as long as He complies with the rules and doesn't make too many demands upon the day-by-day, practical, down-to-earth reality of living. When God intrudes Himself upon the congregation, insisting upon the application of the ethical precepts and the moral values so fervently professed, then God is to be "put in His place," which is a far-distant heaven, with the warning that He should mind His own business or face the consequences of abandonment or summary dismissal. This is a respectable and accepted blasphemy.

We are shocked when we hear men take the name of the Lord in vain. We are revolted when we hear irreverent words defaming the divine. Are we equally shocked and revolted by *actions* that repudiate God? Are we disturbed and agitated by deeds that make a farce out of prayer and a mockery out of worship? Mature religion contends that it is even more blasphemous to act against God than to speak against God. To verbalize our love of God even as we ignore or violate His commandments is the supreme blasphemy.

"Men have been urged to pray," writes H. G. Wood, "when they would have done better to think, observe and act."[6] This indicates the fallacious thinking that there is a disparity between prayer and action. Prayer should never be a substitute for moral action. Prayer should motivate, compel, and inspire man to take action against evil, injustice, greed, hatred, prejudice, and ignorance. The purpose of prayer is to enable man to go beyond himself, to transcend his weakness and apathy, in order to obey God's commandments and build his society in accordance with the will of God. The Jewish sages recognized this when they pointed out that the Hebrew word for worship, Avodoh, has its root meaning in the verb "to work or to serve." Worship is putting our faith to work. Worship is service in behalf of God's children.

The prophets of Israel excoriated those who substituted prayers for deeds, who offered God sacrifices instead of righteousness. The prophet Micah declared: "It hath been told thee, O man, what is good, and what the Lord doth require of thee: only to do justly, to love mercy, and to walk humbly with thy God" (6.8). God requires ethical action. God wants to see prayers walking and moving. God does not require words alone or verbal prayers alone, rites, creeds, or dogma, but living prayers equated with social action.

Accordingly, the mature faith looks upon prayer as religion in action. It suggests that we cannot invite God into our lives until we make the effort to walk in His ways. Prayer is the sacred invitation to God to enter our ways by inspiring us to a divine imitation. The belief that God requires justice sensitizes us to the divine mandate to worship God with acts of justice. The belief that God requires mercy must inspire us to worship God by acts of mercy and love.

We, like Abraham, must dedicate ourselves to destroying the false gods that enslave man to ignorance and superstition; to shattering the image of the kindergarten God we and our fathers have created and perpetuated—a primitive God that is insatiably hungry for words of praise and rites of adoration. We must hear anew the admonition of God addressed to our generation, through Isaiah:

[6] H. G. Wood, *Christianity and Civilization* (New York, The Macmillan Company, 1943), p. 61.

"Yea, when ye make many prayers,
I will not hear;
Your hands are full of blood.

.   .   .   .

Cease to do evil;
Learn to do well;
Seek justice; relieve the oppressed,
Judge the fatherless, plead for the widow."

To obey these commandments is to offer prayers that walk with God.

If prayer is the invitation to God to intervene in our lives so that we may walk in His ways, how are we to ascertain the ways of God? If prayer is to motivate us to imitate the divine attributes of God, how can we know what these divine attributes are? The reply to that question is the subject of the next chapter.

12

The Book of Books

Let truth and falsehood grapple.
—JOHN MILTON, in *Areopagitica*

Burn, Bible, Burn!

Our generation is being called upon to choose sides in the struggle over Holy Scripture, identifying itself with either the fundamentalists or the modernists. The fundamentalists insist that every word of the Bible is literally true, revealed at one time and one place—the irrefutable, undeniable revelation of the will of God. The modernists contend that the Bible evolved over a long period of time and that it may be interpreted allegorically as well as literally. To the modernist, the Bible is a dynamic, progressive revelation of man's quest for God —an evolving compilation of religious history, folklore, law, literature, and morality.

With the publication of the New Revised Standard Version of the Bible in 1953, the fundamentalists mobilized to resist the incursion of modernist thought. A mass meeting was held in Rocky Mount, North Carolina, to protest the elimination of the word "virgin" in the prophecy of Isaiah. The dramatic high light of this meeting was the public burning of the Book. A minister thundererd that "the new version is a deliberate attack on our historic Christian faith," and protested against the substitution of "young woman" for "virgin" in Isaiah 7.14: "Behold the Lord shall give you a sign: the virgin shall conceive and bear a son, and shall call his name Immanuel." While plans were being made for the public burning, a scholar who directed the preparation of the new Bible, Dr. Luther A. Weigle, Dean Emeritus of Yale University Divinity School, insisted correctly that the Hebrew word used in Isaiah was *almah*, which means "young woman," and that the corrected text should read, "A young woman shall conceive and bear a son."

Despite the objection of other ministers to the proposed book burning, the minister who summoned the people to the mass meeting proceeded with his plans and before an audience of two hundred he ripped the paper covering off the Bible, revealing the word FRAUD on the leather covers. Each member of the congregation assembled was given a Bible and a flag, and a page was torn from the Bible and cast into the flames. Describing the new Bible as a master stroke of Satan, the minister cried out: "Some say that this Bible came out of the belly of a crocodile. I say it came out of the belly of hell!" Another fundamentalist minister averred that the cover of this new version of the Bible is appropriately red to indicate that it is Communist-sponsored.

Such a public book burning evokes disturbing memories of the burning of the Talmud in the Middle Ages, the auto-da-fé of the Spanish Inquisition where not only books but human beings also fed the flames of bigotry and ignorance, as the fanatical inquisitors watched and complimented themselves on their religiosity and devotion to God. Such public burning is reminiscent of the burning of witches in Salem and the Nazi conflagration of the wisdom and culture of the ages, with books consigned to the flames as the hysterical mob roared a *Sieg heil* of devotion to Adolf Hitler.

The unconscionable burning of the Bible reveals more than the combustible hysteria of religious incendiaries. It reflects the irrational fanaticism of kindergarten religion. In the cries of "Burn, Bible, burn," we hear again echoes of the din of an ancient and yet modern battle, the sound of the permanent war between wisdom and ignorance, light and darkness, understanding and intolerance, truth and falsehood. Repercussions of that battle were heard in the war between the conservative doctrines of the church and the Copernican theory of astronomy in the sixteenth century. The battle cry resounded in the conflict between the fundamentalists and the Darwinian theory of evolution in the nineteenth century, and now we hear the continuing sound of war in the ideological battle for the mind of man in the twentieth century. Bibles may be burned, but no fire can destroy truth. Hysteria, fear, coercion, reactionary opposition may impede the march of freedom—but there is no power on earth that can eradicate or extinguish the spark of freedom that ignites the flame of the human soul, as man endeavors to throw off the shackles of ignorance in his quest for the presence of the living God.

The Modernist Approach to the Bible

To the modernist the Bible is a sacred testament, a record of man's religious growth from religious infancy, through childhood and adolescence to the threshold of maturity. It is through the modernist approach to the Bible that we mature in our faith, a faith that enables us to say with Heine: "What a book! great and wide as the world, rooted in the abysmal depths of creation and rising aloft into the blue mysteries of heaven. . . . Sunrise and sunset, promise and fulfillment, birth and death, the whole human drama, everything is in this book. . . . It is the book of books, Biblia."

Everything is in this book: man in search of God, God in search of man, a panoply of history, law, poetry, drama, wisdom, morality, love, hate, laughter, and tears. It influenced art and architecture, music and drama, law and literature—but more than anything else, it has enabled man to wrestle with the enigma of being and emerge with blessed religious convictions, a blueprint of morality to guide and instruct him to fashion and create the good society, God's kingdom on earth. Here he beholds the progressive revelation of God to man. Through its sacred pages he witnesses the ascent of man as he gropes his way through darkness into the light—as he grows in spiritual stature.

The modernist does not accept the Bible in its totality as the word of God but regards it as the record of man's quest for God and the continuous revelation of God's will to man. He accepts the findings of science and archaeological discovery, distinguishes between allegory and literal fact, and looks upon the Bible as the most exalted and morally true of all sacred literature. Such an approach in no wise detracts from the holiness of the Bible, but rather enhances it as a testament of Divinity.

The modernist finds no essential conflict between the Bible and science. The creation story, unequaled in majesty and sublimity, is viewed as the answer to early man's question: How did the world come into being? He accepts the hypothesis of science that the age of the earth's crust may be estimated as 5,000,000 to 10,000,000 years. He is not concerned to lift Scripture out of its context to prove that there is no conflict with the scientific account of the evolution of the earth and the ascent of man from lower forms of animal life. What concerns him is not the mode of creation, but the significance of the revealed truth that man was created in the image of God, and thus endowed with divinity. He is not driven to casuistic arguments to explain the enigma of Cain's wife, nor does he have to justify the vengeful God who commands Moses to rip up the bellies of women with child. These are myths, fables, and distortions of an infantile conception of God and a kindergarten view of religion.

It is unimportant to the modernist whether Sodom and Gomorrah were actually destroyed, or whether these cities ever existed. What is important is the belief that Abraham pleaded with God in behalf of the people. He invoked an ethical God, saying: "Wilt Thou indeed sweep away and not forgive the place for the fifty righteous that are therein? That be far from Thee to do after this manner, to slay the righteous with the wicked, that so the righteous should be as the wicked. . . . Shall not the Judge of all the earth do justly?" (Genesis 18.23-25). This indicates religious growth as man groped his way to a glimpse of a God of compassion. Abraham did not plead and intercede for his friends, but for his enemies who had harassed him and his servants for many years. Here indeed is a magnificent description of a religious man pleading in behalf of his enemies, urging a God of justice to do justly and to exercise the attribute of compassion.

The modernist accepts the narratives of the Book of Genesis as imaginative stories, and agrees with the professor of journalism who told his students, "If you want to read examples of the best short stories ever written, then turn to the book of Genesis." To the modernist, however, these are more than short stories to be evaluated in terms of literary merit. They reveal man in search of morality. They adduce moral lessons and spiritual values precious and sacred to mankind.

Because through archaeological research he knows the crude Babylonian creation myth of Tiamat, and the Chaldean Gilgamesh epic of the flood, the Sumerian account of paradise, and the other parallels to the stories in Genesis, the modernist appreciates all the more the beauty, the skill, the spiritual sensitivity, and the moral fervor of the Hebrew version of creation and the emergence of man.

Because he knows of the Babylonian laws of Hammurabi and the Greek laws of Draco, and compares these laws with the humane legislation of Exodus, his reverence for Scripture is increased, not diminished. To him it isn't important whether the Ten Commandments were revealed at one time and place, whether through Moses or another God-inspired prophet. He is not concerned about the exact date or the circumstances that attended the revelation. What enthralls him is the unparalleled truth and sanctity of the moral revelation itself, and the uncontested validity of the Ten Commandments as ethical exemplars to infuse life with holiness both then and now.

Revelation—Divine and Human

More than its chronicle of man's quest for God, the Bible reveals God's will to man. To declare that the totality of the Bible has been revealed by God is to ignore the evidence of archaeological research, the conclusions of higher biblical criticism, and the hypothesis that Holy Scripture is a cumulative testament of the evolutionary, progressive account of man's growth from religious infancy to religious maturity. To declare that the Bible is literature written entirely by man, devoid of the revelation of God to man, not only detracts from the divine authority of the moral laws of Scripture, but also leaves unanswered the question: How were the lawgivers, the prophets, the psalmists, at a time of brutality, savagery, and religious infantilism, inspired with the knowledge of God's will? Even if we should concede that the people of Israel had a genius for religion, how do we account for the anomaly of a people promulgating moral laws and prophetic doctrines thousands of years ahead of their time? Without historical precedent, without a process of moral conditioning, why were they so spiritually and ethically different from their contemporaries?

It has been argued that the nomadic Israelites were a desert people, and thus were not inclined to the practices and the institutions identified with the fertility cult and sex rites of an agricultural civilization. But other peoples were nomadic and observed folkways and more similar to those of the Jews. Why didn't they offer a moral and ethical code of compassion and righteousness? Why and how did the people of Israel come to the belief in one God of morality? Why did they promulgate laws of mercy and justice at a time when their contemporaries were impervious to mercy, justice, and consideration for the rights of others? Even if the Ten Commandments were not given at one time and one place but represent a summation of older laws, how and why did they come into being? Assuming that the prophets and psalmists were hypersensitive men, attuned to Divinity, are we to conclude that their religious teachings, thousands of years ahead of their time, were acquired *de novo*, without divine inspiration?

This writer has struggled with these questions for many years, searching for a rational explanation that would obviate the supernatural. He has studied the findings of anthropology, archaeology, sociology, and psychology, seeking a tenable, natural explanation for the moral truths revealed through the Bible. His studies afford no conclusion other than the belief that God reveals His will to religiously sensitized men who have entered into communication with Divinity, men who are receptive to supernatural inspiration. The

Bible, therefore, in his opinion, reflects a revelation that is both human and divine.

The story of Jephthah sacrificing his daughter because of a rash vow is a human revelation of religious infantilism. The Ten Commandments, the biblical laws of compassion and justice, the eternal truths of social justice proclaimed by the prophets, the vision of a future society of brotherhood and peace, are revelations of Divinity that lead man toward religious maturity.

The moral laws were to distinguish man from the beast, to elevate him above the jungle of animal depravity. The law of the jungle dictated the commandment to kill; the law of Sinai declared, "Thou shalt not murder." The law of the jungle is amoral, impervious to purity, fidelity, or ethics among beasts. The law of Sinai declared, "Thou shalt not commit adultery," and imposed moral restraints upon man. The law of brute survival permitted man to steal, assuming the right of the strong to rob the weak. The law of Sinai commanded clearly and unequivocally, "Thou shalt not steal." It imposed upon man not only a regard for the sanctity of property, but also the obligation of protecting the weak, of seeking justice in behalf of the exploited, and providing for the orphan, the widow, the poor, and the afflicted. These are laws revealed to man by God.

At a time when other peoples were offering their first-born as human sacrifices, casting them into the furnaces of Moloch; at a time when other peoples were contemptuous of the weak, the afflicted, the poor, how did the children of Israel establish and adhere to the Holiness Code of Chapter 19 of Leviticus that commanded: "Ye shall not steal; neither shall ye deal falsely; nor lie one to another. . . . I am the Lord. Thou shalt not oppress thy neighbour nor rob him. . . . Thou shalt not curse the deaf, nor put a stumblingblock before the blind. . . . I am the Lord. Ye shall do no unrighteousness in judgment . . . but in righteousness shalt thou judge thy neighbour. Thou shalt not go up and down as a talebearer . . . neither shalt thou stand idly by the blood of thy neighbour: I am the Lord. Thou shalt not hate thy brother in they heart. . . . Thou shalt not take vengeance, nor bear any grudge . . . but thou shalt love thy neighbour as thyself" (vs. 11-18). Did the children of Israel codify these laws and formulate such patterns for moral conduct apart from God's influence?

The Bible offers an exalted testament of human ethics for man to emulate. These ethics were not promulgated for the sake of social expediency, but because they were regarded as the will of God. No matter in what period of early history the biblical scholars may place the laws found in Deuteronomy, Chapter 21 and following, we cannot help expressing wonder and awe at the ethical sensitivity of a code that declares:

"Thou shalt not see thy brother's ox or his sheep driven away and hide thyself from them; thou shalt surely bring them back unto thy brother. . . .

"If a bird's nest chance to be before thee . . . thou shalt not take the dam with the young.

"When thou buildest a new house, then thou shalt make a parapet for thy roof, that thou bring not blood upon thy house, if any man fall from thence.

"Thou shalt not plow with an ox and an ass together." (Because they differ greatly in their nature, size and strength.)

"Thou shalt not oppress a hired servant that is poor and needy, whether he be of thy brethren, or of the strangers that are in thy land.

"Thou shalt not pervert the justice due to the stranger, or to the fatherless; nor take the widow's raiment to pledge."

These are typical of the numerous provisions made for the afflicted and the needy. This is the biblical welfare legislation decreed in the infancy of civilization. It is difficult to believe that such legislation could come to fruition out of man's natural inclinations.

Two other passages indicate the command to love even those who were enemies of the children of Israel: "Thou shalt not abhor an Edomite, for he is thy brother." These were the descendants of Cain, the enemies of Israel, and yet the children of Israel were admonished against hating an Edomite, "for he is thy brother."

"Thou shalt not abhor an Egyptian, because thou wast a stranger in his land." The Israelites, but recently liberated from the slavery in Egypt, emancipated from the torture and the humiliation of the taskmaster's whip, are urged to remember that the oppression was the act of Pharaoh rather than the will of the Egyptian people. Israel had found a home in Egypt. Joseph and his brethren had been received as guests, fed and sustained. Therefore, the Egyptian must be remembered with gratitude, and to hate him is to disobey the commandment of God.

Spokesmen of God

In the Hebrew tradition, the prophet never spoke in his own name. It was always "Thus saith the Lord." Each prophet regarded himself as the means by which God spoke to man, as the channel for divine communication. The sacred mission of being called by God to reveal His will to man was a compulsion over which the prophet had no control. Jeremiah clearly reveals this when he declares:

> "And if I say: 'I will not make mention of Him,
> Nor speak any more in His name,'
> Then there is in my heart as it were a burning fire
> Shut up in my bones,
> And I weary myself to hold it in."
> —JEREMIAH 20.9

The prophets were spokesmen of God endowed with a blessed insight, sensitized to a divine communication. Aflame with Divinity, they showered religious sparks upon mankind to ignite a burning passion for justice. They feared neither priest nor king. Nothing could dissuade them from their prophetic mission because they were agents of the Lord. The prophet Nathan courted death as he pointed a finger of accusation against David and cried out, "Thou art the man!" (II Samuel 12.1ff.) Elijah stood in the shadow of destruction when he cursed King Ahab for his wickedness. Amos was abused by the priests of Beth El because of his impassioned protest against the hypocrisy of solemn assemblies and burnt-offerings when God demanded, "Let justice well up as waters, and righteousness as a mighty stream" (Amos 5.21-24). Micah faced an angry mob when he insisted that the Lord requires man "to do justly, and to love mercy, and to walk humbly with thy God" (Micah 6.8). They cursed him. They jeered, laughed, and mocked him, insisting: We are religious. We give God what he wants—sacrifices. Who is this man to tell us what is right? Justice, mercy, humility—what do they have to do with God? The prophet, undaunted by opposition or threat, had to speak out because he was articulating the ethical will of God.

The scrolls of Jeremiah were torn into pieces and burned by King Jehoiakim. The prophet was hounded, put into stocks, tortured, beaten, flung into prison, lowered into pits of filth while his tormentors demanded: "Tell us what we want to hear. Prophesy success, victory and joy for us!" Jeremiah answered even from the pit, "Nay, but if ye thoroughly amend your ways and your doings; if ye thoroughly execute justice between a man and his neighbour; if ye oppress not the stranger, the fatherless, and the widow, and shed not innocent blood . . . then will I cause you to dwell in this place" (Jeremiah 7.5-7). It was not Jeremiah who set forth the moral requisites or enunciated the stubborn denunciation of the king. It was God who spoke through the prophet.

When the King of Judah built a great palace by means of the forced labor of his subjects, exploiting God's children, the prophet Jeremiah went to the very door of the king's palace and cried out:

"Woe unto him that buildeth his house by unrighteousness,
And his chambers by injustice;
That useth his neighbour's service without wages
And giveth him not his hire;

. . . .
He shall be buried with the burial of an ass,
Drawn and cast forth beyond the gates of Jerusalem."
—JEREMIAH 22.13, 19

It was God speaking with the voice of Jeremiah.

One cannot help asking with the sages of Israel, "Did the prophets speak their own wisdom gained through observation and study, or did they not speak as God commanded them?" In pondering this question, Jewish scholars have contended that God did not dictate each word or phrase, but communicated His will to the prophets. The belief in ethical monotheism, the worship of a God of justice, holiness, and compassion, committed the prophets to the demand for justice, holiness, and compassion in the affairs of men and nations.

Israel did not and does not have a monopoly of God's truth or exclusive rights to the channels of divine communication. Unquestionably other religious cultures and the sacred literature of other peoples reveal the ethical will of God. No other prophetic tradition, however, has had such a profound moral impact upon the religious thinking of mankind. The ethics of Judaism were incorporated into the ethics of Christianity and were thus disseminated throughout the world. To divorce the phenomenon of the prophets from the mystery of divine revelation leaves unanswered the question of how these spokesmen of God arrived at their unprecedented concepts of morality, ethics, and social justice at a period of civilization characterized by brutality, immorality, and religious infantilism.

Egyptian history discloses that under Pharaoh Necho, 120,000 laborers were worked to death building a canal connecting the Nile and the Red Sea, yet we do not read of one word of protest or one sentence of condemnation from the Egyptian seers and sages. At a period of history contemporary with Pharaoh Necho, when children were flung to the crocodiles or cast into the furnace to appease the god Moloch, when men and women of other cultures participated in abominable sex rites in honor of the gods and goddesses of fertility, the prophets of Israel exhorted their people to sexual purity, moral righteousness, social justice, and a consideration for the rights of the needy, the oppressed, and the afflicted. The Holy Scriptures reveal man in search of God and God in search of man. Amos, Isaiah, Jeremiah, Micah, Malachi, and Jesus, a galaxy of God-intoxicated men thirsting for Divinity have bequeathed to mankind the concept of an ethical God who cannot be separated from the realities of life, a God of justice and compassion who has given man the freedom of will to glorify Him through a divine imitation, by manifesting love, justice, and compassion to His children.

Progressive Revelation

Progressive revelation enhances rather than detracts from the divinity and the humanity of Holy Scripture. Through the stories, history, struggles, aspirations, poetry, law, and religious sensitivity of the prophet we behold the evolving drama of man in search of God, and the gradual revelation of God to man. "Thus saith the Lord God" has been the prelude to the loftiest social ethics ever promulgated. Through the struggle and groping for religious maturity, man speaks to man, and God speaks through man.

Frank W. Moyle, in *About the Bible*, was right when he declared:

"The question of the authority of the Bible need not trouble the humblest reader. It is not, as a recent writer has said, 'a code which fell from the sky, guaranteed by a celestial imprimatur,' but a collection of writings which still breathes upon us the only authority which is worth regarding, the authority of power of the Spirit."[1]

The puerile question "Where did Cain get his wife?" is unimportant when compared with the eternal question asked by Job, "Why do the righteous suffer?" We need not disturb ourselves debating whether or not Cain and Abel were historical personalities, when we understand that the story of Cain and Abel was the first intimation that man is his brother's keeper and that one human being is responsible for the welfare of another. What if the story of the burning bush is proved to be a myth, an optical illusion in the desert? The Bible teaches that God is in every aspect of life and that even a humble thornbush may be aflame with Divinity. What if the story of Joshua commanding the sun to stand still cannot be validated by archaeologists, if we know that Amos poured out his soul in the hills of Tekoa and that Isaiah preached by the waters of Shiloh?

It was not with the resonance of human speech that God spoke to the psalmist. It was not by ecclesiastical pronouncements that He revealed His Presence. The heavens declared the glory of God without a word. The firmament was a living proof of divine artistry. The wonder and beauty of a single day spoke without words of the majesty of the Creator. The speechless night articulated the language of revelation.

Is it more important to believe that Eve was created from the rib of Adam, or to plead with the psalmist: "Create in me a clean heart, O God, and renew a steadfast spirit within me"? It is not more important to believe that Samson was shorn of his strength by Delilah than that a psalmist, whatever his name, displayed the strength of an indomitable will to love when he prayed:

"Thou hast no pleasure in burnt-offering.
The sacrifices of God are a broken spirit;
A broken and a contrite heart, O God,
Thou wilt not despise."

[1] New York, Charles Scribner's Sons, 1956, p. 182.

The Bible is the Book of all books—the revelation of man's groping for religious maturity, the revelation of the moral will of God. In the dispute over whether the totality of the Bible is the revealed word of God or not, and in the childish insistence that myth is fact and allegory is history, we obscure the glimpses of Divinity that are afforded to man in the most sacred of all religious literature.

Here are adventure, storytelling, the bitter pessimism of Ecclesiastes—"Vanity, vanity, all is vanity under the sun." Here are joy, ecstasy, doubt, and above all, an insatiable hunger for God.

We may not know how the psalmists gained their divine insights, but we are confident that their sensitive spirits enabled them to commune with a Power greater than themselves, and permit that Power to fill their souls with a rapturous song of holiness.

We may never know how the authors of the Book of Proverbs acquired the practical wisdom that has instructed generations of God-seeking men and women in their quest for morality. Rather than debate the means of revelation, we should strive to accept their wisdom: "Better is a morsel with quietness therewith than a house full of feasting with strife"; "Reverence for God is the beginning of wisdom"; "A soft answer turneth away wrath"; "A tranquil heart is the life of the flesh, but envy is rottenness of the bones."

Do we want wisdom, we turn to the book of Proverbs. Do we yearn for a greater vision of God's love, we read the poignant story of Hosea who forgives his faithless wife, Gomer, and receives her back in love, just as God received Israel back in forgiveness and in love, after betrayal and infidelity. The concept of Israel as a bride of God, wed to the Most High, could only be revealed by a divinely inspired prophet. The same Bible that describes a jealous and vengeful God also depicts a God who declares unto Israel: "I will betroth thee unto Me for ever;/Yea, I will betroth thee unto Me in righteousness, and in justice,/and in lovingkindness, and in compassion" (Hosea 2.21). Both concepts of God are revealed in the same sacred literature. One bespeaks the infancy of a childlike religion, and the other manifests the maturity of that same religious spirit. Was it God who revealed Himself as a vengeful, jealous, demanding deity, or was this the miscalculation of man not yet in mastery of the God-man communication?

The Bible not only reflects the religious growth of man, but his emotional experiences also: love, fear, sorrow, perplexity, frustration, and aspiration. Who speaks of love poetry without recalling the tender words of the Song of Songs: "I am my beloved's, and my beloved is mine"? In every generation lovers have said to each other:

"Set me as a seal upon thy heart,
As a seal upon thine arm;
For love is strong as death . . ." (8.6)

Who speaks of sadness and human misery without the dirge of Lamentations:

"How doth the city sit solitary,
That was full of people!
How is she become as a widow!
She that was great among the nations . . .
My inwards burn;
My heart is turned within me. . . .
They have heard that I sigh, there is
none to comfort me." (1.1, 20, 21)

How often through the millenniums have men and women appealed unto God with the psalmist: "Out of the depths do I cry unto Thee, O Lord"? Is it important when this psalm was written or the name of the man who wrote it? Is it essential for us to know whether he addressed God as Yahveh, Elohim, Adonoi, or El Shaddai? What is important is the expression of appeal to God made by man who cries unto the eternal Mystery for help, for solace, for spiritual strength to bear his suffering.

The Book of Ruth was written as an answer and a refutation to those who made of God a limited, nationalistic tribal deity. It breathes the spirit of liberalism and religious resiliency that enables man to extend his concept of God beyond tribal and national boundaries to a belief in a universal Father of infinite love for all His children.

A senior student in a theological seminary was denied ordination solely because he would not profess the belief that the whale swallowed Jonah. The examining committee did not ask whether he would dedicate himself to the service of God and man, to love the stranger, seek justice, practice mercy, and consecrate himself to the ethical and moral teachings expounded by Jesus. Being a man of gentle, loving character, completely devoted to the cause of justice, he would have answered "Yes" to all these questions.

He enrolled in another seminary, and in the years that he has served as a minister of God, his love of his neighbors, his unassuming humility, and dedication to Christian ethics have brought many to understand and revere the Bible as the testament of God.

While we argue over whether Jonah was swallowed by a whale and give all manner of reasons and adduce specious proof to substantiate the claim that it is possible for a man to be swallowed by a whale and live, we sometimes ignore the prophetic meaning and the purpose of the Book of Jonah: to indicate the infinite love and compassion of God. Who can speak of a vengeful God after reading the Book of Jonah and the concept of a God who had compassion on "Nineveh, that great city, in which are more than a hundred and twenty thousand people who do not know their right hands from their left; also much cattle"? Why should the magnificent lesson of God's forgiveness be swallowed up in the belly of a whale?

This is the Bible: adventure, poetry, song, sorrow, joy, love, hate, wisdom, foolishness, fable, fact, history, allegory, law and legend, pain, pleasure, holiness, custom, superstition, and an unequaled passion for justice. Here are prophets and psalmists, lawgivers and poets, men of vision, giants of the spirit. In the midst of desolation and suffering, of oppression and greed, they saw hope; in war, the ways of peace. In the perennial processes of nature, the treasuries of the snow, the rain, the waste places of the deep, the singing of the morning stars, they were close to God and reached up to bring the sublime values of God to man. The Bible is the Magna Charta of the soul, the autobiography of the human spirit groping for Divinity.

Progressive revelation does not detract from the divinity or the humanity of Holy Scripture. Through the stories, history, struggles, aspirations, poetry, religious groping of a people, we find revealed the evolving drama of man in search of God—and what is even more sacred, the gradual revelation of God being made manifest to man. The Bible is sacred not only because it is so divine, but also because it is so human.

Progress in Righteousness

Matthew Arnold declared that "as long as the world lasts, all who want to make progress in righteousness will come to the Bible for inspiration." It is the Bible that is the blueprint for the building of God's kingdom on earth, a society of justice, brotherhood, and peace. That is why it is not only futile but sinful to debate its divine authorship while we ignore the implementation of its eternal truths. For too long we have believed in the Ten Commandments without practicing them. We have extolled the Sermon on the Mount without adhering to its sacred admonitions. This is the greatest of all blasphemies—to revere a book in theory and repudiate its precepts in practice. The Bible offers us more than belief. It offers us ethical and moral commitment. Our love for the Bible is not to be determined by fanatical claims for its divine authenticity, but by the extent to which we accept and apply its spiritual truth to our lives and to our society.

Quentin Reynolds said: "If I were a dictator the first book I would burn would be the Bible. I'd burn it because I'd realize that the whole concept of democracy comes from this book." Rabbi Abba Hillel Silver asserted: "The Bible nowhere calls upon men to go out in search of peace of mind. It does call upon men to go out in search of God and the things of God. It challenges men to hunger and thirst after righteousness, to relieve the oppressed, to proclaim liberty to captives, and to establish peace in the world. These objectives must be elaborately sought. As often as not, such enterprises are attended by persecution and suffering. Judaism as a prophetic religion could not offer its faithful the compensation of peace of mind, except insofar as the confidence of faith lessens the tensions of doubt and despair; but it did offer them other and more precious compensations—the nearness of God, an uplifting interest in life, a nourishing pride and dignity and, on occasion, the ineffable ecstasy that derives from moments of spiritual daring and adventure. There is a lyrical vibrancy to such moments when man drinks of the wine of life and partakes of the very manna of Heaven."[2]

The Judaeo-Christian ethical tradition revealed through the Bible

[2] *Where Judaism Differed* (New York, The Macmillan Company, 1956), p. 143.

is a potential source of inspiration for the effort to build the future and establish a just society, a democratic philosophy of government, and God's kingdom on earth. The effectiveness of the Bible in contributing to human progress and social justice depends upon how seriously, rationally, radically, and maturely its moral and ethical principles are activated and applied to the society of the future and the world to come.

III

The World to Come

《 》

13

The Daring Dream

What a wonder it is—the great fact, or hope, or daring dream of immortality.—WILLIAM PIERSON MERRILL

Dust Returneth to Dust

Jeremy Bentham, the famous English jurist, has been dead since 1832, but he still sits at all meetings of the Council of the University of London. His entire fortune was bequeathed to the university with instructions that his body be given to the medical department and dissected in the presence of his friends, his bones joined together, and the skeleton clothed with his own clothing, to be given a wax face and be brought in to sit at meetings of the council. These instructions were followed, almost to the very letter. Ordinarily, Jeremy sits in a cabinet, which is carried into the council room when conferences are held.

The image of the physical Jeremy Bentham sitting in at all meetings of the Council of the University of London will appear to most of us as incongruous and gruesome. We rebel at the preservation of a body beyond death, and accept the familiar dictum of traditional religion: "Dust returneth to dust."

Kindergarten religion, however, perpetuates the myth of physical life after death, and contends that not only will the soul persist in eternal life but that the physical body will also continue to exist beyond the grave. While such a belief is vague and nebulously uncertain, any effort to limit immortality to the soul will frequently elicit the most passionate and articulate opposition.

A bereaved mother whose heart was crushed with the burden of grief for her eight-year-old daughter asked her minister: "Will I ever see my little girl again in the next world? Tell me, I must know. It is my only hope and comfort."

The minister answered: "The soul is immortal and cannot die. You will be reunited with your little girl in the next world."

"But I'm not talking about souls," said the mother. "I want to see my little girl again. I want to put my arms around her and know that we can live together again. You can't put your arms around a soul. You can't caress a spirit. I want to touch her golden curls again. I want to hold her close and cradle her in my arms. Will I be able to do this?"

The minister spoke gently to the distraught woman: "I understand your yearning to see and touch your little girl again; and my heart goes out to you, but I cannot tell you that her body is immortal. 'Dust returneth to dust.' It is her immortal soul that lives on with God. Her spirit can never die, and—"

"You are no comfort to me at all," interrupted the mother. "I'm not interested in your talk about souls. I'm going to find another church and another minister who really believes in what the Bible teaches about life in the next world. All your theological talk may impress others, but I have come to you for comfort in my sorrow and you have failed me."

The above is not a fictional dialogue, but a true, actual conversation that reflects the yearning not only for the immortality of the soul, but also the hope for the continuation of the body after death. Inherent in the dialogue is the contrast between the kindergarten and the mature approach to the problem and the question of immortality.

The kindergarten image of immortality where one lives happily ever after continues even when the child has grown chronologically into adulthood. Just as the child envisages the continuation of the body, and finds it difficult to comprehend the abstraction of the immortality of the soul, so many adults maintain the image of a physical life after death and tenaciously cling to the assurance that those who are good "go far, far away, and live happily ever after."

Why does man insist upon what William Pierson Merrill called "the great fact, or hope, or daring dream of immortality"? To our present knowledge, man is the only living being who conceives of the idea of immortality. His desire for eternal life has had a profound impact upon his theology and has influenced the history of religious thought.

As man gropes toward a mature religious faith he must ask himself:

Is this ubiquitous belief in immortality instinctive and inherent? Does man carry the proof of immortality within himself? Can immortality be proved, or is it a conviction, a belief that derives from faith and thus transcends rational proof and empiric knowledge? Is there a life beyond the grave and what is the nature of that "life"? Can it not be that the conviction of immortality derives from the inherent unlearned will to live, the yearning for continued and unending existence? Isn't it possible that the belief in immortality is the instinctive response to the contemplation of the extinction of the ego, the terrifying fear of the unknown, and the necessary rationalization that enables man to derive solace and comfort when bereaved and spiritually crushed by the loss of loved ones?

Even though man may never know with certainty what awaits him after death, he continues to search and quest for an answer to the mystery beyond the grave. If his quest is to be supported by reason, then man must forsake his yearning for the continuation of the physical body in the world beyond the grave. It is not only childish and immature; it is contrary to reason. We cannot believe that finite matter, subject to deterioration and decay, will persist as finite matter without yielding to the inevitability of organic change and physical disintegration. If anything persists in the next world it will be that which is incorporeal. The religious dictum that "dust returneth to dust" may be supplemented with "and the spirit returneth unto God who gave it." If dust returns to dust, then man cherishes a vain hope when he insists upon the continuation of the physical body in a life after death.

Dostoevski graphically described "the will to live" when he wrote, in *Crime and Punishment*, "Some one condemned to death says or thinks, an hour before his death, that if he had to live on some high rock, on such a narrow ledge that he'd only room to stand, and the ocean, everlasting darkness, everlasting solitude, everlasting tempest around him, if he had to remain standing on a square yard of space all his life, a thousand years, eternity, it were better to live so than to die at once! Only to live, to live and live! Life, whatever it may be!"[1]

There is a desperate urge for life even when we cry out most passionately for death. Jewish tradition tells of a poor man, afflicted with pains and sorrow, who had to carry an unbearable load on his back.

[1] New York, The Macmillan Company, 1927, p. 147.

One day when it seemed that he could carry it no farther, he took the sack from his shoulder and cried in despair: "Oh, death, come and free me!" In a flash, the angel of death was at his side, inquiring politely, "You called me?" "Yes," the poor man answered hastily. "Please help me put my load back on my shoulders." Man yearns for survival. He instinctively strives for the preservation of life. Men, however, have given up their lives for great causes and sacred objectives. The will to live may be subjugated by the willingness to offer one's life for noble ideals and cherished principles. A mother will overcome the will to live in order to save her child. A soldier will overcome the will to live for the sake of his family, his country, and the freedom he regards as more precious than his own life. It may be argued that one who contemplates or commits suicide is mentally and emotionally ill. Nonetheless, the will to live in such cases proves weaker and less dominant than the will to die.

The fact that there is a will to live offers no proof that physical life continues beyond the grave. The fact that men believe in a physical life after death does not adduce irrefutable evidence that such a belief has a basis in truth.

Hope Sees a Star

The belief in immortality is strengthened not only by the will to live but also by man's yearning for eternal life when the shadow of death lengthens over those he loves.

There is no pain more devastating, more intense, more prolonged, more difficult to accept than the pain of grief. With all our wonder drugs, what medicine is effective against the pain of bereavement and the excruciating torture of sorrow? With all the advances made in modern surgery, who can mend a broken heart?

Those who have suffered the anguish of sorrow understand what the prophet Jeremiah meant when he said:

> "Oh that my head were waters,
> And mine eyes a fountain of tears,
> That I might weep day and night." (8.23)

Those who have lost dear ones know what he meant by this. During those trying hours when grief lacerated our souls, with all our maturity, with all our knowledge, with all our experience, we were helpless—we were like infants crying in the night of despair, in the darkness of sorrow, as we appealed out of the depths for comfort and consolation. No matter how old we are, no matter what our age, sorrow makes each of us an infant crying in the night, with no language but a cry.

And yet, there is a language other than a cry. There is a language that speaks to us with accents of comfort, assurance, and peace—and that is the language of faith, a deep and abiding faith in the existence of an immortal God who has endowed man with an immortal soul. Even when we cannot understand, even when we hurl our protest at the universe, and ask: Why? Why must this be? Why must one so young, so good be taken from us? it is then that we must listen to that language of faith, and even though we cannot understand, we must believe, believe with all the power and sincerity of our hearts that there is a life beyond the grave. Even though our finite minds cannot comprehend or solve the mystery of the unknown, we must believe that God is love and that the souls of our dear ones have been summoned from this earth to life everlasting with God.

At this point the reader may question this language of faith and inquire how we can have the assurance and the proof that there is a life beyond the grave and that there is an immortal God to whom the immortal soul returns and with whom the immortal soul unites. A friend who read the manuscript of this volume asked: "What does reason have to say about this? Isn't it just as irrational to conceive of the immortality of the soul as it is to conceive of the immortality of the body?"

There is no proof of the immortality of the soul. Religion, even mature religion, is not to be entirely and totally equated with science. There are similarities and differences between science and religion. Science proceeds from the known to the unknown. So does religion. Science accepts theories on faith as it awaits demonstrable proof. So does religion. Agnosticism is a concomitant of science, as it is of religion. The mature faith accepts the findings and discoveries of science, but goes beyond science. Reason is a handmaiden of science, as it is of religion. The mature faith must apply the requisites of reason to its doctrines and convictions, but does not require proof for that which is consistent with reason but has yet to be validated by science. The mature faith weds hope to reason whenever it asserts a belief in the immortality of the soul.

One of the most beautiful and meaningful statements on the subject of immortality came from the pen of a famous agnostic and freethinker, Robert G. Ingersoll. Here was an iconoclast, a doubter, who ripped apart the bulwarks of respectable religion. He refused to accept the fundamentalist doctrines of the Bible, of God, of prayer, and even of immortality, and yet, standing at his brother's grave, he said: "Life is a narrow veil between the cold and barren peaks of two eternities. We strive in vain to look beyond the heights. We cry aloud, and the only answer is the echo of our wailing cry. From the voiceless lips of the unreplying dead there comes no word; but in the night of death—hope sees a star and listening love can hear the rustle of a wing."[2]

The last lines are captivating and elevating, not only in the poetic grandeur of expression, but in the truth conveyed. Hope sees a star even in the night of death. Hope gives us the vision to see in the night—even in the night of sorrow, and listening love gives us the acuity to discern even the rustle of a wing. It is this hope that sustains man's belief in the immortality of the soul.

The Immortality of the Soul

The religious belief in the immortality of the soul is predicated on the teaching of Scripture that man is created in the image of God and endowed with an immortal soul—a soul that is incorporeal, imperishable, and eternal—a soul that can never die.

When Sir Arthur Keith, one of the great British scientists, stated that at death a man goes out like a candle, Professor Arthur H. Compton replied that the candle does not go out; its energy goes on and on to the farthest reaches of the universe.

Professor Ashley Montagu, in his lecture series on immortality given to the Brooklyn Institute of Arts and Sciences in 1951, stated that "the law of conservation of energy, which states that energy is neither created nor destroyed, in any of its transformations, and the fact of the continuity of the germ plasm, constitute a scientific basis for the

[2] C. H. Cramer, Royal Bob (Indianapolis, The Bobbs-Merrill Company, Inc., 1952), p. 263.

belief both in the indestructibility of energy or matter, and of the imperishability of life; in other words, the basis for our belief in the immortality of different levels of integration of energy relations."

Not even the most reputable evidence from science could support the belief in the eternality of the spirit. A mature religious faith does not demand proof to explain the mysteries of the unknown. It asks only that a belief help us to sanctify life in this world. It asks only that poetry and science supply the beauty and power to sacred convictions. Faith supplied the vision that hope may see a star even in the dark night of death. Faith enables us to hear the rustle of a wing that lifts expectant man to unprecedented heights of holiness.

In his book *Why We May Believe in Life After Death*, Charles Edward Jefferson writes: "Science has no authentic and satisfying word to speak on the subject of Immortality. She cannot prove life beyond death, neither can she disprove it. She has no warrant for condemning those who believe it, and she can furnish only a dubious support to those who deny it. She has much to say about many things, but not about Immortality. Her instruments of research are powerful, but they are impotent in the realm of the dead."[3]

Whether we turn to science or poetry, art or religion, we cannot believe that death is the end of life. Nor can we accept the specious arguments that immortality is man's projection through children, memory, or influence. When we speak of immortality we mean that man contains within himself something other than the material. This "something" survives physical disintegration of the body. Furthermore, this essence is more than intelligence, and more than an ethical or moral potential. It is part of God, eternal, deathless, Divinity within man. With the dissolution of the body, this "something" we call the soul transcends the plane of living to enter the wholly other realm of immortality. The immortal soul of man returns in oblivious unity to become reunited with the immortal soul of souls we call God.

The belief in the immortality of the soul is not without insoluble problems, perplexing mysteries, and inherent dangers. Even those who adhere to the belief in the immortality of the soul are hard put to answer the following questions: When does the soul enter the body, at conception, at birth or at some period intermediate? When does the soul depart from the body? Do animals have souls? Is the soul identi-

[3] Boston, Houghton Mifflin, 1911, p. 115.

fied with consciousness, and if so does damage to the brain do damage to the soul? If soul is identified with a moral potential, does this mean that environmental and hereditary factors can influence the soul? How can we believe that degenerates and criminals, perverts and ruthless dictators responsible for the extermination of millions are created in the image of God, endowed with immortal souls? To what extent does the soul influence the body, and the body influence the soul? If the soul is to be equated with constant energy, isn't this a matter of physics rather than religion? If survival after death is nothing but the energy within man becoming one with the supreme and divine Energy, do we have the right to dignify such energy-survival with the status and designation of immortality?

Here is where the mature faith is driven to a retreat from pure reason and is compelled to seek refuge in faith and belief. When confronted with such questions, some devotees of the mature faith shrug aside these tormenting queries and surrender to agnosticism, declaring that we cannot know the mystery of the soul any more than we can completely comprehend the mystery of God.

The Sadducees taught that the soul becomes extinct when the body dies and that death is the final end of the human being. The much maligned and greatly misunderstood Pharisees attached great importance to the doctrine of immortality, and made it a part of the "Eighteen Benedictions" of daily prayer. The Samaritans agreed with the Sadducees in denying the dogma of the resurrection of the body and the immortality of the soul.

The mature faith cannot look upon life or death with the blithe denial of immortality of the Sadducees. It does not regard death as sure doom that falls pitiless and dark. It cannot equate man with omnipotent matter that rolls on its relentless way. Mature religion does not presume to ally itself with pure reason and offer answers to all the mysteries of life and death. There is a point where man must go beyond reason, although he may never controvert it with religious theories and hypotheses that are obviously at variance with science or objective truth.

In essence, however, the mature faith does not place a primary emphasis upon speculation about the nature of the soul or the world to come, but stresses the importance of "one world at a time," with the objective of sanctifying and perfecting this world, the world in which we live. An eighteenth century rabbi became weary of meta-physical theories and esoteric conjecture, and said, "In the time that I devote myself to thoughts of the next world I could be stringing pearls for the sake of heaven." His statement was interpreted to mean that the time that he was exploiting for speculation about the next world could be better used for good deeds, acts of kindness to the needy, and the perfection of this world for the sake of God and for the sake of man.

Living Memorials

It is in this spirit that sages throughout the centuries have sug-gested that we should honor our departed and manifest our belief in the immortality of the soul, not by a tribute of tears, but by a tribute of deeds; not by weeping for them, or mourning for them, but by liv-ing for them. It is not by monuments of stone that we sanctify the memory of our dear ones, but by monuments of constructive and creative service that serves the living.

Several years ago, an article by Robert O'Brien, "In Memoriam," appeared in a Temple bulletin. It reflects the worth and religious significance of living memorials:

"Some twenty years ago, two elementary school boys established a friendship that was destined to last until death. They were insepara-ble during their grade school years, and, later, through their high school years. After their graduation they shook hands and said good-by for they wouldn't be seeing much of each other from then on. One of them came from a well-to-do family; he was to start his pre-medical training at the University of California in the fall. The parents of the other boy were poor; he was going to work.

"And that's the way it went, and things went along like that until the war came. The pre-medical student left the university and joined the Air Force. The other shifted to a vital war industry job and kept plugging. One day, the flyer's mother received a War Department telegram. It was bad news. The hospital plane her son had been fly-ing was shot down. Her son was dead.

"He was an only son, and it took his mother many months to get over it. Not to get over it exactly, but to accept the fact of his death, to adjust herself to his never coming back. When she could look ahead again, an idea began to turn in her mind. An idea for what would, in a way, be a living memorial to her dead son. She sat down and wrote a letter to his boyhood friend.

" 'Dear Joe: By now, you must have heard of Arthur's death in action. I remember you when you were playmates together, and I remember how fond you were of each other. And now he is gone, living on only in the heart of a loving mother. But I have thought of a way in which he can live on in another sense, a broader, more unselfish sense. Like him, you wanted to be a doctor, to ease human pain and suffering. But your family was too poor to pay, or even to help pay, your way through the long years of university training. They needed your help, so you did the only thing you could. But now they are in better circumstances, and you are more free. If you are still interested in being a doctor, I want you to be one. I want you to take Arthur's place at the university. Nothing would make me happier than to pay your way, every bit of it, and thus do for Arthur's best friend what I had so hoped to do for him. I have thought of it as a sort of living memorial to him, and I know it is what he would want. . . .'

"Humble, grateful and determined to live up to the faith placed in him, Joe entered the pre-medical school at the University of California two months later, and, ordinarily, that would be the end of this story. But there's something to add, and it's this: the dead pilot was a Jew. His boyhood friend, the one who's carrying on in his place, is a Negro."

The rabbis in the Talmud ask, "Why is the water of the eyes salty?" "Because," said a sage of old, "when a person weeps for the dead constantly he becomes blind, but since tears are salty, and make his eyes smart, he stops weeping."

Our tears sometimes do make us blind—blind to those who need us, our smiles, our laughter, and our joy; our tears blind us to the real meaning of a faith that reaches beyond this life to eternal life with God; our tears blind us to the obligations we owe to the living in this world who look to us for direction that will lead them on paths of hope and love and light.

It is our service to the living that helps us to understand the language of faith, and sensitizes us to the voice of God telling us how to find comfort. A traveler was crossing mountain heights of untrodden snow alone. He struggled bravely against the sense of sleep which weighed down his eyelids. He knew that if he gave in to despair and yielded to sleep, death would be inevitable. Just then his foot struck against a heap lying across his path. Stooping down, he found it to be a human body half buried in the snow. The next moment he held him in his arms and was rubbing the frozen man's limbs. The effort to restore another unto life brought back to himself warmth and energy, and was the means of his own survival.

"Heaven's gate is shut to him who comes alone./Save thou a soul, and it shall save thine own."[4]

By the effort to create living memorials—by turning away from ourselves to the needs of others, we not only pay tribute to our dear departed, but we also find comfort and peace.

The University of Michigan created a memorial for students and faculty members who died in World War II by establishing a research institute to find ways of using atomic energy for peaceful and humanitarian purposes.

In the State of Israel, a middle-aged couple suffered the loss of their only child, a little girl. In order to find comfort, they went to the adoption center and saw a lovely girl who touched their hearts. The little girl refused to go with them unless they also adopted her little brother. They took the children home with them, and after the exciting day the children were put to bed. A few minutes later they heard the youngsters screaming hysterically. Rushing into the room they found that the girl had taken a picture of the woman's sister off the wall and was clutching it—the picture of their own mother. Thus these kindly people found that they had adopted the child of a sister who had remained in Poland and had been exterminated by the Nazis. They had given a home to their own niece and nephew, and it was through their love of these children that they found healing, consolation, and peace.

If we can believe in constant energy that never dies, why can't we believe in the theory of the conservation of love? The love we perpetuate can never die, and when we identify ourselves with loving-kindness and loving service we identify ourselves with immortality.

The belief in the immortality of the soul in the next world must never permit us to deviate from our objective of sanctifying this life

[4] Rabbinic tradition, cited by Rabbi Joseph Hertz.

by destroying injustice and evil, and perfecting our world under God. Whenever a religious denomination cavalierly shrugs off the primacy of this world and defaults in its responsibility to seek the solution of social problems, it partakes of the characteristics of a kindergarten faith.

The writer was discussing world peace and justice with a friend, analyzing the effectiveness of the United Nations and the hope of achieving a society of righteousness and brotherhood, when the friend's wife interrupted the conversation by saying: "You're both wasting your time discussing the hope of a good society. It is only when this world comes to an end and God supernaturally brings about His kingdom that we will ever solve the problems of injustice, hatred, and war. This world is hopeless and evil. It can only be redeemed by God's grace in sending the Messiah again. Our salvation is of the next world, and not this one." This, too, is an indication of kindergarten religion.

The Daring Dream

As we yearn for immortality, we may find ourselves in the position of the rabbinic scholar who dreamed one night that he had entered Paradise. There, to his surprise, he found the sages discussing a difficult academic problem. "Is this the reward of Paradise?" the sage cried out in angry astonishment. "This is exactly what they did on earth." "Foolish man," admonished a voice, "you think the sages are in Paradise. It is just the opposite. Paradise is in the sages." He discovered, as may we, that the Paradise for which we quest may be found in the divine nature of man himself.

There is a dream more daring than the dream of the immortality of the soul and life in the world to come. It is the dream of establishing God's kingdom on earth, building a just society of brotherhood, love, and peace. This dream is more daring than the hope of redemption through the supernatural intervention of God. We can believe that an omnipotent God can create a perfect society by means of supernatural salvation. Can we believe that finite man, limited and fallible, has the power and the ability to create a just society and a kingdom of God on earth by activating and implementing the ethical and moral principles and precepts of a mature religious faith? Which is the more daring dream, a just and a moral society compelled miraculously by God, or a just and a moral society created religiously by man acting as a co-partner of God?

If this daring dream is to be transmitted into reality, then we shall have to concur with Ernest Renan that "the aim of humanity is not repose; it is intellectual and moral perfection. How can people talk of repose, I should like to know, when they have the infinite to traverse and the perfect to reach? Humanity will only repose when it has reached the perfect. It would be too strange if a few profane persons could from mercenary motives or personal interest, arrest the progress of the mind, the true religious progress. The most dangerous state of humanity would be that in which the majority, finding itself quite at ease and not wishing to be disturbed, should retain its repose at the cost of thought and of an oppressed minority."[5]

If this daring dream is to become a reality, then man must minimize the contemplation of immortality in the next world and give an exalted primacy to the improvement, the perfection, and the sanctification of this world. Man must bring God from heaven to earth. The mature faith must be based on this-worldliness that requires the application of moral and ethical values to this life. Our religious institutions must teach its devotees that the best preparation for death is life and that we prepare for eternity through our efforts to apply the moral truths of God to this world.

A student of Rabbi Pinchas (eighteenth century) once came into his teacher's room and found him lying down and playing with his watch. He was surprised because it was almost noon and the rabbi had not yet uttered his morning prayers. Just then the rabbi said to the student: "You are surprised at what I am doing? But do you really know what I am doing? I am learning how to leave the world." It is through the contemplation of time, and by the realization that the precious hours given to us are gifts of God to be used for the perfection of the world, that man prepares for death and learns the glorious lesson of how to leave the world.

In a similar spirit, Rabbi Israel, known as the Baal Shem Tov (the founder of the Chassidic movement dedicated to the joyous application of God's commandments to life), once contemplated his own unworthiness. He concluded that he wasn't righteous enough to earn

[5] Ernest Renan, *The Future of Science.*

eternal life in the coming world. Then he said to himself: *"If I love God what need have I of a coming world?"* and he resolved to dedicate himself to the sanctification of life on earth.

This is the essence of the daring dream: To believe in the immortality of the soul and in eternal life with God, but to make the love of God such a factor in our lives that we don't need a coming world; to recognize that our most exalted immortality is sharing here and now the life of God. In order to learn how to die, we have to learn how to live—to live meaningfully and religiously with God. The more holiness, justice, mercy, and love we bring into this world, the more we assure ourselves of the sacred possibilities of the daring dream.

14

Tranquilizers of Faith

No religion is a true religion that does not make men tingle to their finger-tips with a sense of infinite hazard.
—WILLIAM ERNEST HOCKING

Social Action and Religious Struggle

The daring dream of building God's kingdom on earth will not be achieved through peace of mind, the cult of comfort, security, and respectable conformity, or by the tranquilization of faith. If the just society of the future is to be attained, it will be through the application of mature religion to life, narrowing the gap between faith and works, theoretical theology and the dictates of social action. The attainment of the exalted dream of the future requires constant and consecrated effort, the determination to transcend conformity, unceasing opposition to the stereotypes of comfortable and respectable religion, and the blessing of discontent.

It is hazardous to contemplate the advance into the future with the objective of clearing away a wilderness of ignorance, treacherous obstacles of prejudice, and successfully combating the formidable resistance of conservative, respectable religion. Winston Churchill once offered the people of England "blood, sweat and tears" for the victory against the Axis powers in World War II. The prophetic faith offers to clergy and laymen alike: anxiety, creative nonconformity, insecurity, abuse, discontent, and unceasing struggle as requisites for the realization of the daring dream. Those who pioneer into new frontiers of religious faith will be harassed, persecuted, maligned, and despised. With indomitable courage and stubborn resolve, they will have to persist in overcoming apathy, indifference, hostility, and the most invidious of all spiritual evils: the disposition to tranquilize religious faith into social passivity, political acquiescence, and intellectual conformity.

On a Sunday morning in May, 1956, the minister of a Presbyterian church in a South Carolina community delivered a sermon on "Our Racial Problem." He did not speak in favor of or against segregation. His only reference to the desegregation problem was that a white supremacy group was being organized in the community, and he urged his congregation not to join any organization or any group that would bring prejudice, anguish, and dissension into the community.

When he completed the sermon there was an uncomfortable silence. The Reverend Sidney Riegel said, "Come on now—all those of you who agree with me, please rise." Again a deadly silence, followed by a shuffling of feet as someone in the last pew got up.

Mr. Riegel studied the congregation for a moment, and said, "I will not let my wife stand alone." The minister left the pulpit and walked down the center aisle to stand beside his wife. The religious services ended—and so did the pastorate of Mr. Riegel. The board of deacons dismissed him that same afternoon.

Would such drastic action have been taken if he had limited himself to generalizations about the nature of original sin or arguments for the existence of God? Would he have experienced trouble if he had preached on immortality or the Ten Commandments or religious ethics? Who gets upset about God? Who becomes agitated over sin or immortality or ethics? But when this churchman had the temerity to disgress from pulpit palliatives, peace of mind, barbiturates of the spirit, and sedatives for the soul, to come to grips with the specific issue of race prejudices that spread anguish and dissension in the community he served, then he was summarily dismissed because he had exerted a disturbing influence upon his congregation—a congregation that didn't want the teachings or the preachments of religious morality, but wanted, instead, to be lulled and soothed by tranquilizers of faith.

Those who are emotionally disturbed, the mentally ill, and the physically tense may be helped by tranquilizers. A society where men and women are driven by the tensions of an industrial, mechanized age, where people are sucked into a neurotic whirlpool of frenzied competition because of a market-place orientation, a society haunted by the fears and phantoms of hydrogen warfare, may need happiness pills and tranquilizers. When, however, we apply tranquilizers to a religious faith, when we apply ecclesiastical Equinil, ministerial Miltown, and theological Thoracin to the religious problems that challenge our thinking and our society, we negate the dynamics of the social gospel and repudiate the sacred purpose of a meaningful, living, and ethically motivated religious faith.

The purpose of mature religion is to agitate rather than to tranquilize, to arouse us from our dogmatic slumber, to jolt us and even disturb us so that we may confront the injustices and inequalities of life, in order to bring the full impact of God's moral law to the society in which we live and to enable us to perfect our world under God.

The prophets of Israel did not exhort the people in behalf of peace of mind or tranquillity of soul. Jeremiah never offered any happiness pills. Isaiah didn't propose neat theological rationalizations that soothe the soul and calm the conscience; but, speaking in the name of God, he didn't ask—he demanded:

> "Cry aloud, spare not,
> Lift up thy voice like a horn,
> And declare unto My people their transgression,
> And to the house of Jacob their sins.

.   .   .   .
Will thou call this a fast,
And an acceptable day to the Lord?
Is not this the fast that I have chosen?
To loose the fetters of wickedness,
To undo the bands of the yoke,
And to let the oppressed go free.
Is it not to deal thy bread to the hungry,

.   .   .   .
When thou seest the naked, that thou cover him,

.   .   .   .
Then shalt thou call, and the Lord will answer;
Thou shalt cry, and He will say: 'Here I am.' " (58.1,5-9)

How do you think a congregation would respond to this prophet of God if he spoke to us about the crucial and controversial social issues of our day? In all likelihood he would be excoriated because he disturbed our tranquillity; he would be labeled and smeared as a radical because he refused to tranquilize his prophetic faith.

There are many ministers and rabbis who have become casualties of this tranquilizing trend—good men, devoted and consecrated men, who have been driven from their pulpits because they had the courage to insist that their congregations apply their religious faith to the controversial problems of contemporary society, because they dedicated their lives to the daring dream of building God's kingdom on earth. There are ministers and rabbis who have been ordered by their boards of trustees to avoid even the mention of a controversial issue and who are told categorically that people come to a religious service to be soothed and assured and not to be disturbed or agitated by the realities of life.

Displaced Parsons

In South Carolina five ministers—three Episcopalians, a Methodist, and a Presbyterian—put together a paperback book called *South Carolinians Speak*. The ministers persuaded twelve South Carolina citizens to express "moderate" views on race relations.

As a consequence, one of the five ministers who sponsored the book, John Lyles, minister at the Presbyterian Church in Marion, South Carolina, according to the *Wall Street Journal* of February 14, 1958, was politely told he should look for another congregation because of his involvement in the book. He did so, and now has a church in West Virginia.

A prominent Presbyterian in Marion, and an elder in the church, said: "We had to get rid of him. Mind you, I liked John personally, a fine young man. But people stopped coming to church. We told him when he first came we couldn't have any agitating on the race issue. We're a small church and we just couldn't stand our minister speaking out on controversial issues which tear up his people."[1]

An official of the Southern Regional Council in Atlanta said: "In the South we have a new class of D.P.'s—displaced parsons. Since 1954, we have been in touch with at least a dozen ministers who lost their churches for supporting the Supreme Court decision, or for protesting against violence."[2]

At a session of the Central Conference of American Rabbis, a group of southern rabbis met to consider the question of controversy resulting from the support of the Supreme Court decision on integration. The chairman pointed out that during a period of tension in a southern community, not one rabbi, not one priest, not one minister dared to speak out on this subject. The rabbi who served this community wept as he said: "I have served my congregation for twenty-three years. If I spoke on the Negro question or even implied justice for the Negro, despite my twenty-three years of service, I would be fired the next day."

This is the tragedy of the tranquilized faith. Ministers, rabbis, and priests are tempted to forsake the prophetic faith for the sake of personal security and popularity. The voice of prophetic religion does not speak in terms of security, but rather in terms of commitment— not a commitment to preserve and maintain a superficial popularity, but a commitment to the eternal teachings of the prophets, a commitment to the moral will of God.

Dr. Albert P. Shirkey of Mount Vernon Place Methodist Church of Washington insists: "Christianity is not here to lull the minds and souls of men to sleep, but rather is the bugle call to action against

[1] Ed Cony, "Religion & Race," *Wall Street Journal*, Feb. 14, 1958.
[2] Used by special permission.

every wrong to any life anywhere. God pity America when the pulpits no longer speak out against such ingrained wrongs."[3]

Our generation cannot afford the luxury of a tranquilized religion today, no matter how unpopular the cause of social justice may be. We cannot afford to take the attitude of two women who attended a performance of a Shakespeare play at the Memorial Theater, a play in which the actress Vivien Leigh appeared on the stage with her tongue and her hands supposedly cut off, and one of the elderly women, aghast at the terrifying scene, whispered to the other: "I didn't realize it was this kind of a play. We will just have some tea and forget it." Is this so amusing? It is frightening and tragic because all too often when we are forced to witness some of the tragedies of life we say to ourselves, "I didn't realize it was this kind of world. We will just have a nice tranquilizer—and forget it."

Can those who call themselves religious forget discrimination against racial and religious groups, the violation of civil liberties, the Ku Klux Klan riding throughout the South, holding meetings, burning crosses, distributing handbills, declaring Klanism to be a religion, declaring: "Please remember that every Roman- and Jewish-controlled newspaper is fighting the Ku Klux Klan religion. Shall you exchange your birthright for a mess of Romanism and Talmudism?"

A newspaper headline in the Columbus, Georgia, *Enquirer* blazoned forth: "KLAN EFFORT TO REGULATE CHURCHES SHOULD STIR AUTHORITIES TO ACTION." The editorial declared: "Judging from incidents reported in Sylacauga, members of the Ku Klux Klan of Alabama have taken upon themselves the duty of regulating the churches. They are proceeding in their endeavor by burning crosses and by threatening acts of terrorism.

"Crosses were burned in the vicinity of Methodist and Baptist churches in Sylacauga Saturday night while Klansmen held a rally in the high school football stadium. Just where the Klan obtained the authority to use the stadium of the public school system for the staging of a rally is not clear. Indeed, it is not known whether or not the KKK went through the formality of requesting permission.

"The associate pastor of the Methodist Church had the courage to

[3] A statement made concerning the conditions found in the Second Precinct when it was known as the wickedest precinct in Washington, D.C. (used by permission).

defy the Klan by kicking over the cross that was placed across the street from the church.

"The Rev. Newton Malone also stood briefly in front of a car occupied by Klansmen, halting it for about 30 seconds. Later, Mrs. Maloney received a telephone call in which a man's voice warned that unless the Maloneys and the Rev. Dan Whitsett, pastor, and his family are out of town in ten days 'your house and your child will be blown to bits.' The Maloneys have a child 18 months old.

"The Rev. Mr. Whitsett recalled that other threats had been received. In one call his wife was told that the KKK was going to tear their 17-year-old son 'limb from limb.' A short time later, a caller told Mrs. Whitsett the Klan had her son. This proved to be a hoax, but it followed a pattern of terrorism through which the Klan was hoping to run the pastor out of town."

The newspaper article continued: "Whitsett's endorsement of moderation in race relations and the adoption by the Southern Baptist Convention of a report dealing with the race issue were believed to have been the basis of the action of the Klansmen in their effort to intimidate the preachers.

"The whole thing was disgraceful in the extreme. It was cowardly and inexcusable. When the time comes that the Klan thinks it has the duty to regulate the churches of the community, the authorities should take over and do something. Such conditions are intolerable in a community. Such acts of intimidation against the clergy should call for immediate action. If they are allowed to continue, law and order will give way to mob rule."[4]

Complacency soothes us, saying: "We have always had discrimination and we shall always have it. If we remain quiet enough and obscure enough it will all blow over and be forgotten and sooner or later all Americans of every race and religious faith will live together in peace and harmony." That is what tranquilizers of faith would induce us to believe and accept. But it will not be, it cannot be, unless we arouse ourselves from religious passivity to combat injustice and discrimination, and identify ourselves with a militant concept of religion that must not stand aside when the great problems of humanity that are born in every age struggle in the minds of men.

[4] The Columbus (Ga.) *Enquirer*, June 12, 1957.

We must live by the precepts of a religion that stirs and activates the conscience of mankind.

Here Am I

In a day when the moral law is flouted and tablets of aspirin are more acceptable than the tablets of the Ten Commandments, the prophetic faith must proclaim once more: "Thus saith the Lord." In an age fast succumbing to escape by tranquilizers, the adherents of the prophetic faith must affirm religion's universal mission—to make the right go forth unto the nations and to make the right go forth according to the truth. If we are to make the daring dream an imminent reality, and if we are to be zealous for the mission of a dynamic, disturbing, and prophetic faith, then, as Abraham, Moses, Samuel, and Isaiah, answered, "Here am I; send me," those who would build the future under God must be more concerned with commitment than with comfort, with dedication to a sacred cause than with security, with disturbing than with soothing, and with religious action than with religious dogma.

The Reverend Fred Shuttleworth said, "Here am I; send me," to his God as he went forth to protect four little Negro children who were being attacked by a group of bullies. He was mauled savagely with fists and lacerated by a piece of chain. The Reverend Mr. Shuttleworth went to the hospital, but his assailants went free.

It was prophetic faith that compelled the Reverend Martin Luther King, Jr., of Birmingham, Alabama, to say, "Here am I," subjecting himself to personal violence and vitriolic hate, as he walked forth with his Negro brethren to meet the threatening mob.

It was a divine confrontation of God that inspired the Reverend Paul Turner of Clinton, Tennessee, to respond, "Here am I," when his conscience demanded that a white minister accompany Negro children to school.

It was the courage of a ministry of action that made the Reverend Mr. Kelly, of the Negro Church in Nashville, stand with the children of his church before a menacing mob that literally measured him for a coffin.

It was prophetic courage that challenged a Negro layman, a deacon of a church in Little Rock, Arkansas, to be mauled and choked and smashed into a bloody pulp, while other ministers, white and Negro, and other rabbis and other priests, lifted their voices in safe, carefully worded prayers to their congregations, fearful of offending the agitators and rabble rousers, the forces of Governor Orville Faubus, without personal commitment, without saying, "Here am I," to the voice of God.

It was the love of God that expresses itself through service to man that motivated 312 pastors to issue the Atlanta Manifesto. It was a commitment to a prophetic faith that demanded of Pastor Robert E. Lee, of the Church of the Redeemer in Atlanta, that he preach a classic sermon, "Take Your Choice: Brotherhood or Violence," on October 19, 1958, the Sunday after a Jewish Temple in Atlanta had been bombed.

"Where are the voices," asked Pastor Lee, "that honestly believe that America can remain great—and achieve new heights of greatness in world leadership—only if it lives up to the ideals of the Declaration of Independence and the Constitution—both of which are a political expression of the Christian gospel with its insistence upon the dignity and the sacredness of human personality? The moment we say the rights of one group are more important than the rights of another, we open the door to demagoguery—and ultimately to hatred and violence. . . .

"We have to take our choice—just one of two: Brotherhood ultimately, or violence ultimately.

"If a man saith that he love God and hateth his brother, he is a liar—for if he loves not his brother whom he hath seen—how can he love God whom he hath not seen!

"Inasmuch as ye do it not unto one of the least of these, my brethren, ye do it not unto me!

"Do unto others as ye would have them do unto you.

"Thou shalt love the Lord thy God with all thy heart, and with all thy soul and with all thy mind—and thy neighbor as thyself!

"It doesn't leave us much choice, does it? You may get rid of the clergy who are bold enough to speak—but you cannot get rid of the gospel of Jesus Christ."[5]

Thus speaks a Christian. Thus speaks a man who refuses to permit the tranquilization of his prophetic faith.

It is not to be expected that every layman, even if allied with the

[5] Quoted by special permission of Pastor Robert E. Lee.

prophetic faith, must face howling, hysterical mobs for the sake of religious convictions. Not everyone is expected to perform exploits of courage and heroism, but the question that must burn itself into our souls is: How do we, *in any way*, respond, "Here am I," to God, for service in behalf of the daring dream of the future?

We have enough rebels without cause. The Judaeo-Christian ethical tradition needs—the world needs—those who will rebel against prejudice, rebel against ignorance, rebel against bigotry for the sake of great and sacred causes of social and religious justice.

The Sin of Indifference

It was Edmund Burke who said that "all that is necessary for evil to triumph in the world is for good men to do nothing." There are sins of omission as well as sins of commission. By doing nothing a man or woman may be contributing to the triumph of evil in the world. Hence, the tranquilizing of faith to lull us into passivity makes good men and women accessory to crime, corruption, the degradation of man, and the desecration of the divine within man.

In *The Divine Comedy,* at the very beginning of Dante's progress downward into the Infernal City, the First Circle of the Abyss, he and Virgil find themselves in the Vestibule of Hell, wherein "lamentation, groans, and wailings deep" resound throughout "the starless air." Dante is at first astonished by the "cries of pain and rage" and by the "tumult" which "nothing could assuage." He asks his guide, "Who are these that seem so crushed beneath their plight?" And Virgil replies:

> "These miserable ways
> The forlorn spirits endure of those who spent
> Life without infamy and without praise.
> They are mingled with that caitiff regiment
> Of the angels, who rebelled not, yet avowed
> To God no loyalty, on themselves intent.
> Heaven chased them forth, lest their allegiance cloud
> Its beauty, and the deep Hell refuses them,
> For, beside such, the sinner would be proud."[6]

[6] *The Portable Dante,* Laurence Binyon verse translation (New York, The Viking Press, 1947), pp. 15-16.

Here are people who in this life spent their days discussing things but never arriving at any conclusions. They were reluctant to abandon themselves wholeheartedly to anything. They were never willing to stand up and be counted. They always avoided the necessity of committing themselves. They condemned nothing and they praised nothing. Indecisive and vacillating, they "rebelled not, yet avowed to God no loyalty." Having been rejected both by heaven and by hell, for all eternity, it is their fate aimlessly to chase back and forth, back and forth, without purpose, direction, or meaning.

In our own generation we find those who rebel not, but avow to God no loyalty. In our own time we find what Professor David Riesman calls the "other-directed" man, the man whose goals and whose principles are given him not by tradition or by his own conscience and imagination, but by his immediate social group. According to Professor Riesman, the inner-directed man is guided by a kind of built-in gyroscope that keeps him steadily on his course, whereas the other-directed man is guided by a kind of built-in radar apparatus that receives signals from his immediate social group and adjusts him to the situation indicated by those signals. The greatest horror of the other-directed man is that of failing to adjust and of being regarded by his peers as "unsociable." He is a man who "rebels not, yet avows to God no loyalty," lest, in taking a stand, he plead guilty to the charge of nonconformity.

Ardis Whitman in A New Image of Man quotes the class historian of the 1954 class at Yale as saying: "We did not condemn, but neither did we judge—we listened and did not challenge. We heard a thousand truths and did not shoulder a single cross. . . . We had no ebullience, no spontaneity, no enthusiasm. . . . We did not create and there was no laughter in us. . . . We stood particularized and alone. . . . We were the numb men."[7]

This statement bears a striking similarity to the utterances of those who "rebelled not, yet avowed to God no loyalty." This is further evidence of the phenomenon of men and women tranquilized into apathy, incapable of anger, indifferent to the most flagrant abuse of justice. If we want to build God's kingdom and make the daring dream come true, then the prophetic faith must stir us to anger and

[7] New York, Appleton-Century-Crofts, 1955.

divine discontent. It must motivate us to become God's angry men and women, stirred up and agitated, incensed at the fear-ridden faces of little children bravely running the gantlet of abuse, curses, and physical blows. Anger should surge within us at the picture of Dorothy Counts, a fifteen-year-old Negro girl from Charlotte, North Carolina, pelted with stones, who comforted her friends saying: "They didn't hurt me. They only hurt themselves. I feel sorry for them." Anger should dominate our souls at the hateful, leering faces of students harassing Elizabeth Eckford who tried to pass through the line of National Guardsmen at Central High School in Little Rock, Arkansas. She felt that she had a cause, and she was willing to subject herself to abuse, vilification, and physical injury for the sake of her beliefs. Are we willing to subject ourselves to abuse, calumny, and recrimination for the sake of our convictions and in behalf of our dreams?

There is so much that should make us angry. There is so much that should stir us, animate, challenge, and compel us to resist, to take action, to eradicate the evil that contaminates our world. Is it not a sin against the divine image within to be indifferent to corruption in labor and management, juvenile delinquency, crime, racial and religious bigotry, and war? There is so much that must be done to bring food to the hungry, light to those who walk in darkness, education to the ignorant, and justice where corruption and bigotry walk unhindered and unopposed. How can anyone who calls himself "religious" have the presumption to be bored, apathetic, or indifferent, "rebelling not, yet avowing to God no loyalty, on themselves intent"? Do we have the right to be complacent and indifferent to the bombing of churches and schools; to the slaughter of the innocents in Communist nations, to the inequities and injustices that belie the moral principles of our democracy, to the divisiveness and enmity that threaten the peace of the world?

The prophetic faith is summoning religious men and women to aggressive deeds in behalf of the daring dream, to resist the tranquilization of religion, to fight evil, to identify themselves with the principle of light, and to allow divine discontent to motivate them to religious action.

The Blessing of Discontent

It is creative discontent that has been the motivating factor for all progress, whether scientific, religious, or political. The hope of a life free from all anxiety is doomed to frustration. When a patient asked Sigmund Freud, "Will I ever have peace of mind and freedom from my nervousness?" Freud replied: "We can work together to remove your symptoms but not all of your anxiety. That is our lot as men."

Normal anxiety is essential for the preservation of life. It enables us to exercise restraints and protect ourselves from disaster and destruction. To be without anxiety is to be tranquilized into a bovine complacency that is dangerous—to ourselves and to the progress of religion. Tranquillity, contentment, and complacency constitute the death of prophetic religion, and doom the daring dream to a vague, inchoate yearning that never finds fulfillment. Unrest, struggle, doubt, discontent, and dissatisfaction with the status quo lead to progress, scientific, political, and religious.

It was the blessing of discontent that motivated Anton van Leeuwenhoek, a lens grinder, to develop the first microscope that he might see the minute organisms, the bacteria responsible for disease and the destruction of human life. It prompted Louis Pasteur to work with molds and fermentation to conceive of the germ theory of disease. It spurred Madame Curie to work with pitchblende to discover and extract precious radium. The discovery of penicillin, sulfas, and antibiotics came about because of the dissatisfaction and discontent of medical science with human suffering. It was discontent that prodded Jonas Salk to work desperately to discover a vaccine to prevent polio, that little children might not have to hobble through life with withered limbs and twisted bodies. What is driving scientists everywhere to work day after day with the hope of discovering cures for tuberculosis, cancer, rheumatic fever? It is not the blessing of contentment; it is not satisfaction; it is not smug self-complacency; it is the blessing of discontent that is spurring scientists on to new and wondrous vistas of scientific progress and achievement.

The great religious teachers and leaders of mankind were motivated by the blessing of discontent. A Moses was dissatisfied with the religious concepts of his era, and a new birth of freedom, a new code of morality came about as a result of that divine discontent. The prophets of Israel, Amos, Isaiah, Jeremiah, were perhaps the most discontented men in the history of religious civilization. They were not content with immorality, injustice, and deceit; they were not satisfied with the offering of animals for sacrifice while the people perverted justice and despised truth. They thundered forth their discontent in sublime and courageous protest as they spoke in the name of God, summoning mankind to live in peace, justice, and truth. Joshua of Nazareth was not satisfied with the prevailing religious mood of his era. It was the blessing of discontent that motivated him to drive out the moneychangers from the Temple. He was not satisfied with the pious protestations of those who spoke glibly of the fatherhood of God and the brotherhood of man, while they repudiated these ideals by their actions. It was discontent that made him assert that a man who says he loves God and hates his brother is a liar.

It took discontented teachers and prophets to rebel against established traditions, and it was the blessing of discontent that motivated these spiritual pioneers to clear away the jungle of ignorance and advance to new and exalted frontiers of religious thought.

America has been built up from coast to coast by men and women dissatisfied and discontented. We may hate communism for many reasons, but foremost we must despise communism because it has made it unsafe and unpopular to be a discontented American, when it is discontent that has made our country great. In recent years the fears, the apprehensions, the loyalty tests, the terror of being stigmatized as a Communist or a radical have in large measure inhibited the right of Americans to express their constructive discontent with government, with law, and with every facet of American life—a discontent that is prompted by a great and overwhelming love of America and a sense of pride in the democratic way of life.

We may doubt the loyalty of a completely contented American. Loyal to what? Can any American be content while there are dangerous Communist and Fascist organizations soaring through our nation on wings of terror, desecrating every sacred principle of Americanism? Do we have the right to be smug and satisfied as long as the beauty and magnificence of the American dream are ignored?

Can we as Americans ever be satisfied and content with bigotry, hatred, and prejudice? We can not afford to be content and satisfied. Who loves America the more, one who is content, or one who is discontented and never ceases striving to make of America not only the greatest, not only the most powerful economically, but the most exalted morally and spiritually of all nations of the world? It is the blessing of discontent that makes us Americans.

James Russell Lowell gives us an exquisite parable of a dissatisfied pilgrim who started out to find the mountain of God. He traveled for many months until at last he reached the goal of his search. He climbed to the mountaintop and stood at the summit; but because there was no sign that God was present he prayed that God might show him some visible token of His divine presence. In answer to his prayer, a rock broke open at his feet to reveal a beautiful white flower. He picked it up tenderly, and saw to his amazement that it was the same flower that his child had plucked from his own back yard and had given to him as he began his pilgrimage. While we search for God everywhere, while we look to distant goals and faraway places for the visible signs of God's presence, we sometimes forget that God may be present in our own back yard, with our dear ones; in our homes and in our hearts. We need not look to a world beyond the grave for the presence of God. The blessing of discontent must spur us on, prod us, torture us, disturb us to seek the presence of God in this world and to perfect our society in consonance with the moral mandate of prophetic religion.

This is what the poet meant when he prayed:

"God, though this life is but a wraith,
    Although we know not what we use,
Although we grope with little faith,
    Give me the heart to fight—and lose.

"Ever insurgent, let me be,
    Make me more daring than devout;
From sleek contentment keep me free,
    And fill me with a buoyant doubt.

"Open my eyes to visions girt
  With beauty, and with wonder lit—
But let me always see the dirt,
  And all that spawn and die in it.

"Open my ears to music; let
  Me thrill with Spring's first flutes and drums—
But never let me dare forget
  The bitter ballads of the slums.

"From compromise and things half-done,
  Keep me, with stern and stubborn pride;
And when, at last, the fight is won
  God, keep me still unsatisfied."[8]

How can we ever be satisfied and content with ourselves until we behold the living presence of God, until we bring divinity and holiness into our lives, until we behold the realization of the daring dream. We should thank God for the material blessings He has bestowed upon us, but in fervent gratitude we should also lift our eyes and our voice and our heart in thanksgiving to God for the dissatisfaction that spurs science on to new discoveries, for the divine restlessness that torments religious teachers to give us divine truth, for the impatient stubbornness that strengthens us to resist tranquilizers of faith, and forces us to make our covenant with the prophetic religion that demands social action, religious struggle and the application of the moral principles of religion to life.

Kindergarten religion identifies itself with myth and magic, security, conformity, comfort, popularity, and peace of mind. The prophetic faith is identified with ethical commitment, moral challenge, unpopular causes, insecurity, creative nonconformity, anguish of heart, social discontent, and struggle. Just as Jacob had to wrestle in the night, emerging wounded and crippled, to force a blessing in order to become Israel, so the adherents of the prophetic faith must constantly struggle in the night of conflict, castigated as disrespect-

[8] From *Challenge* by Louis Untermeyer, copyright, 1914, by Harcourt, Brace & World, Inc.; renewed, 1942, by Louis Untermeyer. Reprinted by permission of the publishers.

able, wounded in prestige, unpopular and rejected, but blessed by the sublime knowledge that they are spiritual combatants in an unending battle against evil, injustice, and man's inhumanity to man.

In the nineteenth century Karl Marx was regarded as a contemptible radical when he epitomized religion as "the opiate of the people." In the twentieth century we have made Karl Marx's strictures acceptable and respectable by condoning the sentiment that "religion is the tranquilizer of the people," lulling their conscience to sleep, dulling, anaesthetizing their sensitivities to injustice and evil, making faith a guardian of the status quo, resisting change, progress, and the dynamics of social action.

Kindergarten religion dreams of the time when supernatural intervention will enable man to live happily ever after. It projects the solution of the world's social problems to the next world whose advent will be heralded by the coming of the Messiah.

The prophetic faith insists that man is God's agent, divinely summoned to make this world a kingdom of God on earth, and that the good society may only be achieved by eradicating the causes of war, poverty, evil, crime, injustice, falsehood, and ignorance. That is why the devotees of the prophetic faith must subject themselves to calumny, unpopularity, and conflict in order to destroy the corrosive influence of racial prejudice, poverty, injustice, religious bigotry, and international hostility. That is why tranquilization of conscience is a deterrent to an active, dynamic, mature, and prophetic faith. That is why the disciples of the daring dream must cultivate the art of being color-blind.

15

Souls Don't Have Color

It will be a sad commentary on our life and time if future historians can write that the last bulwark of segregation based on race and color in the United States and South Africa was God's Church.

—BENJAMIN MAYS

How Many Bubbles in a Bar of Soap?

The survival of organized and institutional religion depends upon the degree to which it will apply the moral requisites of the prophetic faith to social action. Unless there is a transition from the stereotypes of respectable religion to a dynamic, social consciousness that expresses itself in behalf of political and social justice, the Church and the Synagogue will degenerate into atavistic museum-like symbols of the past. Organized religion must direct its efforts to combat injustice, bigotry, discrimination, and the social evils of society.

In an official sworn affidavit, a Negro resident of Mississippi declared that on April 11, 1952, she was deprived of the right to vote. After responding in a satisfactory manner to questions pertaining to the Constitution, she was requested to answer the question "How many bubbles are there in a bar of soap?" Her failure to answer this question to the satisfaction of the officials resulted in a denial of her right to be properly registered as a voter.

Respectable religion would insist that this is a political problem of the state judicial and legislative bodies that guarantee civil liberties. The prophetic faith would insist that this and all other problems that relate to social justice, civil liberties, and human dignity clearly and unequivocally challenge religion to take moral action. Respectable religion withdraws apprehensively from taking a stand on "political" issues. The prophetic faith holds that political and social action are as basic to religion as ritual, worship, dogma, and creed.

It is in the area of race relations and brotherhood that contemporary religion most dangerously reveals the disparity between belief and action. It is apparent that, despite constitutional guarantee of equal rights, the Negro is denied his vote. He cannot send his children to integrated public schools; restrictive covenants exclude him from certain residential districts; he is subjected to discriminatory regulations on buses and trains, and is limited in economic opportunities. All of this persists despite his American constitutional rights and the repeated pronouncements of Church bodies denouncing discrimination and prejudice.

In Mississippi a Negro is taken from his jail cell and lynched. In Florida a Negro co-ed is raped by four white men. In Philadelphia a mob stormed the home of a Negro when he bought an abandoned store in a white neighborhood and made it over into a home. In Chicago a mob hurled bricks and crude bombs at the home of a Negro because he had moved into Trumbell Park, an all-white housing project. In a West Coast city a Negro and his two children were burned to death when neighbors set his house afire two days after Christmas. There have been race riots in Detroit, Cleveland, and St. Louis, eliciting racial prejudice, mob violence, and the assault upon persons and the property of Negroes.

Confronted by this ugly evidence of racial prejudice, what are the moral demands for remedial action imposed upon the Church and the Synagogue?

Prior to the United States Supreme Court decision in behalf of the integration of Negro students into the public schools, various Church bodies made the following official pronouncements:

The Methodist Church, at its 1948 General Conference, issued a resolution stating: "The principle of racial discrimination is in clear violation of the Christian belief in the Fatherhood of God, the Brotherhood of man, and the Kingdom of God. . . . We therefore have no choice but to denote it [racial discrimination] as un-Christian and to renounce it as evil."[1]

The Most Reverend Bernard J. Sheil, Auxiliary Bishop, Catholic

[1] "The Christian Church and Race," *The Methodist Discipline* (Methodist Publishing House, Nashville, 1948), p. 601.

Archdiocese of Chicago, said that discrimination destroys the solidarity of the human race, and mocks the Fatherhood of God and the Brotherhood of Christ: "We have asked the Negroes and the Jews to fight and die for democracy; it would be the basest cynicism to refuse to share with them that democracy."

In 1950 the Commission on Justice and Peace of the Central Conference of American Rabbis reported: "Although we note with satisfaction the progress which has been made in education and rejoice in those judicial decisions that reaffirm the principles of the Constitution, we dare not overlook the fact that conditions under which Negroes live is not in keeping with the spirit of brotherhood enunciated by our religion and in conformity with the spirit of genuine Americanism. Studies and statistics indicate conclusively that Negroes have, to a large degree, been denied the right to life, liberty and the pursuit of happiness. . . . It is our belief that, in order to rectify these injustices and establish the brotherhood of man, it is necessary that certain measures be adopted as law."[2]

In 1952 the general board of the National Council of the Churches of Christ in the United States of America declared: "The National Council of the Churches of Christ in the U.S.A. in its structure and operation, renounces and earnestly recommends to its member churches that they renounce the pattern of segregation based on race, color or national origin as unnecessary and undesirable and a violation of the Gospel of love and human brotherhood.

"While recognizing that historical and social factors make it more difficult for some churches than for others to realize the Christian ideal of non-segregation, the Council urges all of its constituent members to work steadily and progressively towards a non-segregated church as the goal which is set forth in the faith and practice of the early Christian community and inherent in the New Testament idea of the Church of Christ.

"As proof of our sincerity in this renunciation, the National Council of Churches will work for a non-segregated church and a non-segregated community."[3]

These and other statements from Christian and Jewish religious

[2] *Central Conference of American Rabbis* (Philadelphia, Maurice Jacobs, 1950), LX, 160.
[3] Ralph Lord Roy, *Apostles of Discord* (Boston, The Beacon Press, 1953), p. 369.

groups attest to the forthright stand of the Church and the Synagogue against racial discrimination and for the integration of the Negro into churches and schools. These statements were accepted in principle as long as they were not too insistent in demanding action and implementation. The official stand of the Judaeo-Christian morality on racial rights has ever been clear and decisive. We may ask, however, to what extent action has been taken to translate these sentiments into the language of reality.

Souls Don't Have Color

One churchman, Bishop Vincent S. Waters, was not content to ease his conscience with nicely worded statements that charged his parishioners to a theoretical opposition to racial discrimination. Therefore he ordered the two Roman Catholic churches in Newton Grove, North Carolina, one for whites only, Holy Redeemer, and the other for Negroes, St. Benedict, to consolidate.

On May 31, 1953, only 29 of the 80 St. Benedict parish members almost fearfully attended Holy Redeemer services. Of Holy Redeemer's 250 parishioners, only 35 showed up for Mass. About 35 more crowded outside the church while Mass was said by Bishop Waters.

When services were completed, as the bishop left the church to walk to the nearby rectory, an irate crowd of white parishioners surrounded him with bitter and angry protests. Facing them from the rectory steps, Bishop Waters quietly declared, "Souls do not have nationality, race or color."

On June 19th Bishop Waters outlawed segregation in every church in his diocese, which includes all of North Carolina except Gaston County. Attacked as a radical, Communist, and "nigger lover," Bishop Waters moved among his people with quiet dignity, emphasizing: "The Church does not propose tolerance which is negative, but love which is positive. If Christ said love your enemies, we certainly can love our friends. These are our friends, and members of our own body, the Church. It is our duty . . . not only to love them but to serve them, to help them. We need to help them get better educational facilities, better opportunities for culture, better living conditions, homes and families, better civic representation, and better friendliness in the community. All of this presupposes the right to worship God freely with us in the Church anywhere.

"I am not unmindful, as a Southerner, of the force of this virus of prejudice among persons in the South, as well as in the North. I know, however, there is a cure for this virus, and that is our Faith. . . . The virus will not die of itself, it has to be killed by being exposed to the light of Faith.

"I am happy to take the responsibility for any evil which might result from different races worshipping God together. But I would be unwilling to take the responsibility of those who refuse to worship God with a person of another race."[4]

When Bishop Waters, a Southerner by birth, took action against segregation, he did more than contribute to the end of a social evil; he took action in behalf of prophetic religion and the moral precepts of the Judaeo-Christian ethical commitment.

The Most Segregated Hour of the Week

A minister at a church convention held in Cleveland, Ohio, declared: "There is more Jim Crowism in America at 11 o'clock on Sunday morning than at any other time."

During the 1957 school crisis, several Negroes in Little Rock were turned away when they attempted to attend a white church service. An out-of-state writer, in a wry critique, observed that perhaps they "mistook this church for the House of God."

The attitude of the clergy of Little Rock is assessed by Thomas F. Pettigrew and Ernest Q. Campbell in *Christians in Racial Crisis.*[5] The authors classify twenty-nine ministers. Fourteen of them, while generally favoring integration, took little action on it; they were older men in small churches. Seven, averaging about fifty years of age, were influential preachers in high-status churches; but after the first days of the Little Rock crisis they were cautious.

The heroes of the crisis were eight "innovators" who pressed for support of school integration. Most of them were Southern-born and most were in their thirties. Unfortunately, however, several of these courageous ministers have been pressured out of their churches in Little Rock.

The minister, priest, and rabbi find no opposition when they speak

---

[4] "End of Segregation," *Commonweal*, July 10, 1953, pp. 349-350.
[5] Washington, D.C., Public Affairs Press.

in behalf of the abstract principle of the Fatherhood of God and the brotherhood of man. They are applauded for their advocacy of moral values. It is when they attempt to concretize moral values and apply universally accepted ideals to real-life situations that they encounter resistance, hostility, and acrid criticism, and are urged to avoid politics and "stick to religion." This is one of the greatest scandals of contemporary religion.

Taking cognizance of this, the World Council of Churches, meeting at Amsterdam in 1948, declared: "The church knows that it must call society away from prejudice based upon race or colour, and from the practices of discrimination and segregation as denials of justice and human dignity, but it cannot say a convincing word to society unless it takes steps to eliminate these practices from the Christian community because they contradict all that it believes about God's love for all His children."[6]

The majority of churches in the United States are segregated, maintaining a racial exclusiveness that belies the religious inclusiveness of Holy Scripture, theological conviction, denominational pronouncement, and ethical universalism. The Synagogue has not been compelled to wrestle with this problem because there are but few Negroes of the Jewish faith. Because of the fear and timidity manifested when problems of racial justice arise, however, it is reasonable to conclude that the Synagogue would react in the same way as the Church if there were a larger number of Negroes affiliated with the Jewish faith.

Whether a church or a synagogue, when any religious institution maintains barriers of race, it cannot effectively protest or take action against segregation in schools, public transportation, hotels, restaurants, job employment, or any other secular establishment or organization, if it gives sanction to bigotry and rears idols of prejudice on its own sacred altars.

Fervent pulpit pronouncements of the sanctity of man created in the divine image, the universal love of God for His children, and the evil of racial and religious prejudice are mocked by the estimate that approximately 95 per cent of the Negroes and the whites worship the same God, perform the same ritual, read the same Bible, and subscribe to the same denominational disciplines in separate congregations.

[6] *Man's Disorder and God's Design* (New York, Harper, 1949), III, 195.

Benjamin Mays spoke to this point when he said: "In our time where segregation is based on race or color there is nothing one can do to qualify. He cannot qualify even when he accepts the same creed, practices the same ritual, prays to the same God and partakes of the same culture. Segregation based on color or race makes it impossible for the Christian of color to qualify; for one cannot change his color and he cannot change his race. And this restriction is tantamount to penalizing one for being what God made him and tantamount to saying to God, 'You made a mistake, God, when you made peoples of different races and colors.' "[7]

With segregation gradually breaking down in other secular areas of life, Mays indicts the vacillation of the clergy, and asserts, "It will be a sad commentary on our life and time if future historians can write that the last bulwark of segregation based on race and color in the United States and South Africa was God's church."

Religion and the Desegregation of the Public Schools

On May 17, 1954, the United States Supreme Court declared that segregation by race in the public schools is illegal, and called for the integration of Negro students into the public schools at all "deliberate speed." This decision created a furor in the nation, particularly in the South. Bigots, hate mongers, and fanatics gravitated to areas of tension. Organizations were formed to combat the decision of the Supreme Court. Pamphlets, propaganda, and inflammatory literature urged hatred of Negroes, Catholics, and Jews, warned of the insidious dangers of mongrelization, and urged violent resistance to the destruction of "the southern way of life." State legislatures and school boards attempted to find ways and means to circumvent the decision of the Supreme Court legally. Governor Orville Faubus of Arkansas defied court orders and called out the state militia to prevent Negro children from entering white schools. When President Eisenhower sent an armed force to assure compliance with the law, Negro and white children studied together in nonsegregated schools, but at the end of the school year Central High School in Little Rock, Arkansas, and other integrated schools were closed by state law.

[7] *Seeking To Be Christian in Race Relations* (New York, Friendship Press, 1957), p. 35.

Some border and southern states integrated the public schools without incident, but mass meetings, protests, picketing, and propaganda continued to agitate and arouse public opinion in the South. Moderates expressed their disapproval of the Supreme Court decision but yielded to a resigned compliance with law. Extremists vowed a continued battle against integration. Goaded by the fulminations of would-be dictators and racial bigots such as John Kaspar, leaders of the Ku Klux Klan, representatives of white supremacy groups, and rabid but respectable and well intentioned segregationists threatened violence and militant resistance to any effort to integrate the public schools of the South.

During this period of unrest and tension, as the transition from segregated to integrated schools was being effected, almost every major religious denomination spoke forth in favor of compliance with the decision of the Supreme Court.

In 1954 the Second Assembly of the World Council of Churches declared its conviction that any form of segregation based on race, color, or ethnic origin is contrary to the Gospel, and is incompatible with the Christian doctrine of man and with the nature of the Church of Christ. The assembly urged the churches within its membership to renounce all forms of segregation or discrimination and to work for their abolition within their own life and within society.

The American Baptist Convention, meeting in June, 1957, declared that "each Church shall work to assure equality for all people in education, employment, housing and political activity [and that] each Baptist organization, school, home and hospital shall follow practices that are consistent with clear policies of racial nondiscrimination."

The American Lutheran Church stated that "Christian churches unfailingly must condemn segregation and stratification as the evil fruit of natural man's pride and his arrogant assumption of superiority over those who appear to be different from him."[8]

In May, 1956, the American Unitarian Association urged compliance with the Supreme Court decision, and called upon "all governmental officials and agencies . . . to accord the full protection of the

[8] "Protestantism Speaks on Justice and Integration," *Christian Century*, Feb. 5, 1958, p. 164.

law to all citizens in the exercise of their rights, including the right to vote, and the other rights guaranteed by the Constitution."

The Augustana Lutheran Church in 1956 urged its members "to use their influence in the securing of full rights of citizenship for all, and in discouraging any activities in their communities which would seek to circumvent orderly judicial procedure in the implementation of the Supreme Court decisions of segregation."[9]

The Union of American Hebrew Congregations asserted that Judaism is opposed to any form of discrimination because of race, and at its Biennial Assembly in Los Angeles in February, 1955, endorsed the decision of the Supreme Court. The resolution states: "Having consistently opposed every form of discrimination because of our fundamental belief in the equality of all men under God, we rejoice in the unanimous decision of the U.S. Supreme Court in the school segregation cases. . . .

"As proponents of Judaism which first enunciated the concept of the fatherhood of God and the brotherhood of man, we pledge ourselves to do all within our power to make the decision of the highest court in the land meaningful in our respective communities.

"We therefore urge our congregations and congregations in all sections of the country to join with forward-looking racial, religious and civic groups in the community in using their influence to secure acceptance and implementation of the desegregation decisions in every community in our land."

The Southern Baptist Convention, the Protestant Episcopal General Convention, the Presbyterian Church U.S.A., the General Conference of Seventh-day Adventists, the General Conference of the Methodist Church, and almost every major Christian denomination issued statements against racial discrimination and declared in favor of the implementation of the Supreme Court decision; but the question that must be answered is this: To what extent did the clergymen and the churches of these denominations take action to support and activate these resolutions of their national church bodies? The answer to this question indicates in large measure whether or not contemporary religion applies moral principles to social and political problems and makes prophetic faith a total response to life.

Here is where the clergyman found himself gored on the horns of

[9] "Protestantism Speaks on Justice and Integration," *loc. cit.*

the dilemma. If he takes an active part in the struggle for desegregation, he is true and loyal to the resolutions of his denominational body and loyal to his interpretations of the Gospel, but he disturbs and even divides his church and incurs personal resentments. If he remains silent or satisfies himself with vague generalizations and abstract preaching on moral principles, he contributes to unity and peace in his church but does not fulfill the moral mandate of the Gospel and fails to comply with the resolutions of his denominational group.

H. Laurence McNeil, in the *Christian Century*, chastised the Church on its silence when acts of violence against the Negro occurred. "Except in rare instances," he stated, "the leading preachers became as silent as the Sphinx. They go underground. . . . You can do anything to a child of God if he belongs to a minority, without fear."

Wallace Westfeld, a co-author of *With All Deliberate Speed*, referring to various "Communities in Strife," concedes that "the position of the clergy is, so far at least, indecisive."

The issue of *Christianity and Crisis* for March 3, 1958, given over wholly to "The Southern Churches and the Race Question," calls attention to "the moral gap between creed and deed," and chides the churches for their "hypocrisy" and their tendency toward "institutional self-preservation."

Not all ministers and rabbis have taken refuge in silence. The courageous act of the Reverend Paul Turner, a Baptist minister who accompanied Negro children to school in Clinton, Tennessee, and was personally assaulted, will long be remembered as a notable example of courage and commitment to a prophetic faith. Rabbi Charles Mantinband, of Hattiesburg, Mississippi; Rabbi Jacob Rothschild, of Atlanta, Georgia; and Rabbi Emmett Frank, of Alexandria, Virginia, manifested prophetic courage in crisis.

On Sunday, November 3, 1957, eighty ministers in Atlanta representing major Protestant denominations spoke for themselves as ministers, as Georgians, and as Americans, but made it clear that they did not speak for their denominations or for their congregations when they issued a six-point guide for Christian thinking and behavior on the question of segregation. Their code for Christian conduct includes: (1) freedom of speech, without reprisal; (2) an obligation to obey the law, as well as a right to try to change laws by legal means, but never by violence and economic reprisal; (3) preservation of the public schools; (4) a condemnation of hate and scorn as never justified; (5) maintenance of communications between responsible leaders of the races; (6) consistent prayer for God's guidance.

While it is regrettable that these intrepid clergymen could not speak for their denominations and their congregations, they are to be commended for reflecting the power of light in darkness, and the prophetic spirit.

In other areas, churchmen have not only spoken but acted in behalf of desegregation in schools, transportation, and housing, and in behalf of equal economic opportunity. Ronnie Dugger tells of clergymen from Protestant, Roman Catholic, and Jewish faiths, under the auspices of the Texas Council of Churches, uniting in definitive action to oppose racist legislation proposed in that state. Undaunted by formidable opposition from members of their churches, undeterred by protests, abuse, and vilification, the clergymen were successful in opposing and defeating almost a dozen vicious race-baiting bills. Dugger declares that this indicates that "churchmen, less vulnerable than politicians, more trusted as ethical leaders than any other group in the community, have a special obligation in the coming crisis of human rights in America. If those in the South will take an active stand against violence, and thus in favor of the orderly processes of the law, they can do more for equal rights than all the politicians in Washington. We learned again in Texas that men of religion are not always defrocked, transferred or repudiated when they take their own vigorous part in the decision-making of democracy; that they can lead, and lead well, in the times of loneliness for the best and highest principles of man."[10]

Dynamite!

The dynamiting and bombing of schools, synagogues, and churches, during the tense years of struggle over the desegregation issue, not only revealed the violence inherent in the camp of rabid segregationists but also provided clergymen with a welcome opportunity to ex-

[10] "Texas Christians Stem the Tide," *Christian Century*, July 31, 1957.

culpate and denounce extremes of racial and religious hatred without taking a decisive position on the segregation issue. It is in this area of the racial controversy that respectable religion revealed its tragic weakness and manifested a betrayal of the prophetic faith.

Few clergymen in the city of Nashville, Tennessee, unequivocally declared their support of the decision of the Supreme Court. The clergy was silent except for some nebulous and abstract statements about brotherly love and equal rights for the Negro. With the dynamiting of the Hattie Cotton School in September, 1957, ministers, rabbis, and priests were galvanized into action and expressed shame and indignation at this breach of law and order, vigorously protesting against the dynamiting as a criminal act. The record does not indicate that this unconscionable act of violence motivated the clergy to insist upon compliance with the law to the extent of implementing the decision of the Supreme Court and hastening the desegregation of the public schools.

On March 16, 1958, when the Jewish Community Center of Nashville was dynamited, and extremists threatened to shoot Federal Judge William E. Miller in cold blood; when the local rabbi was warned that his Temple would be next, and armed guards were placed at the rabbi's home to protect him and his family, the clergy again protested indignantly, expressed sincere sympathy, and offered to raise funds for the repair of the Jewish Community Center. Ministerial associations met to formulate resolutions, and local clergymen preached angry sermons from their pulpits, deploring and protesting the dynamiting of the Jewish Community Center, and appealed for law and order. The appeal for "law" was interpreted by the laymen as a proper request by the clergy as long as "law" was limited to the orderly processes of averting violence. In few instances were the appeals for "law" interpreted to mean the law as interpreted by the Supreme Court vis-à-vis the desegregation of the public schools.

At 3:30 A.M., on Sunday, October 12, 1958, a blast of dynamite shook the foundations of the Temple in Atlanta, Georgia, causing over $200,000 in damage. The disaster, flashed at first over radio and television, shocked police officials and the citizenry of the city and state into a massive reaction of expressions of goodwill and sympathy.

Atlanta's Mayor William B. Hartsfield, shocked and angry, expressed the opinion that the dynamiting was the work of crackpots, similar to those responsible for synagogue bombings in Nashville,

Jacksonville, and Miami, and offered a reward of $1,000 for the apprehension of the criminals.

In Washington, President Eisenhower angrily condemned the bombing of the Atlanta Temple and called upon FBI Director J. Edgar Hoover for a "full firsthand report." The President declared: "We must all share in the feeling of horror that anyone would want to desecrate a place of religion, be it a chapel, a cathedral, a mosque, a church or a synagogue.

"If we believe in the tradition of freedom of worship, then we must not countenance the desecration of any edifices symbolizing one of the great faiths."

An around-the-clock police security guard was posted Sunday night at the homes of the Temple's leaders, Rabbi Jacob M. Rothschild and William B. Schwartz, Jr., congregation president, after Mrs. Rothschild received an anonymous telephone call at 6:25 P.M. warning: "You'd better get out of the house. It will be dynamited in five minutes."

Ralph McGill, editor of the *Atlanta Constitution*, spoke to the conscience of the people of Atlanta with the statement:

"Let us face the facts.

"This is a harvest. It is the crop of things sown.

"It is the harvest of defiance of courts and the encouragement of citizens to defy law on the part of many Southern politicians. It will be the acme of irony, for example, if any one of four or five Southern governors deplore this bombing. It will be grimly humorous if certain state attorneys general issue statements of regret. And it will be quite a job for some editors, columnists and commentators, who have been saying that our courts have not jurisdiction, and that the people should refuse to accept their authority now to deplore.

"It is not possible to preach lawlessness and restrict it.

"To be sure, none said go bomb a Jewish temple or a school.

"But let it be understood that when leadership in high places in any degree fails to support constituted authority, it opens the gates to all those who wish to take law into their hands.

"This, too, is a harvest of those so-called Christian ministers who have chosen to preach hate instead of compassion. Let them now find pious words and raise their hands in deploring the bombing of a synagogue.

"You do not preach and encourage hatred for the Negro and hope to restrict it to that field. It is an old, old story. It is one repeated over and over again in history. When the wolves of hate are loosed on one people, then no one is safe."[11]

Following the dynamiting of the Atlanta Temple, Rabbi Emmett A. Frank, in Alexandria, Virginia, assailed the segregation policies of United States Senator Harry Byrd and questioned whether "Byrdliness was synonymous with Godliness." The young Virginia rabbi was condemned by members of his congregation and citizens of the community. Eleven Protestant ministers signed a "freedom of pulpit" statement defending Rabbi Frank against organized bigots who demanded that the Alexandria Temple repudiate its spiritual leader or suffer "impairing of friendly Jewish-Christian relations."

"We wish simply to affirm that the remarks of Rabbi Frank have in no manner threatened our friendship with him or with our other Jewish friends in this city," declared the Alexandria ministerial pronouncement.

The declaration of the Alexandria ministers undoubtedly gave support to the young rabbi and discouraged his congregation from requesting his resignation.

The crucial issue, however, from the view of the prophetic faith, was not the harmony of Jewish-Christian relationships, nor was it the preservation of freedom of the pulpit. As far as it can be ascertained, the ministers of Alexandria did not issue a forthright statement requesting full compliance with the decision of the Supreme Court and a demand for complete desegregation of the public schools and constitutional rights for Negro citizens.

On February 24, 1959, the Associated Press reported that a Congregational minister who spoke out for Levittown's first Negro family said that outside pressures were forcing him to resign. The Reverend Dr. Fred Manthey, Jr., of the Plymouth Congregational Church, of Levittown, Pennsylvania, told the Associated Press his church's National Board of Home Missions had declared in favor of church integration but refused to back his stand. He said that "the real reason for my resignation is the reluctance of the Board of Home Missions to shoulder the cost of our action" in running a paid advertisement in the local newspaper favoring integration.

Thirty of the 150 church members walked out in a rift over the

[11] Published Oct. 13, 1958. Used with permission of Ralph McGill.

advertisement and over the welcome extended to Mr. and Mrs. William Myers. The Myerses now attend Dr. Manthey's church but are not members. Their two boys attend Sunday school and Bible school at the church—the only Negroes to do so. It was the Myerses' move into this previously all-white community which touched off nine days of riots, stone throwing, and cross burning.

Mrs. Adolph Mall, a deaconess in the church, said the Board of Home Missioners had declared it would support Dr. Manthey's integration stand but did not. She said that the minister had been the target of many insults.

The rift that split the church after the Myers incident brought about the departure of one-third of the church officers to other churches.

Harvest of Hate

The harvest of hate, the crop of things sown was reaped in bombed temples in Miami and Jacksonville, Florida; Atlanta, Georgia; and Peoria, Illinois; a dynamited Jewish Community Center in Nashville, Tennessee, a shattered school building in Clinton, Tennessee, and abortive attempts to dynamite synagogues in Gastonia and Charlotte, North Carolina, and Birmingham, Alabama. It is reported that over seventy churches, synagogues, schools, and dwellings were dynamited in one year as a result of the race issue.

In the face of this, are we to believe that the controversial subject of desegregation transcends morality and rests on its merit or lack of merit as a political problem?

Is it possible for the Church and the Synagogue to remain "neutral" and fulfill their divine purpose of witnessing to the word and will of God?

While the South has been highlighted as the scene of the most dramatic acts of violence, racial injustice is not regional; it is national and international. Those in the South are most immediately and emotionally affected by the problem of racial conflict, but issues of morality transcend regional and geographic dimensions and summon the adherents of the prophetic faith to resist the allure of comfortable conformity, to slough apathy, and apply the precepts of religion to political problems.

Are the ministers, priests, and rabbis who remained silent on the political question of segregation, and who apprehensively guarded their words lest their congregants take offense, less guilty of destroying law and order and less responsible for the ugliness of racial and religious hatred than the perpetrators of acts of violence?

In assessing responsibility for the dynamiting and the bombing of churches, synagogues, and schools, we may not ignore the well intentioned, respectable men and women who worshiped in churches and synagogues and gave assent to the abstract ethical principles of brotherhood and racial justice; who chanted, sang, and uttered responsive prayers declaring their belief in the sanctity of the human personality, but excluded political issues from the sanctuary, and by their silence, apathy, and neutrality gave wordless sanction to the hands of modern Esaus that kindled the fuse and detonated the dynamite that blasted schools and houses of God.

The Challenge and the Divine Demand

In a message for Race Relations Sabbath, 1959, the Commission on Justice and Peace of the Central Conference of American Rabbis declared: "The unfinished task of securing full civil and human rights for the American Negro is still in 1959 the most urgent social challenge that confronts religious leaders. All the pretensions of American democracy and of the Jewish and Christian heritage to a concern with brotherhood and the sanctity of the individual are tested in our response to this problem. The voice of religion should be heard proclaiming most persuasively and firmly those insights of American faith that brand prejudice and inhumanity as sinful. It should affirm in specific relationships and actual test situations those ethical values which will afford to America the moral leadership she so sorely needs. Church-going and synagogue-attendance without a clearly expressed and sacrificially served dedication to the fulfillment, without reservation, of the ideal of human brotherhood is empty mockery of the fundamental concept of man which is the inescapable consequence of Jewish tradition and Christian belief."

The time has come for the Church and the Synagogue to apply the precepts of social justice inherent in their scriptural, theological, and ecclesiastical sources. This is not only urgent, but mandatory. Much more is involved than justice for the Negro. The specific issue of justice for the Negro will determine the survival and the perpetuation of the prophetic faith. The Church and the Synagogue may continue to exist even with the negation of the moral principles that are advocated. Jews and Christians will continue to attend worship services and perform rituals even if institutional religion retreats from the confrontation of social problems, but the divine potential of the prophetic faith will atrophy and ultimately degenerate.

In "The Role of the American Churches" in the journal of the Perkins School of Theology, Spring, 1958, R. F. Curl correctly contends: "Since the question of race relations is theological, the churches must seek to *discover and declare divine demands.* Any approach which evades God's stake in the issue is inadequate; any humanistic solution, insufficient.

"With rigorous exactitude the churches seek God's will for His children who, although of one blood, are of differing pigmentations. In fact no other issue receives more attention in American churches. . . . although many decided differences of opinion exist in regard to details of timing and application of remedial measures, practically unanimous consensus has been reached in the churches as to the basic demands God lays upon us in our human relationships."[12]

What are the divine demands that challenge the prophetic faith in its relationship to racial justice? The Methodist Church, in *The Bible Speaks on Race,* a pamphlet of the Board of Social and Economic Relations, sets forth the following: (1) "All nations of men have a common origin and in the eyes of God constitute a single family"; (2) "Man was created in the image of God and therefore every human being is of infinite worth"; (3) "God shows no partiality"; (4) "Jesus Christ came to redeem every man regardless of race or nationality"; (5) "Persons who respond to the call of Christ in love and obedience enter a new kind of fellowship in the Church where racial barriers are transcended"; (6) "The Church is called and empowered by God to reconcile a divided humanity and to unite all peoples into one family of God"; (7) "Each member of the Church is summoned by God to work where he is toward overcoming misunderstandings and antagonisms that men may dwell together in unity."[13]

[12] By permission of R. F. Curl.
[13] Pamphlet, Board of Social and Economic Relations, Methodist Church.

The statement adopted by the General Assembly of the National Council of Churches of Christ in the U.S.A. at St. Louis in December, 1957, truly reflects the attitude of Christianity: "Racial segregation is contradictory to the teaching of Jesus."[14] As Harry Ashmore says in *An Epitaph for Dixie*, ". . . not even the most determined bigot can make a segregationist out of . . . Jesus Christ." Judaism would affirm with equal vigor that not even the most rabid and fearful Jewish advocate of white supremacy could make a segregationist out of God.

The Art of Being Color-Blind

The story is current of a little boy from the Deep South whose family moved to Ohio and placed him in the kindergarten of a public school. He kept talking about his new-found and best friend and playmate called Jimmy. One day a neighbor asked the boy's mother if she knew that her son was playing with a Negro boy. She was shocked, but determined to approach the matter carefully. When her son came home that afternoon, she asked him, in a casual manner, "Is Jimmy colored?" Her son looked puzzled for a moment, then said, "I don't know, Mother, but I'll look tomorrow."

The Judaeo-Christian ethical heritage inculcates the unassailable conviction that man is created in the image of God (Genesis 1.26), and is therefore endowed with an immortal soul. Scripture does not state that men of the white race alone were created in the image of God. The irrefutable teaching of Scripture is that man, universal man, is created in the image of God and blessed with a soul.

The exhortation of Leviticus 19.18, "Love thy neighbour as thyself," does not specify the race, religion, or nationality of the neighbor. It does not qualify the color of the neighbor's skin, "Love thy neighbor if he is a Caucasian." The accepted pigmentation of skin is not a requisite for brotherly love.

The scriptural admonition from the Book of Leviticus (19.33) implies no recognition of color: "The stranger that sojourneth with you shall be unto you as the home-born among you, and thou shalt love him as thyself; for ye were strangers in the land of Egypt."

When the prophet Micah proclaimed:

[14] New York, W. W. Norton and Company, 1958, p. 159.

"It hath been told thee, O man, what is good,
And what the Lord doth require of thee:
Only to do justly, and to love mercy, and to walk humbly with
    thy God." (6.8)

he was not addressing himself to those of the black, white, or yellow
races, but setting forth the ethical demands of God for the universal
man. Micah had acquired the art of being color-blind.

The prophet Amos was color-blind when he promulgated the concept of the universal God whose love was bestowed in equal measure
upon all His children. Puncturing the puffed-up arrogance of the
children of Israel who regarded God as the exclusive Sovereign of
one people, he thundered in prophetic cadence:

"Are ye not as the children of the Ethiopians unto Me,
O children of Israel? saith the Lord.
Have I not brought up Israel out of the land of Egypt,
And the Philistines from Caphtor,
And Aram from Kir?" (9.7)

God loved the ignorant, primitive, black-skinned Ethiopians with
the same tenderness as He loved the children of Israel with whom He
had made covenant at Sinai. Just as God, in His providential solicitude, had brought up Israel out of the land of Egypt, so He had
redeemed their enemies, the Philistines, from Caphtor and Aram
from Kir.

Malachi, the prophet, envisaged God as color-blind, impervious to
the distinctions of race, nationality, or denominationalism when he
asked:

"Have we not all one father?
Hath not one God created us?
Why do we deal treacherously every man against his brother,
Profaning the covenant of our fathers?" (2.10)

The rabbis of the Talmud were color-blind when they declared,
in the name of God, "I call heaven and earth to witness that whether

it be Gentile or Israelite, man or woman, slave or handmaid, according to the deeds which he does, will the Holy Spirit rest upon him."

The New Testament teaches that there may be no distinctions of color in the new Community of God. The Pauline tradition declares unequivocally: "Here there cannot be Greek and Jew, circumcised and uncircumcised, barbarian, Scythian, slave, free man, but Christ is all, and in all" (Colossians 3.11; Galatians 3.28, R.S.V.). Onesimus, the slaveowner, is enjoined to receive the slave again into his service and also into the church, "no longer as a slave but more than a slave, as a beloved brother" (Philemon 16).

Paul had acquired the art of being color-blind when he stood in the midst of Mars' Hill and said to the men of Athens that God "hath made of one blood all nations of men for to dwell on all the face of the earth, and hath determined the times before appointed, and the bounds of their habitation" (Acts 17.26, K.J.V.).

Jesus was color-blind as he beheld all men as the children of God. Nowhere is there an indication in the Sermon on the Mount that Jesus was addressing himself exclusively to those of the white race when he taught: "Blessed are the poor in spirit . . . Blessed are the meek . . . Blessed are they which do hunger and thirst after righteousness . . . Blessed are the merciful . . . Blessed are they which are persecuted for righteousness' sake . . . Blessed are ye, when men shall revile you . . ." (Matthew 5.3-11). Here, too, is the exalted universalism that beholds man as the child of God, created in the divine image, and endowed with an immortal soul devoid of pigmentation.

Robert Emmet Lucey, Archbishop of San Antonio, understood this when he said that segregation hurts the white man's conscience because he remembers that what you do to the least of the brethren you do to Christ and that the idea of a segregated Christ seems like blasphemy: "Is it not Catholic doctrine that when a brother is excluded, rejected, segregated, it is Christ who is insulted and humiliated?"

If the nations of the world hope to achieve international peace and universal brotherhood, they must concentrate on the art of being color-blind. The colored people in Africa and Asia are pressing for recognition. Estimates of world population[15] assess the number

[15] Reproduced from *The World Book Encyclopedia* with permission, © 1959 by Field Enterprises Educational Corporation. All rights reserved.

of white people as over 1,492,960,000. Rapidly approaching this figure is the number of colored people: 1,173,040,000. The colored man is no longer the "white man's burden." Prophetic religion must look upon him as the "white man's brother." Doctrines of racial supremacy must give way to a new and radical doctrine of racial brotherhood if man is to achieve peace and build God's kingdom of righteousness on earth.

Whether we are Catholics, Protestants, or Jews, no longer may the matter of race relations be summarily dismissed as a secular political issue. The question of human equality before God is clearly delineated by the Judaeo-Christian tradition as a religious and a moral issue. We can, and must, declare that anything that humiliates another human being or diminishes his opportunity to develop his divine potential is un-Christian and un-Jewish, and calls for decisive, courageous, and prophetic action.

16

Religion in Action

... for centuries religion has taken the minister into the market-place, the forum, the parliament and the street corner, wherever he could strike blows for freedom and aid his fellows to diminish man's inhumanity to man.—THE REV. STEPHEN FRITCHMAN

Keep Religion in Politics

The minister, priest, rabbi, or layman who attempts to take an active part in fighting evil, resisting ignorance, and combating the forces that seek to destroy liberty, justice, and civil rights, must persist in the activation of religious values and precepts despite the opposition of those who regard religion as unrelated to the realities of life.

It is incredible that religion should be divorced from social action, when every major faith is dedicated to the welfare of man, when the Bible articulates the demand for justice and righteousness in behalf of God's children, when the Judaeo-Christian ethical heritage sets forth a moral mandate requiring its adherents to create a just society predicated on the ethical commandments of God.

A letter addressed to a rabbi declared in part: "Ministers should stay out of controversy and refrain from speaking on excitable and delicate matters that cause dissension in the church or synagogue. Above all, ministers and rabbis should not become involved in political matters."

How often does the clergyman concerned with social justice hear the admonition: "Don't make trouble. Don't stir things up. Stick to the Bible, Rabbi! Stick to religion, Reverend! Stick to the recitation of the Mass, Father! Just preach religion, and keep the church and the synagogue out of politics!"

Stick to the Bible, Rabbi! If the rabbi should adhere to the social legislation of Exodus, the Holiness Code of Leviticus, the human welfare commandments of Deuteronomy, and the ethical admonitions of the psalmists and prophets, he is irrevocably committed to improving the economic, moral, cultural, and political status of man.

When the minister is adjured to follow the teachings of Jesus, he is compelled to follow a ministry of social action, devoting himself to the afflicted, the outcast, the stranger, widow, orphan, and all those who have been exploited and oppressed by man's inhumanity to man. He must remember the example of Jesus who was not restrained from involving Himself in the political and social turmoil of His generation; a courageous prophet who excoriated the evildoer, who cried out: "Woe to you, scribes and Pharisees, hypocrites! For you tithe mint and dill and cummin, and have neglected . . . justice and mercy and faith. . . . You blind guides, straining out a gnat and swallowing a camel! . . . Woe to you, scribes and Pharisees, hypocrites! . . . you also outwardly appear righteous to men, but within you are full of hypocrisy and iniquity" (Matthew 23.23-28, R.S.V.).

The great religious teachers of mankind narrowed the chasm between religion and life, insisting that religion must sanctify life. They offered neither opium nor tranquilizers to dull the sensitivities of their adherents. They never suggested that the helpless and the oppressed should be content with their fate. They were not hesitant in involving themselves in the political and social problems of their era. They put their religion to work and applied their prophetic faith to the problems, the evils, the injustice, and the inequities of their society.

Since issues relating to the welfare, progress, and moral status of society affect the welfare of man, the prophetic faith must be vitally concerned with politics. To isolate religion from politics is to divorce religion from life. The Church and the Synagogue must therefore manifest a constant interest in civil liberties, and maintain an active role in the critical issues that relate to the welfare of man and the perfection of society.

If we believe that religion is the ethical relationship between man and God and man and man, then the prophetic faith must actively further and promote a politico-social environment that will enable man to achieve his potential for expressing the divinity within, and exert a moral impact upon institutions, conditions, and attitudes that contribute to man's humanity to his fellow man.

The prophetic faith must be vitally concerned with freedom: freedom of speech, freedom of the press, freedom of and from religion, and freedom of thought. It has been estimated that since the first century only 3 per cent of the people have lived in freedom. Today, about one-third of the world population lives under a dictatorship that limits freedom, controls thought, and exerts a vigorous censorship of newspapers, magazines, books, radio, television, and movies. Trygve Lie, former Secretary-General of the United Nations, has stated that nearly one-third of the entire human family is hungry, with millions upon millions of children born to live their few years of pain and privation and then to die amidst squalor, disease, and misery.

The Church and the Synagogue must be directly concerned with civil liberties, problems of unemployment, housing, crime and juvenile delinquency, prison reform and capital punishment, labor-management relations, health and public welfare, education and recreation.

Hovering ominously over the world is the possibility of atomic fallout, and other grim consequences of nuclear experimentation. International tension, hot and cold wars, clean and dirty bombs threaten the survival of civilization and drive nations to the brink of a conflict too terrible to contemplate. And yet there are those who insist that religion must be kept out of politics, who demand that religion must be respectably concerned with ritual, dogma, and theology to the exclusion of social action, maintaining a cowardly neutrality to issues that will determine the survival or the destruction of religious values.

C. Wright Mills, in *The Causes of World War III*, writes: "But you may say, 'Don't let's get the church into politics.' You might well say that with good conscience were the political role of the church to be confined to what it has been and what it is. But in view of what it might be, if you say that you are saying, 'Don't let's get the church into the world; let's be another distraction from reality.' This world *is* political. Politics, understood for what it really is today, has to do with the decisions men make which determine how they shall live and how they shall die. They are not living very well, and they are not going to die very well either. Politics is the locale of both evil and of good. If you do not get the church into politics, you cannot confront evil and you cannot work for good."[1]

The prophets of Israel did not hesitate to bring God and religion into politics. They identified themselves with political groups, supported and denounced kings, princes, and priests. Amos castigated the corruption of the ruling power who bought the poor for silver and the needy for a pair of shoes. He did not hesitate to predict that

"Jeroboam shall die by the sword,
And Israel shall surely be led away captive out of his land." (7.11)

In his prophetic wrath he excoriated the nobility

"That lie upon beds of ivory
And stretch themselves upon their couches,
And eat the lambs out of the flock,
And the calves out of the midst of the stall." (6.3)

[1] *The Causes of World War III*, p. 155. Copyright © 1958 by C. Wright Mills. Used by permission of Simon and Schuster, Inc.

Amos did not seek popularity and security when he declared in the
name of God:

> "I abhor the pride of Jacob,
> And hate his palaces;
> And I will deliver up the city with all that is therein." (6.8)

The prophets of Israel were vehement and uncompromising in
their condemnation of the political evils of their era. They went into
palaces, market places, into the fields, the streets, the homes of prince
and peasant alike to demand righteousness for those exploited by injustice; they asked bread for the poor, housing for the homeless,
mercy for the widow, the orphan, the stranger, and the afflicted. They
concerned themselves with commerce, labor, graft and corruption
in high places, idolatry, sexual purity, prosperity and depression,
national morality and international concord. Nothing political was
alien to the prophet who beheld religion as inextricably a part of
life, and the ethical relationship of man to his fellow man as a
requisite for a holy covenant with God.

What is true of the teachers and sages of the Old Testament is
equally true of the teachers and prophets of the New Testament.
The social gospel of Christianity is revolutionary and radical. James
Russell Lowell understood this when he wrote: "There is dynamite
enough in the New Testament if illegitimately applied, to blow all
our existing institutions to atoms." To adhere to the teachings of
Jesus is to dedicate oneself to political issues that relate to the welfare of man. When Jesus proclaimed:

> "The Spirit of the Lord is upon me,
> because he anointed me to preach good news to the poor.
> He hath sent me to proclaim release to the captives
> and recovering of sight to the blind,
> to set at liberty those who are oppressed,
> to proclaim the acceptable year of the Lord"
> —LUKE 4.18-19, R.S.V.

he was challenging his adherents to identify political and religious
action as one. No one can be a sincere Christian or a sincere Jew

and accept a passive attitude toward the social and political evils that desecrate society and repudiate the moral and ethical demands of the Judaeo-Christian ethical tradition. No amount of rationalization can justify silence, indifference, insensitivity, and cautious regard for personal security on the part of those who are determined to meet the challenge of the prophetic faith.

Christianity and Judaism must take a gigantic "leap of action" to bring the moral demands of religion into politics. The cult of comfort must be abandoned in behalf of a radical dedication to civil rights and liberties predicated on the fatherhood of God, the brotherhood of man, and the sanctity of the human personality.

Civil Rights and Liberties

More than 2,200 years after the prophet Habakkuk declared, "The righteous shall live by his faith" (2.4), the essayist Charles Caleb Colton wrote: "Man will wrangle for religion; write for it; fight for it; die for it; anything but live for it."[2]

It is in the refusal to live for and by a morally compulsive faith that respectable religion manifests its greatest weakness, and prophetic religion finds its greatest challenge.

The revered teachers and prophets of the Judaeo-Christian tradition were motivated by the Voice that declared, "Thus saith the Lord." They were compelled by the force of divine commandment to apply the moral and ethical precepts of their faith to every aspect of life. Their belief in the sanctity of man imposed upon them a mandate to seek justice for the oppressed and the afflicted. Rights and liberties were not granted by governments. They were conferred by God as a precious legacy derived from the inherent Divinity in man. Consequently, the protection of man's liberties and the assurance of his right to live in peace and dignity were elevated to essential objectives of prophetic religion. "Thus saith the Lord" was regarded as the prefatory summons to social action in behalf of human rights.

In the twentieth century we are inclined to regard civil rights and liberties as political guarantees granted by government rather than religious values demanded by God. As a result, respectable religion has, to a cowardly extent, surrendered and retreated from the battle

[2] *Lacon* (New York, Charles Wells, rev. ed., 1836), p. 30.

against social injustice, allowing the political to corrupt the religious, permitting the liturgical amens and hallelujahs, the reading of prayers, and the articulation of dogma to obscure the Voice that declares, "Thus saith the Lord."

The clarion call to religious action must again resound in our churches and synagogues, summoning the adherents of the prophetic faith to reject the ecclesiastical dross, to strip away the liturgical veneer, and to strive anew to restore the preservation of man's civil rights and liberties as an essential and primary objective of religion. This objective will be attained when the "righteous will live by their faith" and will join forces with the devotees of democracy in keeping religion in politics.

The political definition of "civil rights and liberties," particularly the definition offered in the context of our American democracy, is basically the same as the religious definition. Both the political and religious definitions derive their essence from the belief in the sanctity and the dignity of the human personality.

"Civil rights" refer to those rights that are the heritage of every human being, affording him the right to work, to education, to housing, of health and welfare services, the right to live in peace and dignity without discrimination or segregation based on religion, race, ancestry, or national origin.

"Civil liberties" refer to those freedoms of the individual which are guaranteed by the federal and state constitutions. They include freedom of speech, press, assembly, religion, the right to bear arms, to petition for redress of grievances, and to security against unlawful searches and seizures, double jeopardy, excessive bail, cruel or unusual punishment or forced self-incrimination. They assure trial by jury, the right to confront witnesses, and all the safeguards of the individual as enumerated in the various "bills of rights."

With the advent of the Communist regime in Russia and the Fascist totalitarian doctrine in Italy, Germany, and Spain, civil rights and liberties were suspended or eliminated. In the main, the Church and the Synagogue made feeble whimpers of protest and then capitulated to coercion and fear. The Voice was silenced by the raucous screaming of dictators and the frenzied roar of hysterical multitudes chanting slogans of worshipful obeisance to the uniformed superman. "Thus saith the Lord" was supplanted by "Thus commands the

Fuehrer." The sanctity of the state was substituted for the sanctity of the individual. The religious rationale gave way to political expediency. The moral law was replaced by the law of the jungle. Might made right, and the religious values of mercy, justice, purity, fidelity, honor, and brotherhood were swept away as refuse of an obsolete and decadent Judaeo-Christian ethical tradition to be disdainfully thrown into the garbage pits of ancient history.

Those who had insisted that religion must be kept out of politics now found themselves victims of the most monstrous and evil political philosophy ever witnessed by history. Fearful of controversy, apprehensive about religion encompassing the realities of life, they were now compelled to give assent or acquiesce silently to mass murder, concentration camps, crematoria, lethal chambers, the deprivation of civil and human rights, the sanction of sexual immorality, and the desecration of cherished values and beliefs.

One may only conjecture as to the impact of religion upon history if the Church and the Synagogue of Russia had been dedicated to social action in behalf of the oppressed and the afflicted, and consecrated to social justice. If those who called themselves religious had really lived by their faith and implemented the moral requirements of their religion, would atheistic communism have taken root and flourished? We may only wonder what would have happened in Germany if a united Church and Synagogue, and if the men and women affiliated with religion, had brought the force and the power of moral righteousness to the fore. If they had applied the teachings of social justice to the political life of Germany, would Nazism have been aborted as a degenerate offspring of evil?

The Church in Germany did resist, sporadically and sometimes heroically, but when it was too late. After World War II, Professor Albert Einstein offered an encomium to the Church when he wrote:

"Being a lover of freedom, when the revolution came in Germany, I looked to the universities to defend it, knowing that they had always boasted of their devotion to the cause of truth, but no, the universities immediately were silenced. Then I looked to the great editors of the newspapers whose flaming editorials in days gone by had proclaimed their love of freedom; but they, like the universities, were silenced in a few short weeks. Then I looked to the individual writers, who, as literary guides of Germany, had written much and often concerning the place of freedom in modern life; but they, too, were mute. Only the Church stood squarely across the path of Hitler's campaign for oppressing truth. I never had any special interest in the Church before, but now I feel a great affection and admiration because the Church alone has had the courage and persistence to stand for intellectual truth and moral freedom. I am forced to confess that which I once despised I now praise unreservedly."

Despite Professor Einstein's tribute to the Church, and despite the martyrdom and heroism of many clergymen and laymen who resisted the attack on human rights and endeavored to salvage remnants of the victims of Nazi oppression, the Church as a religious institution did not take a united, active, and forceful stand in behalf of civil rights and liberties. The adherents of respectable religion did not put religion into politics with the intent of averting the evil of Nazism. With all its pious pronouncements of dedication to human rights and reverence for the sanctity of the human personality, the devotees of respectable religion throughout the world issued sporadic protests and offered vacuous resolutions of sympathy and indignation, and then took happy refuge in the tranquilizing comfort of ritual, verbalized prayer, and the anticipated bliss of the world to come. Because of apathy and indifference to religion in action, the values of institutionalized religion were sucked into the maw of the totalitarian horror, even as the Church became an impotent and subservient adjunct of the Superstate.

The power of prophetic religion has never been put to the test in our age. We cannot know the extent to which religion in action might deter the evil of communism and fascism, protect civil rights and liberties, and contribute to international peace in contemporary society. What of the present and the future? Have we learned any religious lessons from the holocausts of history? Are we sufficiently convinced of the need for religion in action to put our prophetic faith to work in our own age and in our own nation? Are we ready and willing to accept the moral challenge of an atomic age, and respond to the Voice declaring, "Thus saith the Lord"?

In the midst of the Nazi and Communist horror, the United States stood out as a bastion of freedom, and as the great proponent of civil rights and liberties. Beginning in the 1930's, however, a new and dangerous trend developed in the United States which threatened the historic guarantee of civil rights and liberties and controverted the spirit of freedom that has always characterized our nation.

Reacting to the threat of Communism and the need for national security, "loyalty oaths" were instituted, congressional committees assessed the patriotism and loyalty of government employees and men and women in public life, guilt by association ruined the reputation and endangered the security of the innocent, and civil rights and liberties of American citizens were endangered.

In 1945 Justice Black of the Supreme Court stated that "Test oaths, designed to impose civil disabilities upon men for their beliefs rather than for unlawful conduct, were an abomination to the founders of this nation. . . . Under our Constitution men are punished for what they do or fail to do and not for what they think and believe."[3]

He declared, in the case of American Communications Assn. v. Douds: "Guilt should not be imputed solely from association or affiliation with political parties or any other organization, however much we abhor the ideas which they advocate. Like anyone else, individual Communists who commit overt acts in violation of valid laws can and should be punished. But the postulate of the First Amendment is that our free institutions can be maintained without proscribing or penalizing political belief, speech, press, assembly, or party affiliation. This is a far bolder philosophy than despotic rulers can afford to follow. It is the heart of the system on which our freedom depends."[4]

In 1949 Dorothy Bailey was dismissed from a government position as a loyalty risk after a hearing before the Loyalty Review Board where no one testified against her and no affidavits were presented against her. She was not given the names of those who had informed against her.

Contending that "dismissal for disloyalty is punishment and requires all the safeguards of a judicial trial," Judge Edgerton dissented against the judgment of guilt. He pointed out that in the loyalty hearings employees have been asked questions such as the following:

Do you read a good many books?
What books do you read?

[3] *United States Reports* (Washington, D.C., U.S. Government Printing Office, 1946), Vol. 325, pp. 576, 578.
[4] *Ibid.*, Vol. 339, pp. 452, 453.

What magazines do you read?
What newspapers do you buy or subscribe to?
Do you think that Russian Communism is likely to succeed?
How do you explain the fact that you have an album of Paul
Robeson records in your home?
Do you ever entertain Negroes in your home?
Did you ever write a letter to the Red Cross about the segregation
of the blood?

In 1917 the Communist regime initiated the destruction of organized, institutional religion by restrictive laws, rules, and regulations. In the 1930's Hitler placed padlocks on the doors of churches marked "By Order of the Fuehrer." In the summer of 1953, the churches in California were endangered when the California Legislature passed a law requiring every church enjoying tax exemption to sign at least once a year a declaration that the person or organization does not advocate the overthrow of the Government by force or violence or other unlawful means nor advocate the support of a foreign government against the United States in event of hostilities.

This was the first effort in any of the states to destroy the tax-exemption rights of the Church. Failure to sign the declaration would deprive the Church of tax exemption.

The Executive Director of the Los Angeles Church Federation, Dr. Forrest C. Weir, called the law "an attempt on the part of the state to control the conscience of the church and to pre-determine conditions for its membership."

Despite the gravity of the threat, only a dozen California churches refused to sign. Twenty other churches signed under protest. In Northern California the American Civil Liberties Union filed a writ of mandamus with the State Supreme Court on behalf of the San Leandro Methodist and the San Jose Unitarian-Universalist churches requesting immediate higher court review of the basic constitutional questions involved.

What troubles us is not only the effort to impose thought control and loyalty tests upon the Church and the Synagogue, but even of greater concern is the indifference of clergymen to the threat of the denial of civil liberties and the apparent acquiescence of the Church and the Synagogue to the menace against basic American freedom.

Archibald MacLeish, former Librarian of Congress and Pulitzer Prize winner, correctly said: "A man who lives, not by what he loves, but by what he hates, is a sick man. And so, too, a nation. We know it all of us. The revulsion against our fears and hatreds, and against those who have exploited them for political or economic advantage, is mounting throughout the country. We are coming to know the worth of that winter patriotism which measures itself not by its love for America and all that America means but by its cold passion against the Soviet Union. . . . Above all, we find it hard to believe that that man is an American patriot who would sacrifice to his hatred of Russia the heart of what America is: the freedom of the individual mind and soul and conscience."[5]

In an address at Harvard University, in the spring of 1954, Adlai Stevenson warned that the very existence of the Communist threat "has created strains and tensions, anguish and anxiety, which beat upon the free mind, surround it, torment it, and threaten to smother it. . . . In recent years we have seen the contagion of unreason and anti-intellectualism spreading among ourselves, inhibiting thought and initiative in government, distorting the emphasis in our public affairs, moving groups to extremes of intolerance, diverting attention from our great concerns and provoking division among us."[6]

That is what Justice William O. Douglas meant when he wrote an article called "The Black Silence of Fear." In part, he said:

"Irresponsible talk by irresponsible people has fanned the flames of fear. Accusations have been loosely made. Character assassinations have become common.

"Suspicion has taken the place of good will. . . . Once we had confidence in each other. Now there is suspicion. Innocent acts become tell-tale marks of disloyalty. The coincidence that an idea parallels Soviet Russia's policy for a moment of time settles . . . an aura of suspicion around a person."[7]

When Justice Douglas wrote that article on January 13, 1952, there was an atmosphere of suspicion and fear in America. Committees set themselves up as authorities, and removed books from public libraries, burning the volumes as dangerous and seditious. Teachers and pro-

---

[5] Quoted by permission of Archibald MacLeish.
[6] *Call to Greatness* (New York, Harper and Brothers, 1954), p. 100.
[7] *New York Times Magazine*, Jan. 13, 1952.

fessors were afraid to speak out on controversial subjects, because of the fear of being labeled radicals and poor security risks. State and government employees were compelled to take "loyalty oaths," and even the churches and synagogues in some states were asked to take loyalty oaths as a requisite for tax exemption.

The situation became so serious that President Dwight D. Eisenhower urged the American people:

"Don't join the book burners. Don't think you are going to conceal faults by concealing evidence that they ever existed. Don't be afraid to go in your library and read every book as long as any document does not offend your own ideas of decency. That should be the only censorship.

"How will we defeat communism unless we know what it is? What it teaches . . .

"Now we have got to fight it with something better. Not try to conceal the thinking of our own people. They are part of America and even if they think ideas that are contrary to ours they have a right to have them, a right to record them and a right to have them in places where they are accessible to others. It is unquestioned or it is not America."[8]

Fortunately, the American people refused to be pressured into hysteria and fear. Men and women in every profession spoke up in protest against book-burnings, censorship, and the deprivation of civil rights and liberties. Some courageous ministers, priests, and rabbis raised their voices in prophetic opposition to the climate of suspicion and fear. The Church and the Synagogue, however, did not reflect credit upon contemporary religion because of timidity of action, cautious vacillation, and the reluctance to enter into areas of controversy because of the possibilities of being castigated as radical, nonconformist, and different.

The battle for civil rights and liberties is not over. The victory must still be won. If the prophetic faith yields to fear or the urge to conform, and ceases to fight, pray, work, and take moral action to protect and enhance the sanctity of man, it will repudiate its holy purpose and merit the contempt that will ultimately designate it as an outmoded anachronism and a sacred relic that has no place or purpose in the realistic and practical effort to build God's kingdom on earth.

[8] "Fun and Courage," *Vital Speeches*, July 1, 1953.

The survival of religion is not of the essence unless there is a consecrated and exalted purpose to survival. The Voice is calling to us, summoning religion to action, to the fulfillment of divine purpose, demanding that we sensitize our souls to hear and respond to "Thus saith the Lord."

The prophetic faith must be put in its proper perspective as a religion of social action. Much more is involved than the preservation of civil rights and liberties. What is of related concern is the preservation of the Church and the Synagogue because of the immediacy of its purpose and the urgency of its ethical and moral message.

The Social Message of Prophetic Religion

At a Sunday morning service, on June 21, 1959, in his farewell sermon to his congregation, Dr. John W. Rustin told the membership of the Belmont Methodist Church in Nashville, Tennessee, that "if a church has no message, it should close its doors and quit pretending that it does. It should know what it stands for, and should not be afraid to stand up and be counted. It is important what church people say and do about slum clearance, racial discrimination, social snobbery, better schools, sanitary conditions, better religious education and recreational facilities."

Dr. Rustin asserted: "We are in the midst of a world revolution. Some church people recognize the confusion and social strain but say, 'We can do nothing about them. We'll wait until Jesus comes.' Of all the pious pap ever uttered, that is it."

If a minister spends his time being careful, popular, and trying to please, Dr. Rustin said, he won't be prophetic. "A minister should rebuke, reprove, stir up and strike people out of their lethargy."[9]

It takes courage for a minister, rabbi, or priest to follow this exhortation of Dr. Rustin, and interpret the prophetic faith as a religion of action. Freedom of the pulpit is not always accorded to clergymen. Dedicated ministers, rabbis, and priests are being driven from their pulpits because they dare to preach and act in behalf of civil rights and liberties.

In June, 1959, a judicial commission of the Southwest Georgia Presbytery announced that the Reverend Robert B. McNeill was

[9] Quoted in *Nashville Tennessean*, June 22, 1959.

being relieved of his pastoral obligations because "the interests of religion imperatively demand it."

What are the interests of religion served by the dismissal of Robert B. McNeill? On May 28, 1957, he had published an article in *Look* magazine under the title "A Georgia Minister Offers a Solution for the South." In the article he stated a theory of "creative contact" as a road to the solution of the racial problem lying between integration and segregation. He declared that southern whites and Negroes should establish points of contact that are creative despite the conflict between state and federal laws on the segregation issue.

By "creative contact," he said, he meant that "our contact with the Negro people can become creative if we will sit with their leaders at the council table, listen to them with respect and share with them the responsibilities as well as the privileges of living together."

Because of this article proposing mutual discussion and communication, the Reverend Robert McNeill became the center of a controversy that resulted in his dismissal because "the interests of religion imperatively demand it." This is a graphic example of the pious pap that endangers the prophetic faith.

When the Reverend Mr. McNeill was ousted from his pulpit, he was told bluntly that a preacher is bound to say what his congregation wants to hear—not the truth, not the word of God as he interprets it, but what he thinks his congregation wants!

The eight-man commission designated to study and act on reports of dissension in McNeill's church in Columbus, Georgia, at first issued a statement that "the Christian pulpit must never be muffled or silenced by threats of any description, for to do so would be to write a death sentence for freedom and to sound the funeral march of the Christian Church."

Later, the commission seemed to reverse itself when the man stated: *"The Commission feels that the voice of the pulpit should be the voice of the congregation."*[10]

This happened in a Presbyterian church. It could have happened in a Methodist church, a Baptist church, a Jewish synagogue, or a church of any other denomination. What jolts and dismays us is the dangerous implications of the lay insistence that the voice of the pulpit should be the voice of the congregation rather than the

[10] *New Christian Advocate*, August, 1959.

voice of God. The recognition that freedom of the pulpit is one of the cherished fundamentals of our whole concept of religious and political freedom, makes the statement all the more shocking and inimical to the objectives of the prophetic faith.

A few hours after his arrest as a leader of Negro passive resistance against the city's bus lines in Montgomery, Alabama, the Reverend Martin Luther King, Jr., issued the following statement: "We have known humiliation, we have known abusive language, we have been plunged into the abyss of oppression, and we decided to rise up only with the weapon of protest. It is one of the greatest glories of America that we have the right of protest.

"If we are arrested every day, if we are exploited every day, if we are trampled over every day, don't ever let anyone pull you so low as to hate him. We must use the weapon of love. We must have compassion and understanding for those who hate us. We must realize so many people are taught to hate us that they are not totally responsible for their hate. But we stand in life at midnight; we are always on the threshold of a new dawn."[11]

We can only bow our hearts in reverence and lower our heads in shame before the exalted spirit of such a statement. At a time when his people are victimized by hate, a minister of God urges love. At a time when those of his race are being exploited, harassed, and brutally exposed to cruelty, a modern prophet exhorts his people to compassion and understanding for those who hate them. At a time when a religious teacher might have become embittered by the violation of civil rights guaranteed by American democracy, he urges the use of the weapon of protest as one of the greatest glories of America.

"The righteous shall live by his faith!" Which statement will future generations of Americans assess as the most representative of prophetic religion—the statement of the commission that declared "the voice of the pulpit shall be the voice of the congregation," the statement of an Atlanta clergyman, "God put a curse on Ham and his descendants, turning them black and placing them in a servile position," the statement of ministers advocating segregation, discrimination, and racial supremacy in the name of God, or the statement of Martin Luther King, Jr.?

The survival of a meaningful, sacred, dynamic, and prophetic religious faith is predicated upon the consecrated endeavors of the Church

[11] Quoted with permission of Martin Luther King, Jr.

and Synagogue to bring their message to bear upon the socio-political problems of our age. Religion must have a voice in determining the political climate that affects civil rights and liberties. It is the purpose of the Church and the Synagogue to intensify man's capacity for moral indignation and summon their adherents to social action. What are we doing through our churches and synagogues to organize social-action committees to support legislation that protects the weak and affords justice under law? What are we doing as religious men and women to work in our own communities to protect the sanctity and the dignity of human beings—the weak and the oppressed, the different and the maligned? These are questions that must be answered if we are to fulfill the prophetic faith.

Our generation is sated with the pious platitudes that soothe the conscience and render us insensitive to the moral imperatives of society. Religion must be girded with strength of purpose, revitalized for the struggle, for the eternal contest with evil, for ceaseless battle against the ubiquitous forces of ignorance, bigotry, darkness, and despair.

The devotees of the prophetic faith must mobilize for a religious war against ignorance, bigotry, racial and religious discrimination, poverty, disease, and despair for the purpose of implementing the values and precepts that will enable man to create a moral society that will fulfill the commandments of God.

Religion in action must be vitally concerned with housing projects, slum clearance, mental health, employment, and the menacing evils of crime and juvenile delinquency in all levels and income groups of society.

Special congressional committees have been studying the effects of comic and crime books, television and the motion pictures upon juvenile delinquency. Special juvenile-court judges and family courts have been set up to combat the alarming spread of juvenile delinquency. Social scientists offer us the results of their findings and research. Criminologists present learned papers on the causes of juvenile delinquency. To what extent are churches and synagogues concerned with programs of study and action in the area of social maladjustment and antisocial behavior? It is not enough for ministers to preach against the evils of broken homes, divorce, alcoholism, the desecration of the sanctity of the family, and crime. Clergymen and religious laymen must be actively concerned with participating with social agencies in the effort to prevent crimes before they occur, devoting their efforts to eliminating the causative factors that contribute to delinquency and crime.

Rackets, confidence men, and swindlers take millions from the public every year. Innocent people are preyed upon and compelled to pay "protection" to operate their businesses. The selling of dope, especially to minors, demands the continuous vigilance of narcotics agents. Gambling syndicates, bookies, lottery and numbers rackets, prostitution, and the corruption of our youth are evils that must be stamped out. If the prophetic faith is to survive and contribute to the "good society," then it is incumbent upon clergymen and laity alike to take action by means of political effort, the support of social legislation, and a positive intervention in the concrete and practical problems of community, state, and nation.

Religion must get into politics in order to allow the message of the prophetic faith to be heard and obeyed, even though the voices of the Church and the Synagogue may engender violent controversy, frenzied opposition, and bitter attack.

A Fair Housing Practices Act, introduced on January 7, 1959, in both the Senate and House of Representatives of the Rhode Island General Assembly, declared its intent "to assure to all individuals regardless of race or color, religion or country of ancestral origin, equal opportunity to live in decent, safe, sanitary and healthful living quarters in order that the peace, health, and safety and general welfare of all inhabitants of the state may be protected and insured." The proponents of the bill believed that "no one could quarrel with that purpose." The bill, however, was defeated. It was stated by advocates of the Fair Housing Practices Act that the proposed legislation might have been approved if the Church and the Synagogue had taken a more active role in its favor.

Until 1921 the famous words of Emma Lazarus on the pedestal of the Statue of Liberty, "Give me your tired, your poor, your huddled masses yearning to breathe free," gave an accurate picture of the American attitude toward immigration. Since then our present law, through its national origins quota system, is strongly weighted toward so-called Anglo-Saxons. In 1921 Congress passed the first major law in our country's history limiting new immigration. In 1924 the law was revised until 1929, when a system fixed a ceiling of a little over 150,000 for immigrants from countries outside the Western Hemisphere to be admitted annually. In 1952 the policy of 1924 was continued by the McCarran-Walter Act.

A new, enlightened policy of immigration is needed to remedy some of the restrictions and effect a more just basis for the admission of those seeking the hospitality of our nation. George Washington said: "The bosom of America is open to receive not only the opulent and respectable stranger, but the oppressed and persecuted of all nations and religions; whom we shall welcome to a participation of all our rights and privileges, if by decency and propriety of conduct they appear to merit the enjoyment." What do the Church and the Synagogue have to say about the problem of immigration, and the historic American policy of offering refuge to the persecuted, the afflicted, "the huddled masses yearning to breathe free" and to find a new life of justice as citizens of our nation?

Religion in action requires the Church and the Synagogue to take part in issues and problems affecting labor-management relations, fair labor standards laws and minimum wage legislation. The prophetic faith must be vitally concerned with protecting management from racketeering, corruption, and graft in labor. It must be equally vigilant in protecting workers from exploitation and assuring them an income sufficient to maintain health and human dignity.

The General Board, National Council of the Churches of Christ in the U.S.A., in 1959 resolved: "The principle of minimum wage legislation, federal and state, should be supported as a practical and proven means of assuring at least the minimum standard of living necessary for the maintenance of health and decency for family living today, and should be extended to all workers and that the general board authorize representatives of the National Council of Churches to testify at hearings in support of the principle of the extension of the minimum wage legislation to include groups not now covered."

Monsignor George G. Higgin, Director, National Catholic Welfare Conference, said: "It is sometimes forgotten that the historic encyclical of Pope Leo XIII, the 'Rerum Novarum,' not only endorsed the right of workers to organize, but also called for state intervention to remedy injustices in the field of wages, hours and working conditions." In effect, then, the Catholic Church has been in favor of wage-hour legislation since 1891, or nearly half a century before the first such law was adopted by Congress.

The Very Reverend Francis B. Sayre, Jr., Dean of the Washington

Cathedral (Episcopal), stated: "It is distressing to realize that even in the times of our prosperity there is a large and growing group of wage-earners who are losing the race for bare subsistence. These are the workers whose earnings are keyed to the present federal minimum wage law, or who are not protected by any law at all.

"Legislation has been introduced in the Senate by Senators Kennedy, Morse and others, and in the House of Representatives by Representative Roosevelt and others, that would raise the federal minimum wage to $1.25, and extend the law's coverage to some 7½ million non-agricultural workers.

"Anything that Congress can do to give a hand up to the underpaid and often hopeless men and women at the foot of American life will give strength to us all—for no nation has the right to allow suffering to exist in the midst of plenty."[12]

Speaking for the Commission on Social Action of the Union of American Hebrew Congregations, Rabbi Eugene Lipman stated: "As far back as 1918, the Central Conference of American Rabbis called for a legal minimum wage and a limitation on hours of work. This position has been restated and amplified repeatedly over the last 40 years. . . .

"The evidence is clear that unorganized and legally unprotected workers have not shared in the economic gains won by industrial workers as a whole, especially in the last 10 years. Thus there are millions of our fellow citizens to whom the 'American way of Life' means grinding toil and desperate poverty.

"There are many reasons why this social and economic blight demands prompt correction. Our society, which claims to be founded on religious principles of equality and justice and decency, mocks its essential principles so long as these conditions continue. This mockery has had its inevitable negative effect upon our position as exemplar of the free world in the world-wide struggle against communist tyranny. If we do neglect the least among us, the appeal of democracy to the underprivileged peoples of underdeveloped countries will be weak indeed."[13]

Fair employment practices and policies are not so exciting nor do they have the dramatic impact of issues of civil rights and liberties,

[12] Used by permission.
[13] Used by permission.

but they are integral to the principles of social justice set forth by our American democracy and promulgated by the prophetic faith.

During the period from July 1, 1956, to June 30, 1957, the contracting agencies of the Federal government examined the employment practices and policies of more than five hundred plants of business concerns holding government contracts. The survey was undertaken as part of a program initiated by the President's Committee on Government Contracts concerned with policing compliance with the nondiscrimination clause required to be in all contracts entered into by government agencies for materials and services.

The survey indicated that although equal job opportunity is being extended in production work and the skilled trades, less progress has been made in the white-collar areas, and particularly in professional-technical and clerical jobs. The breakdown indicated discrimination against Negroes, Jews, Catholics, and persons of various nationality groups.

They Are Slaves Who Fear to Speak

There are many other areas of social welfare and human relations that must be influenced constructively and humanely by the efforts of clergymen and the message of prophetic religion committed to social action. One out of every five citizens will at some time occupy a bed in a mental institution. Constructive and liberal legislation is urgently needed in behalf of a nation-wide program of mental health. Our schools are neglected and education is in desperate need of Federal aid. Hospitals and clinics are not numerous enough or adequately financed to meet the needs of the physically ill who are desperate for diagnosis and treatment. The problem of the aged cries for research, facilities, and therapy. The unwed mothers and their tragic offspring, stigmatized by archaic attitudes of contempt and rejection, require a "new look" by society and compassionate efforts to provide maternity care, foster homes, and adequate case-work study and help. How is it possible, in the name of God, for religion to stay out of politics? How is it possible, in the name of a prophetic faith, to ignore the cries of the oppressed, the afflicted, the homeless, the naked, the hungry, and the ill, and soothe our conscience by the declaration that religion has no place in the controversial issues of society, retreating into ritual and taking refuge in liturgical prayers and theological dogma?

Any minister, rabbi, or priest who, by reason of timidity or fear, rationalizes his indifference to social action must examine himself in the light of the prophetic requisites of his faith and subject himself to the verdict of conscience. James Russell Lowell would castigate the modern clergyman as a slave to conformity or a servant of cowardice if he defers or ignores the activation of his religious faith because of the comforting security of respectable religion:

> "They are slaves who fear to speak
> For the fallen and the weak;
> They are slaves who will not choose
> Hatred, scoffing, and abuse,
> Rather than in silence shrink
> From the truth they needs must think;
> They are slaves who dare not be
> In the right with two or three."[14]

The religious layman is not exempt from attending to the Voice. He, too, is committed to obey the divine commandments that begin with "Thus saith the Lord." If the men and women who call themselves "religious," who worship God, who strive for the sanctification of life, shut themselves off from the Voice, ignore the challenge of the prophetic faith, and reject the summons to apply religion to the problems, issues, and requirements of society, the threat of nuclear war, and the efforts for world peace, the future may compel them to listen to another voice—a voice that bespeaks the obsequies over the atrophied corpse of religion and the nuclear-contaminated remains of civilization. This may be the Second Male Voice in the Third Chorus of the pageant-play *The Rock* by T. S. Eliot. It will be:

> "A Cry from the North, from the West and from the South
> Whence thousands travel daily to the time kept City:
> Where My Word is unspoken
> In the land of lobelias and tennis flannels

---

[14] "Stanzas on Freedom," *The Complete Poetical Works of James Russell Lowell* (Boston, Houghton Mifflin Co., Cambridge ed., 1896), p. 55.

The rabbit shall burrow and the thorn revisit,
The nettle shall flourish on the gravel court,
And the wind shall say: 'Here were decent godless people:
Their only monument the asphalt road
And a thousand lost golf balls.' "[15]

17

The Sensitization of Man

The desensitization of twentieth-century man . . . represents the
loss or impairment of the noblest faculty of human life—the ability
to be aware both of suffering and beauty; the ability to share sorrow
and create hope; the ability to think and respond beyond one's wants.
—NORMAN COUSINS

Tolerance for Evil

"Help! Help! For God's sake, can't you hear me?" These were the
words that Mack Parker is said to have shrieked to his cellmate when
the lynch mob burst upon them in an unguarded jail in Poplarville,
Mississippi. His cellmate heard him cry, and listened in terror as a
hooded mob dragged Parker, his head bumping sickeningly, down
the concrete steps, leaving a trail of blood. The screaming Parker
disappeared into the night. Several days later his battered body was
found in Pearl River.

Mack Parker was a Negro—a victim of mob hatred. The governor

[15] From "The Rock," copyright 1934 by Harcourt, Brace and Company, Inc.
Reprinted from *Collected Poems 1909-1935* by T. S. Eliot, by permission of the
publishers.

of the state deplored the foul deed. The President of the United States condemned it. Decent citizens of the South and the North castigated it. Anger flared up and then died down. Editorials were written; some organizations issued protests. There was talk of instituting and strengthening antilynch laws. Indignation subsided, and the public, inured to violence, brutality, and death, turned its attention to labor-management disputes, murders, political polls, the cold war with Russia, baseball scores, and personal events relating to the private lives of motion-picture and television celebrities.

This is another area of human relations that requires the prophetic faith to take moral action. Not only must the Church and the Synagogue use their influence in behalf of strengthening and enforcing existing antilynch laws, and encouraging and working for the institution of antilynch laws in states that have resisted such legislation, but prophetic religion is challenged to combat the moral lethargy that nurtures social injustice, violence, brutality, and man's inhumanity to man.

The efforts of prophetic religion must be directed to the resensitization of man in order to reduce his saturation level of cruelty and his tolerance for evil.

In a perceptive editorial in the May 16, 1959, issue of the *Saturday Review*, Norman Cousins wrote of "the Desensitization of Twentieth-Century Man." His thesis is that the individual is being desensitized by living history. "He is developing new reflexes and new responses that tend to slow up the moral imagination and relieve him of essential indignation over impersonal hurt. He is becoming casual about brutality. The range of the violence sweeps from the personal to the impersonal, from the amusements of the crowd to the policies of nations. It is in the air, quite literally. It has lost its sting of surprise. We have made our peace with violence."

Mr. Cousins believes that an individual who has lived in an era of two world wars; seen cities ruined by dynamite hurtling down from the heavens; witnessed nations being destroyed; seen millions of people exterminated in gas chambers; and governments compete with one another to make weapons which even in the testing put death into the air—such an individual must be affected by the horror, brutality, and violence of his age.

It is not an easy matter cavalierly to dismiss this thesis of Norman

Cousins. Man is affected physically, morally, and spiritually by his environment. He cannot remain insensitive to the climate of his social milieu. He does not escape the immoral contamination of an ethically desensitized society. The desensitization of twentieth-century man "represents the loss or impairment of the noblest faculty of human life—the ability to be aware both of suffering and beauty; the ability to share sorrow and create hope; the ability to think and respond beyond one's wants."[1]

The resensitization of man is a requisite for the attainment of the full sanctity of man, the quest for political morality, the achievement of international unity, the realization of the hope of the good society, and the fulfillment of God's kingdom on earth. This is the most difficult and yet the most exciting challenge of the twentieth century. The challenge will be met, not by education, political science, or psychotherapy, but by a radical, revolutionary application of the precepts of prophetic religion to the society in which we live.

Religion must emerge from the warmth and security of the theological womb into a world of reality. Religion must advance from superstition, myth, fantasy, security, adolescent stereotypes, and a preoccupation with the irrational, to a maturity that insists upon the requisites of struggle, controversy, reason, social justice, and consecrated action for the sensitization of man.

No longer may ecclesiastical religion take refuge in external forms, ritual, or creed with the expectation that these alone will sensitize man to hear the Voice and respond to the "Thus saith the Lord." Religion can no longer hide its inadequacies behind the imposing façade of its buildings and institutions. A religious revolution is in the making. It has come upon us quietly and almost imperceptibly. This revolution demands not only the sensitization of man to resist evil, brutality, and tyranny, but calls for the evaluation of such terms as "spiritual," "moral," "soul," "holiness," "piety," "God," and "religious" in the practical context of man's social, political, national and cosmic environment.

A new generation is asking questions, expressing doubts, calling for a reappraisal of the meaning and validity of religion in an atomic age. The polls and surveys that attest to the revival of religion are being critically assessed by those who utter a loud "So what?" to the

[1] Cousins, *op. cit.*

statistics of attendance at churches and synagogues. Perceptive men and women are asking, "What if more people are affiliated with religious institutions, and if our churches and synagogues are active in the proliferation of programs? What are the churches and synagogues doing about the evils that plague our society? What are the churches and synagogues doing about the horrible possibility of nuclear warfare? Are the churches and synagogues reconciling their doctrines with the discoveries of science? To what extent are the churches and synagogues preparing man to take his place in a new age that will witness interplanetary travel and the conquest of outer space?"

Respectable religion cannot answer these questions, nor can it offer a rationale for the faith of the future. A radical and prophetic religion can project a program of social justice that will meet the religious demands of the present and the future by its emphasis upon deed rather than creed, action rather than dogma, and human and civic rights rather than ceremonial rites. Prophetic religion is committed to direct its efforts to the extirpation of those social, economic, and political conditions that detract from the sanctity of the human personality and contribute to the desensitization of man. Prophetic religion is as much concerned with the material as with the spiritual, with legislation as with liturgy, with social welfare as with theology, and with the divinity of man as with the divinity of God.

It follows, therefore, that prophetic religion must reinterpret "sin" as something more than sexual immorality or theological deviation. "Sin" is that which contributes to the desensitization of man. "Sin" is the attitude of mind that permits an individual to ask, "Am I my brother's keeper?" "Sin" is the rejection of responsibility for one's fellow man. "Sin" is the anaesthetization of conscience, the ability to "stand idly by the blood of thy brother." "Sin" is indifference to social injustice. "Sin" is that which limits or deprives man of the opportunity to express his potential as a human-divine being. "Sin" is the desecration of the sanctity of the human personality.

With such an interpretation of sin, prophetic religion must go beyond the confines of the church and the synagogue, to sensitize man to hear the Voice in the market place, the public forum, the school, the home, the halls of Congress, and from the podium of the General Assembly of the United Nations. "Thus saith the Lord" must be heard in its application to civil and human rights in the twentieth century, as much as it was heard by the prophets who walked the paths of God in ancient Israel.

The prophetic faith is itself guilty of sin if it permits and tolerates evil, allows society to increase its saturation level for cruelty, and isolates itself from the practical realities and political considerations that effect the desensitization of man.

Cry Aloud, Spare Not!

This desensitization of man summons the adherents of the prophetic faith in our generation; just as it summoned Isaiah to

"Cry aloud, spare not,
Lift up thy voice like a horn,
And declare unto My people their transgression" (58.1).

And yet, how tragically silent is religion when its voice should be heard crying aloud against injustice and evil! How traitorous is religion to the moral mandate of being "a light unto the nations" when it permits darkness, evil, and brutality to desensitize men and nations and obscure the luminescent glory of God's presence in man's tortuous ascent from the jungle to the stars.

It is futile to castigate religion for its sins of omission and commission, excoriating it for its failures, condemning it for its cowardice, without setting forth a constructive program of social action that will enable the prophetic faith to fulfill its sacred purpose of sensitizing man to divinity. Before efforts are made to apply the moral precepts of religion to the future, however, it is necessary to review the psychological process by which man is desensitized, and assess some areas of history and human relations where religion might have successfully combated the efforts to render man callous, insensitive, and indifferent to the degradation of his fellow man.

The desensitization of man begins by a process of conditioning that enables him to accept ever increasing acts of cruelty and evil with diminishing resistance. His toleration of minor and trivial injustice enables him to increase his acceptance of ever more unconscionable acts of injustice and unspeakable manifestations of evil. In time, his conscience is anaesthetized to the degree that he accepts injustice, cruelty, and evil without indignation and moral rebellion. He is able to rationalize his doubts with the assurance that what is happening is inevitable, and that persistence on his part is both futile and dangerous. He becomes a part of a social pattern that adjusts morals and ethics to the demands of expediency. The abnormal becomes normal. The great lie becomes truth. Conformity is less disturbing than nonconformity, and the assurance that he is a part of a statistical majority contributes to his comfort and security. By this process of conditioning to evil, man becomes desensitized to the recognition that what he is accepting without protest is evil. This is what the sages of Jewish wisdom meant when they taught that "the real slavery of the children of Israel in Egypt was that they learned to endure it."

Man's capacity to endure and accept evil was graphically and horribly illustrated in the 1930's and 1940's when the Nazis in Germany, following the monstrous leadership of Adolf Hitler, undertook the persecution and the systematic extermination of the Jews of Europe. When the first reports reached the world that Jews were being driven from government positions, expelled from the universities and colleges, deprived of civil rights, and oppressed by discriminatory laws, the people of Germany and the nations of the world reacted with shock and moral indignation. As the Nazis continued their acts of brutality and injustice and Jewish children were forced to leave their schools, when the government took over Jewish-owned plants, factories, and businesses and mobs painted mocking signs on Jewish homes, smashed the windows of Jewish stores, and compelled all Jews to wear yellow badges of shame, the people of Germany and the nations of the world expressed cautious sympathy. In time, by reason of the frequency of the acts, we became desensitized and needed ever more horrendous incidents to arouse our sympathy and elicit our protests.

The first reports of bearded Jews forced to scrub sidewalks in Germany, of indignities imposed upon Jewish women and children, and then the news releases that ten Jews were killed, and then fifty, and then one hundred, brought cries of indignation and expressions of anger. Following the Nuremberg Laws, synagogues in Germany were burned, thousands of Jews were herded into concentration camps, and the statistics of Jewish deaths mounted, but the world was becoming used to such reports of discrimination and mass murder. Our toleration for evil was increasing.

As Hitler marched into Austria, Poland, and Czechoslovakia, the Jews were no longer interned. Instead, Hitler announced a policy of wholesale extermination. Names of death camps were emblazoned in headlines: Dachau, Bergen-Belsen, Maidenek. Jews by the hundreds of thousands were being burned alive in furnaces, gassed in lethal chambers, the fats of their bodies converted to soap, their skin made into lampshades; children were crushed to death before the eyes of their parents; Jewish girls were torn from the arms of their families to be requisitioned for brothels.

In Czechoslovakia 260,000 Jews were killed. In Rumania 425,000 Jews were killed. In occupied portions of Russia, 1,500,000 Jews were killed. In Poland 2,800,000 Jews were killed. This does not include the number of Jews slaughtered in Hungary, Lithuania, Holland, France, Latvia, and Germany itself. Horror was added to horror, statistics were added to statistics, and by 1945 the Jewish dead had increased to 6½ million, men, women, and children.

In the Kishinev Massacre of 1903, forty-seven Jews were killed. The nations of the world were shocked and indignant. Mass meetings, protests, resolutions expressed the sense of shame and revulsion at the massacre of forty-seven people. Forty years later, the figure of six million Jewish dead became a nameless, faceless abstraction. The tragedy of an era of human butchery revealed that the world was able to accept these statistics with increasing tolerance and diminishing indignation.

Even as millions of Jews and Christians were being slaughtered in the human abattoirs of Europe, respectable religion separated itself from concern with political issues, international law, and human rights, and clergymen throughout the world delivered learned theological discourses on the commandment "Thou shalt not kill." Politics was still a dirty word in the vocabulary of religion. Law was still a secular concept without relevance to international butchery. Respectable religion did not see itself or its adherents as accessories to the monstrous crimes of murder, because of the toleration for evil, the refusal to "cry aloud," the indifference to social injustice that should have caused the advocates of the moral law to lift up their voices like a horn, the timidity and withdrawal from the affairs of men that should have compelled ministers, priests, and rabbis to declare unto the people their transgression.

Man was in the process of being desensitized for centuries before Hitler. The Church and the Synagogue tolerated the process with but feeble and sporadic protest. Political and religious anti-Semitism, the most vicious propaganda against Jews, and discriminatory measures limiting the rights of Jews had been tolerated by Church and State for over a thousand years prior to the Nuremberg Laws of Germany, and now moral passivity had borne its rotten fruit. Ethical apathy had increased man's capacity for brutality. The priority given liturgical ceremonial rather than applied social justice had rendered man impervious to the anguished pleadings of the Voice. History, at last, shook and rocked the pietistic structure of respectable religion. Mounting statistics of the butchered became so astronomical that religious men and women were forced to recognize that much more had been lost than 6,500,000 Jews. Man had lost his capacity for moral indignation. He had learned to endure mass murder and accept the desecration of the dignity and the sanctity of the human personality, the rejection of compassion, and the domination of unspeakable evil. The desensitization of man had been accomplished.

Not until it was too late did the adherents of respectable religion in Germany recognize that the first intimations of the persecution of Jews and the violation of civil rights were portents that prophesied the ultimate persecution of liberals, the state control of education, the attack upon ministers and priests, the authoritarian control of the press, the radio, the persecution of and the murder of Christians, and a malevolent determination to destroy the values and moral precepts of Christianity. Not until it was too late did the adherents of respectable religion throughout the world behold in the persecution of Jews the premonition of a terrible and devastating war that was to encompass the world and desensitize man to permit him to kill, bomb, burn, and mutilate the divine image within.

When we learned to accept the fascism of Italy under Mussolini, we prepared ourselves to accept naziism under Hitler. In our own generation, we have learned to do business with Perón in Argentina, Tito in Yugoslavia, Franco in Spain, Batista and Castro in Cuba, and Nasser in Egypt. We have become conditioned to totalitarian governments despite the evil they may represent.

Fortunately, we have not learned to accept the totalitarian menace of communism because of the recognized threat to democracy and the survival of the United States as a free nation. There was a period of history, however, when the nations of the world learned to tolerate the evil of communism with political equanimity. The revolution in Russia in 1917 evoked interest, but the slaughter and massacre of millions were accepted without violent indignation. From 1917 to the present day, the Communist regime has deprived the people of Russia of civil rights, imposed thought control, persecuted minority groups, exiled political deviationists, destroyed religion, exercised censorship of the press, radio, textbooks, art, literature. The people of Russia have been so morally desensitized that they are able to tolerate evil, to endure tyranny, and to accept the degradation of man.

When there appeared to be no threat to our own security as Americans, we were quite content to accept the persecution and the mass murder of millions of Russians, farcical trials, brainwashing, and the evil of totalitarian tyranny without horror. In so doing, we contributed to our own desensitization and moral acceptance of in- cipient efforts to impose thought control in our American democ- racy.

To a lesser degree we have witnessed in our own nation the en- largement of the capacity for evil and the process of moral decondi- tioning whereby man is not only able to endure but accept without protest the deprivation of civil rights and liberties.

When the era designated as the era of McCarthyism began in the 1940's in the United States, the American people were at first shocked and indignant at the imposition of loyalty oaths, the dis- missal of government employees on flimsy suspicion of Communist sympathy, guilt by association, character assassination, censorship, and thought control. In time we became less shocked and less in- dignant. We shrugged off the headlines and accepted congressional investigations as part of contemporary American life. The American citizen gradually became desensitized to the heritage of freedom and liberalism that has characterized our nation.

The prophetic faith is charged with the protection and the preser- vation of the sacred principles of American democracy. In 1952 the National Council of Churches in a resolution adopted at Denver declared that the Christian churches "have a prophetic role to play within the national life. It is their duty . . . to sensitize the conscience of the nation and of all classes and institutions within it." Religion in action must address itself to the recognition that the American mind is in the process of being desensitized to freedom of thought, the right to be different, the expression of creative nonconformity, and stubborn resistance to censorship and any restriction to freedom of access to information and communication. To what extent have the Church and the Synagogue taken an active and dynamic role in alerting their constituents to the creeping menace of thought control? Have the Church and the Synagogue joined in crying aloud, sparing not, declaring unto state and national government their transgressions against the unique and precious heritage of American freedom?

The Rabbits' Wedding

As a result of twenty years of attempted thought control, loyalty tests, and the violation of civil rights and liberties without the articulate and impassioned protest of religion, the American mind has been so conditioned and desensitized that it has become impervious to subtle but dangerous limitations placed upon freedom of access to information and communication. In May, 1959, the acceptance and toleration of censorship were indicated by the ludicrous effort to suppress a children's book on animals because of its devious racial implications. An innocuous children's story, "The Rabbits' Wedding," was attacked by racial segregationists in Alabama. Since one of the rabbits was white and the other black, some segregationists saw in this a calculated propaganda effort for miscegenation.

State Senator E. O. Eddins declared that the book "should be burned." Attacks against the book prompted Miss Emily W. Reed, Director of the State Public Library Service Division, to withdraw "The Rabbits' Wedding" from general circulation, saying: "We had to make a choice because of the aroused feelings to stop peddling the book." In a directive to the state's public libraries, Miss Reed stated that "in view of the troubled times in which we live we decided to withdraw the book from circulation."

The noted artist Garth Williams, who wrote and illustrated the book, reacted with surprise to this eugenical nonsense. "I am completely unaware," he said, "that animals with white fur . . . were considered blood relations of white human beings. I was only aware that a white horse next to a black horse looks very picturesque and my rabbits were inspired by early Chinese paintings of black and white horses in misty landscapes." He insisted that the book was about a soft furry love and had no hidden message of hate.

On June 2, 1959, the Associated Press reported that a Miami segregation leader leveled a blast at "The Three Little Pigs" and said that he was trying to get the Florida legislature to have it removed from the state's bookshelves.

David Hawthorn contended that clever integrationists had got hold of the story and were trying to brainwash American youngsters with a version that pictured a black pig as superior to a white pig. Hawthorn said that originally all the pigs were white, but that about seven years ago the book began appearing with two of the pigs in color.

Is this lugubrious intrusion of racial doctrine into the animal kingdom too petty and ridiculous a matter to merit the attention of the disciples of prophetic religion? A children's animal book was removed from general circulation by order of the State Public Library Division of Alabama with little protest from the official religious bodies of America. Does this indicate that we are becoming desensitized to the spirit of American freedom?

Much more is involved than states' rights and the whimsical indignation of a state senator. A basic principle of our American democracy is endangered. The cherished right to free access to books is being denied because of a fantastic charge of racial propaganda. While we laugh with contemptuous amusement at the strictures of racial fanatics that a book about rabbits is endorsing miscegenation and that the story "The Three Little Pigs" is an invidious attempt to insult the white race, we forget the wisdom of James Madison who argued that freedom of access to information and its publication "is the only effectual guardian of every other right." If books are banned by edict of a Director of a State Public Library Service Division, not because they are licentious or prurient, but because they injure the feelings of the advocates of racial supremacy, what is to stop the banning of other books for reasons of political and religious prejudice? If an innocuous book relating the story of rabbits is banned, is there not the imminent danger that a controversial book such as the Bible may be censored, banned, and removed from the bookshelves, charged with being subversive literature or radical propaganda fostered by those who seek sanction for civil rights and divine authority for advocating the concept of the brotherhood of man?

Desensitization to Brotherhood

When controversial issues arise and socially accepted stereotypes are threatened, it is not unusual to discover that even the belief in the Fatherhood of God and the brotherhood of man may be limited, distorted, or denied for reasons of political and theological expediency.

Everett Tilson in *Segregation and the Bible*[2] reports that James L. Fowle, pastor of the First Presbyterian Church of Chattanooga, Tennessee, started a battle royal among the ministers of that city with his criticism of a campaign by the Junior Chamber of Commerce to secure blood-donor pledges on the basis of the brotherhood of man. For several days thereafter, despite the continuation of hostilities in Korea, the citizens of Chattanooga took an uncommon interest in the progress of this theological fracas. This caused much embarrassment to the American Red Cross, the Department of Defense, and the National Conference of Christians and Jews, as well as the Junior Chamber of Commerce, since all these organizations had sought such pledges through the use of a card containing the reminder, "As God is the Father of all men, so all men are brothers."

Denouncing this statement as a Unitarian creed, Dr. Fowle proceeded to deny a place for it in Trinitarian Christianity. "We in Trinitarian faiths," he declared, "believe only in the brotherhood of men in Christ. We are glad to give our blood for our boys in Korea, but to call these Communists brothers when they are killing our men and would destroy our churches and our American way of life is a position we are not willing to take." Robert Cousar, pastor of the Central Presbyterian Church, joined the battle on the side of Dr. Fowle. "We can only be a brother to one who is a son of our Father, and this link is only possible in Christ," he contended.

The first of these assumptions received emphatic support' from an ardent segregationist, who said, in effect, that any Christian who

[2] Nashville, Tenn., Abingdon Press, 1958, p. 54.

knows his Bible, and has not been fed a "diluted, indoctrinated version," is aware that there is only one Brotherhood of Man taught in the New Testament. This is the spiritual Brotherhood of Born-Again Christians. It has nothing to do with sociological reforms. God is the Creator of all, but He is the Father of only those who have accepted His Son as their Redeemer.

Such a sectarian concept of human brotherhood, qualified by dogma, limited by theology, circumscribed by credal arrogance, indicates a kindergarten concept of religion that controverts the universalism and the rationalism of the prophetic faith. It strikes at the very heart of our American democracy, and desensitizes man to an activated recognition of the sanctity of his fellow man as a child of God.

The Constitution of the United States, and principally the Bill of Rights, are predicated upon the religious premise of the sanctity of the human personality and the brotherhood of man without limitations of religious belief, racial identification, or political conviction. To maintain that man as a child of God has civil rights without securing those rights by process of law would relegate our American democracy to a status of a political fraud and would render our philosophy of government a contemptuous and hypocritical mockery. Religion becomes no less a pious fraud and no less a theological mockery when it proclaims the brotherhood of man, and then assumes an attitude of apathy to legislation, the political climate, the social milieu, and the humanitarian environment that affect man's status as a child of God.

Legal Murder

The Church and the Synagogue must be concerned with the controversial questions of capital punishment and prison reform. It is imperative that clergymen and religious laymen take an active role in the radical alteration of an attitude that seeks to penalize by hate rather than rehabilitate by love. If man is to be activated by the moral sensitivities that derive from his divine potential, the prophetic faith must be particularly aggressive in the effort to abolish capital punishment with its concomitants of brutality, vengefulness, ignorance, and disregard for the sanctity of human life. Legally to execute a human being by hanging, electrocution, the firing squad, or dropping pellets of cyanide of potassium into a container of hydrochloric acid in a lethal chamber is to contribute to the desensitization of twentieth century man and perpetuate a barbaric, vicious, and primitive attitude toward justice.

Those who have never witnessed a legal execution may advance objective arguments in behalf of the merits of capital punishment. Observers of such executions, however, have recoiled in horror at the protruding eyes, the blackened face of the victim who has been hanged by the neck. Witnesses to electrocutions have told of the sickening reaction to watching a man being burned alive, the jolt of a human body hurled against the straps by thousands of volts of electricity, the nauseating odor of burning flesh, and the startling realization that the state has just committed a legal murder. The sweating terror of a human being placed in a lethal chamber to inhale the deadly fumes of gas attests to the tragic evidence that despite the technical advances in civilization, our society is still following the primitive principle of *lex talionis*, emulating the medieval methods of execution refined by modern electronics and chemistry, and adhering to a punitive attitude of hatred and revenge that renders man insensitive to the divine nature of his fellow man.

The late Benjamin Cardozo, Associate Justice of the United States Supreme Court, offered a challenge to the prophetic faith when he wrote: "The next generation may look upon the death penalty as an anachronism too discordant to be suffered, mocking with grim reproach all our clamorous professions of the sanctity of life."

The death penalty does mock our claim to being civilized, and impedes the effort of religion to sensitize man to compassion and love. To perpetuate legal murder is to strengthen what Henry Weihofen calls "the urge to punish,"[3] and to condone the famous remark of Sir James Stephen, who said in 1883: "I think it highly desirable that criminals should be hated, that the punishment inflicted on them should be so contrived as to give expression to that hatred, and to justify it so far as the public provision of means for expressing and gratifying a healthy natural sentiment can justify and encourage it."[4]

[3] *The Urge to Punish*, Henry Weihofen (New York, Farrar, Straus & Cudahy, 1956).
[4] *History of the Criminal Law of England* (1883), Vol. II.

The argument that the biblical admonition of "an eye for an eye, a tooth for a tooth, a life for a life" is a divine sanction for capital punishment is both specious and unsound. The rabbinic exegetes interpreted this biblical verse in terms of adequate monetary compensation. Moreover, such a verse is indicative of human vengeance rather than divine compassion. It is in no way binding upon the prophetic faith.

The number of nations abolishing the death penalty is increasing from year to year. Holland has not executed any criminals since 1860, Belgium since 1863, Norway, 1875 and Denmark, 1892. Eight countries have abolished capital punishment in South America. In the United States, of the eight states having the lowest murder rates, five have no death penalty. The state with the very lowest murder rate is Maine, which abolished capital punishment in 1870.

In the light of modern scientific knowledge and concepts of humanity, the resort to capital punishment either by a state or by the national government is morally unjustifiable and reprehensible. There is no crime for which murder by society is justified.

More essential than statistics in behalf of the abolition of capital punishment is the need for revolutionary action in behalf of an enlightened, humanitarian, and religiously sensitized attitude toward the criminal, and the causative factors that contribute to crime.

The criminologist Bernard C. Glueck, Jr., has said: "It is my personal opinion, based on the examination of men in the death house at Sing Sing, that no person in our society is in a normal state of mind when he commits a murder."[5] Who is to judge whether a person is mentally responsible for his crime? By what criteria is he adjudged to be mentally responsible or legally insane?

We would not think of applying the medical standards of 1843 to our society, and yet the rule utilized to judge legal insanity in the United States, with few exceptions, is the M'Naghten Rule handed down by the presiding judge in a murder case in England in 1843, declaring: "To establish a defense of insanity, it must be clearly proved that, at the time of the committing of the act, the party accused was laboring under such a defect of reason, from disease of mind, as not to know the nature and quality of the act he was doing;

[5] *Changing Concepts in Forensic Psychiatry* (Boston, Little, Brown and Company, 1916).

or if he did know it, that he did not know what he was doing was wrong."

How many offenders afflicted with mental illness have been sent to their death by the state after a cursory diagnosis adjudged them to be legally sane? Who can assess the criminal injustice done to men and women who were not mentally or emotionally capable of comprehending the enormity of their crimes? The eminent psychiatrist Dr. Karl Menninger recently implored: "Abolish the stupid, medieval custom of capital punishment. . . . Capital punishment must be abolished to help the mentally ill, charged with crime."

The Church and the Synagogue may no longer afford to ignore the controversial questions of capital punishment and prison reform. Penologists assert that our prison system is a failure primarily because the objective is punishment rather than rehabilitation and cure. Reform schools, jails, penitentiaries, and detention homes, instead of removing the causes of crime and correcting the causes of social maladjustment, frequently embitter the offender, teach him additional lessons in crime, and contribute to his moral degradation.

Crime and Punishment

In *We Call Them Criminals* by Dr. Ralph S. Banay,[6] there is an eloquent plea for a thoroughgoing reformation of the penal system. He indicates the futility of punitive incarceration and the vindictive attitude of the public toward the convicted felon, and insists that society, and not necessarily the individual, is the patient.

If the prophetic faith is to succeed in the sensitization of man, it must take the initiative in a moral crusade to change the barbaric, archaic, and primitive concept of punishment by law to rehabilitation through understanding, therapy, and compassion.

The history of mankind reveals a progressive advancement from punitive measures to corrective and rehabilitative therapy. There was a time when those who were physically ill were flagellated, tortured, and harassed in order to exorcise the evil spirits. It was believed that they were possessed by demons. They were punished for their illness. In time, man advanced to the conviction that these people that were ill were not guilt ridden, and consequently were not to be punished,

[6] New York, Appleton-Century-Crofts, 1957.

but rather to be healed, cured, and rehabilitated with love. No longer does the stigma of guilt attach itself to those who are ill, nor does society punish the physically afflicted.

What pertained to physical illness likewise was true of mental illness. Those who were emotionally or mentally ill were chained, placed in pits of filth, whipped, and in some cases the top of their head was removed in order to permit the evil spirits to be expelled. As man progressed, he learned that those who are mentally ill are not of necessity guilt ridden; they are not to be punished, but cured and healed through psychotherapy, understanding, and love. Rather than to be incarcerated, they were sent to mental hospitals for diagnosis, treatment, and healing. Society no longer makes mental illness a criminal offense.

What has been true of physical and mental illness is likewise true of social illness and criminal maladjustment, and yet today we stigmatize and punish those who are deviates from norms of social conduct. We prescribe the period of punishment by the regulations of statute books and the designations of law. The offender is released from penal institutions to take his place in society not when he is well and cured, but when he has completed his sentence.

We no longer try to drive out the evil demons or attempt to exorcise malevolent spirits, but the punishment meted out implies that the individual is totally responsible for his behavior, without giving adequate consideration to the environmental and hereditary factors or the complex of mental and emotional tensions that contribute to his asocial actions and criminal delinquency.

Crime has causal factors just as disease, and the way to treat any abnormal condition is to remove the cause. To evaluate a crime committed as a single incident unrelated to the past is absurd. To permit a jury of laymen to diagnose and determine the mental and emotional competence of an offender is to compound the ridiculous. Only the trained and professional expert has the technical capability of inquiring into reasons and conditions that cause a human being to commit acts of violence and abnormal aggression. We would protest vehemently if a group of laymen were charged with the responsibility of diagnosing and prescribing treatment for the physically ill. We accept, without protest, a jury system whereby a group of well-intentioned but professionally incompetent laymen diagnose and prescribe punishment for the mentally, emotionally, and criminally ill.

In the main, the sexual deviate is punished by law instead of being treated by psychiatry. Is this unfortunate individual to be condemned or cured? Is he not compelled by a complexity of factors that make his sexual aberration probable if not inevitable? Isn't it possible that he is driven by compulsive forces that are just as strong as the physical factors that make an individual limp, or fall victim to chickenpox, flu, or a virus?

The arrogance, smugness, and cruelty that permits society to prosecute and punish the so-called juvenile delinquent must be replaced by understanding and kindness. Instead of castigating and punishing the offender for his crimes, through case study, diagnosis, and therapeutic treatment, he should be healed of his illness. To punish a child without ascertaining and correcting the cause of his delinquency is barbaric. To stigmatize the youthful offender for stealing, vandalism, assault, and other crimes without consideration of his intelligence, his emotional age, his family, environment, and the multiplicity of factors that contribute to his maladjustment is ignorant and unsound. The sexually delinquent girl is shunned by society, and condemned as shameful and evil. Do we ever ask what makes her an offender? Do we look to the broken home, the hunger for love, and the other factors that contribute to her delinquency? It is only in recent years that juvenile courts are utilizing the skills of trained social workers and the findings of psychological testing and psychiatric examination in an effort to eliminate the causative motivation for immoral and amoral conduct.

The prophetic faith must endeavor to sensitize society to look upon the social offender, both juvenile and adult, with compassion, and to regard crime as an illness. Instead of sending the offender to a prison for punishment, he should be sent to a hospital for healing. All jails, penitentiaries, and penal institutions should be abolished as primitive anachronisms that reflect an outmoded and insensitive attitude of punishment. They should be replaced by hospitals constructed and ordered for the treatment, rehabilitation, and cure of the socially and criminally ill. Just as those with contagious physical illnesses must be isolated, for the protection of society, so extreme cases of criminal illness may call for isolation, but with the intent of cure and not with the intention of punishment. The criminally ill who may be regarded as violent and incurable are not to be set free to endanger society any more than those who are mentally ill, dangerously, and maniacally abnormal are to be permitted freedom to threaten and endanger others. In all cases, however, the attitude of society should be corrective rather than punitive.

Those who argue that the rehabilitation of criminals is too costly and that we are spending too much money on the prevention and treatment of juvenile delinquency might well attend to the story told by Frank C. Laubach: "In Westphalia, in the town of Bethel, there is located the famous Colony of Mercy. It is a missionary institution dedicated to the care of epileptics and mentally deficients. One department is set aside for babies and young children. A wealthy man was being shown around the institution one day, and was so moved when he came to the children's ward that he could not speak. When he had recovered emotionally, he asked the superintendent how many of the children could be helped enough to live a normal life. The superintendent answered that about one in a hundred was the average. The man broke in impatiently: 'One! Then it isn't worth it.' 'But,' replied the superintendent, 'suppose that one were your son.' "[7] The meaning of the story as applied to the criminal or the delinquent should be self-evident.

The attribute of compassion must be engendered by the prophetic faith as a requisite for the sensitization of twentieth century man. Such an attribute leads to humility and a recognition of the weaknesses, the limitations, and the fallibility, as well as the divinity, of man. We must be wary of applying absolute standards even to morals. Are we to say that man's course is determined and that we must accept the thesis of behavioristic psychology that life is a response to stimuli and that every act, thought, word, as well as the course of human destiny, is determined by what we eat, by our glands, by our psyche, our genes, and our environment? Conversely, do we not have the freedom to make moral decisions, to choose between good and evil? Without freedom of will, man is a robot and not a child of God. Can it not be that man is caught in a vortex of both—churned by the determining factors that compel him and the freedom of will that invites him to resist the compulsion to evil and to make moral decisions that sanctify life with holiness, ennoble his character, and contribute to the welfare of his fellow man?

We are so quick to judge, indict, condemn, and punish our fellow

[7] *Pulpit Digest*, 1953.

man without understanding and with little compassion. Smugly, arrogantly, and self-righteously we excoriate the offender because he has failed to achieve the respectability and the normative standards we have attained. He is no longer a human being in our eyes, but a criminal, a scoundrel, and a menace. We look at him as he is, without consideration of the multiplicity of factors that made him what he is. How frequently are we insensitive to his inner anguish, self-loathing, and the embittered, twisted mentality that compels him to unleash his hostilities toward life and that drives him to a furious resistance to law, order, and society! Do we have the wisdom to know, to understand the frustrations, the rebellion, the ignorance, the misery, weakness, immaturity, and emotional infantilism that result in crime? The mature faith does not ask society to forgive and tolerate criminals. It asks society to replace retributive punishment with attempted rehabilitation and cure. It seeks compassion for those who walk in weakness, the endless parade of men and women who march through life in confusion, bitterness, and shame. God have compassion upon us—but, even more, God help us to find compassion for others, for the rejected, the outcasts, the children of despair, the offenders, delinquents, criminals, the sexual deviates, the prostitutes, procurers, the swindlers, thieves, embezzlers, adulterers, rapists, murderers, who have been desensitized to their divine endowments as children of God!

Our generation needs the wisdom of the rabbinic dictum: "Do not judge your fellow man until you are in his place!" We need the compassion and understanding of the Chassidic Rabbi Israel Baal Shem Tov who once heard of a disciple who used to preach severe sermons admonishing and castigating the members of his congregation as sinners. The rabbi said to his disciple: "What do you know about admonishing! You yourself have remained unacquainted with sin all the days of your life, and you have nothing to do with the people around you. How should you know and understand what sinning is?"

This remarkable homily implies that if the righteous and the self-righteous could really identify themselves with the people, experience their tribulations, encounter their temptations, and live the squalor and misery of their lives, they might more mercifully understand why they succumbed to sin. It is not incumbent upon them to judge and

denounce sinners. Judgment should be left to the mercy and compassion of God.

A man who kills another is sentenced to death. What shall we say
of a society that permits a nuclear experimentation that may result
in not one death, but the destruction of countless millions?

The Control of Nuclear Weapons

The future of our civilization is dependent upon the ability of the
prophetic faith to sensitize twentieth century man to utilize the
power of the atom for world peace and human welfare rather than
for international conflict and the destruction of society. When scientists are warning us of the destructive potential of nuclear fission and
the pregnant possibility of spawning generations of monsters as a result of radioactive influence upon the genes, we may not summarily
dismiss the concern for the survival of civilization as hypothetical,
fantastic, and remote from reality.

The need for national and international control of nuclear weapons
points up why the prophetic faith must enter into politics and
science, in fact, into everything that affects the preservation and the
sanctity of human life. The adherents of respectable religion may
shudder at the contemplation of the Church and the Synagogue entering politics, but do they shudder with equal horror at the knowledge that babies are drinking strontium 90 with their milk? Anything
that affects human life adversely or beneficially is the concern of the
radical and prophetic faith.

The great Christian saint Dr. Albert Schweitzer, together with
other religious leaders, has urged an end to nuclear-bomb tests for
the sake of the yet unborn. In a world-wide appeal against nuclear
weapons, Dr. Schweitzer warned: "Generation after generation, for
centuries to come, will witness the birth of an ever-increasing number
of children with mental and physical defects. We must not assume
the responsibility of the future birth of thousands of children with
mental and physical defects."[8]

If religion has nothing to say about unrestricted nuclear experimentation, fallout, radioactive contamination, and the use of nuclear
weapons in war, then the opponents of religion are strengthened in

[8] *Peace or Atomic War* (New York, Henry Holt and Company, 1958), p. 15.

their strictures against the "opiate of the masses." A silent, cowardly religion that separates itself from the problems and realities of life deserves to atrophy into decadence. A courageous, forthright, prophetic faith demands not only beautifully worded resolutions expressing concern but also an active participation in the effort to control and regulate nuclear power for peaceful and constructive purposes.

The tragedy of our era is that twentieth century man became so desensitized to death, horror, and destruction that he was able to accept the atomic bombing of Hiroshima and Nagasaki as a necessary concomitant of war and an acceptable means of achieving national victory. It is true that he experienced sorrow and revulsion at the destruction of hundreds of thousands of noncombatant men, women, and children. He deplored the number of casualties that resulted from the bombings. He turned squeamishly from the gruesome statistics of incendiary devastation, and the sickening vision of burning and charred human beings running, screaming into the night. In time, however, he learned to read reports of newer, more powerful and devastating atomic and hydrogen bombs as an achievement of science without conjuring up memories of Hiroshima and Nagasaki, and without relating the devastating potential of destruction to himself, his dear ones, or his civilization. Today, through atomic experimentation, radioactive debris is being scattered upon the earth as scientists, legislators, and the man in the street debate the question of tolerable levels of radiation, as casually as they discuss sewage disposal, inflation, stock-market reports, and the advantages of stereophonic music.

The challenge presented by the desensitization of twentieth century man will not be met by respectable religion. Only a dynamic, mature, radical, and prophetic faith, applied to life, can and must sensitize man to fulfill his divine destiny as a child of God and advance into the future with dedicated resolve and abiding hope.

18

Faith for Tomorrow

Who can separate his faith from his actions, or his belief from his occupations?
Who can spread his hours before him saying, "This for God and this for myself; this for my soul and this other for my body"? . . .
Your daily life is your temple and your religion.
Whenever you enter into it take with it your all.
—KAHLIL GIBRAN, *The Prophet*

Hope for Man

Although the radical, prophetic faith is dedicated to the moral sensitization of man to combat the injustices, cruelty, and inhumanity of contemporary society, it is irrevocably committed to the future. It affirms hope for man, intensifying his reverence for life, guiding and leading him in his journey through time beyond the valleys of despair and the shadows of death, until he emerges upon the incipient glow that portends the light and dawn of a moral tomorrow.

"Tomorrow" is one of the most precious words in the vocabulary of man, a word that offers infinite possibilities for the realization of dreams. Predicated on hope, it suggests the dawn of a new day, the renewal of life, and the priceless gift of time. Without the hope of tomorrow, man is powerless and must concede the imminence of death. With such hope, man is invincible, unconquerable, covenanted to an affinity with life, committed to the challenge of the future.

Today there are many voices of doom and prophets of defeatism predicting the end of our civilization. Resigning themselves to the inevitability of atomic destruction and cosmic death, they implore:

> "Let not the atom bomb
> Be the final sequel
> In which all men
> Are cremated equal."

They affirm no hope for man. There is no tomorrow. There is only the night and the promise of death.

Recently, a group of college men and women conducted a symposium on the question "What Does Man Need Most Desperately for the Future?" The answer given by the majority of the students was, "A good, reliable bomb shelter." Instead of stubbornly affirming their faith in tomorrow, bringing the power, enthusiasm, and vigor of youth to the building of a moral society; instead of affiliating themselves with organizations and causes that contribute to world peace and international understanding, they reject the challenge of the prophetic faith, yield to futility, and surrender unconditionally to despair.

The greatest threat to our civilization is not from atomic bombs or guided missiles. Rather, it is to be found in man's acquiescence to doom, his reluctance to struggle against evil, and his loss of faith in tomorrow.

Does the following sound familiar? "It is a gloomy moment in history. Not for many years—not in the lifetime of most men who read this paper—has there been so much grave and deep apprehension; never has the future seemed so incalculable as at this time.

"In France the political caldron seethes and bubbles with uncertainty; Russia hangs as usual, like a cloud, dark and silent upon the horizon of Europe; while all the energies, resources and influences of the British Empire are sorely tried, and are yet to be tried more sorely, in coping with the vast and deadly Indian insurrection, and with its disturbed relations in China. It is a solemn moment and no man can feel an indifference—which, happily, no man pretends to feel—in the issue of events.

"Of our own troubles [in the United States] no man can see the end."

The above, though it sounds current, is from *Harper's Weekly*, October 10, 1857—over one hundred years ago.

From the dawn of human history man has experienced agonizing anxiety about the future, and has articulated his fear and expressed his apprehension about tomorrow by means of prayer, song, art, and story.

An ancient legend culled from rabbinic literature describes the terror that seized Adam when he beheld the sun rapidly descending in the heavens for the first time. As the shadow of evening gradually enveloped the world in its dark embrace, he held up his hands as if to stop the swift march of the night. He whimpered and then screamed to God his fear that the sun would never shine again, that his world had lost the blessing of light forever.

With mercy and compassion, God then gave him the divine intuition to take two stones—one called *Darkness* and the other *The Shadow of Death*, and to rub these stones together, and lo, there was light! In joyous gratitude, Adam uttered the benediction: "Blessed art Thou, Lord, Creator of Light." He was given the assurance that light had not departed from the world, and that his future would not be eternally chained to darkness and despair. Calmed into sleep, he dreamed of the morning. "And there was evening and there was morning, the first day."

Unlike the title of Eugene O'Neill's tragic play *Long Day's Journey Into Night*, with the theme that the ultimate in life is stark tragedy, despair, and darkness, a mature, radical, and prophetic faith insists that life is a long night's journey into day. It teaches that man has been endowed by God with freedom of will, and the ability to act to direct and change his life despite the forces that oppose and harass him.

Beginning with the Genesis story of creation, the progression is not from order to chaos, but from chaos to order, from darkness to light, and at its conclusion this thought is symbolically expressed: "There was evening, and there was morning, the first day." This was a portent of the divine summons for man to proceed in a long night's journey into the day of God, which will be the day of universal justice, brotherhood, and peace.

Thus, in every age of anxiety, there must be those who lift themselves above the despair of their day. In every period of history, there must be dreamers who refuse to surrender to defeatism. In every age of crisis, religiously mature men and women must separate themselves from the doleful majority, and lift their eyes on high. They resist the onrushing tidal wave of pessimism that threatens to engulf their dreams, and insist that it was out of chaos that the world was created and that it was out of the black threads of darkness that a pattern of light was woven into the texture of the universe. They see beyond tragedy to the light and hope of a new tomorrow. These are the pioneers of spiritual frontiers, who declare with the psalmist: I shall not die, but live—live to declare the glory of God.

Even as the literary and intellectual spokesmen of our age write an obituary for life and intone a solemn requiem over the decease of civilization, we ask: But what of our dreams? What of our hopes? What of our future? Will despair enable man to advance into the future? Will pessimism give strength to the weary, hope to the despondent, and assurance to the uncertain? Are the hopes and dreams of man to be cast into a coffin of doom and buried forever? If life is but a jest, a vapor at best—if life is reduced to a macabre dance of atoms, leaping and cavorting in mad and riotous chain reaction, why bother about anything? Why hope or plan or dream? Our hopes are, of necessity, abortive, our plans will miscarry, bringing forth monstrous offspring of futility, and our sublime dreams will multiply into a montage of mocking nightmares from which there is no awakening.

If we believe that there is no hope for man and no future for civilization, then morality is a meaningless illusion; life "is a tale" told by a divine idiot, "full of sound and fury, signifying nothing," and our existence is an obscene and impious joke, jocularly and malevolently formulated by a supreme Demon for the malicious purpose of humiliating and degrading man.

The prophetic faith calls to man to identify his belief in God with meaningful and purposeful universe. It does not say with Tennyson: "Be patient, our playwright may show in some fifth act, what this wild drama means." It summons man to hope, to faith in tomorrow. It sensitizes man to hear, above the voices of doom, another Voice echoing through the ages—the still, small Voice of divinity, summoning man to create and build a future that will reveal God's kingdom of justice, brotherhood and peace for all the peoples and nations of the world. It insists that there is a force in the world that is mightier than the atom. It can have a greater impact than the cobalt bomb. That force is the power of a living, dynamic, radical, and prophetic faith—a faith that enables us to dedicate ourselves to what Ernest Renan called "the passionate search for the future," with the determination to live for that future, to work for that future by a program of consecrated action that will release the potential of divinity dormant within man.

That is why the religiously mature is a prisoner of hope and can never liberate himself from the vision of a better tomorrow. That is why the adherents of the prophetic faith must challenge the pessimism of our era, insisting that man is not a cosmic orphan alone in a parentless universe, but that he is a divinely endowed child of God, blessed with a potential for goodness, holiness, and love—a potential that summons man to enter upon an exalted adventure, pioneering into the future, advancing into untouched and untrodden vistas, struggling to establish new religious frontiers of faith.

Salesmen of Faith

Sholem Asch concludes his book *Kiddush Ha-Shem* (Sanctification of God) with the story of the young man Sholomo, who wanders from town to town in search of his family, following the terrible massacre of the Jews in Poland in 1648. Bereft of his family and friends, he roamed about through the fair of Lublin among the refugees. Listening to the cries and moans of his people—orphans for their parents, wives for their husbands—he yielded to despair and asked himself: Could there be a future for his people?

"He walked in a narrow street in Lublin where the merchants' stalls were located. And he saw standing before an empty booth an old man who was calling buyers into his booth. He marvelled greatly, for the booth was empty, and there was nothing in it to sell. He walked into the booth and asked the old man: 'What do you sell here? Your booth is void and empty, and there is no merchandise in it.'

"And the old man answered: '*I sell faith.*'

"And he looked intently at the old man, and the old man appeared to him familiar as though he had seen him before."

Sholomo had seen him before. He was Abraham, answering "Here am I" to God at Mount Moriah. He was Moses receiving the Ten Commandments at the heights of Sinai. He was Amos demanding justice at Beth El. He was Isaiah comforting the exiles. He was Joshua of Nazareth preaching the Sermon on the Mount. He was the gentle Rabbi Hillel, and Maimonides. He was Paul and John. He was every salesman of God selling faith and hope to a despairing world.

Many devoted young people today are searching for new worlds to conquer, new frontiers to pioneer, new and uncharted continents to explore. Science has opened new vistas of attainment for those who dare to advance into the unknown. Geophysical scientists are endeavoring to solve the mysteries of earth, sea, and space. There is another and even more exciting and challenging endeavor that calls for the vigor, enthusiasm, and stubbornness of youth. It summons the bravest and the most creative of men and women for a hazardous but exalted adventure into the unknown. It beckons them to explore into new areas of human relations, to convert darkness into light, to progress into the future with the objective of building God's kingdom, to lift their eyes and sensitize their souls to behold a vision of a sacred tomorrow that will witness the realization of the ethical ideals and moral objectives of the prophetic faith.

The future is in desperate need of salesmen of faith, men and women who are "sold" on their product, who believe in the worth and importance of their spiritual merchandise, who are willing to work and plan and sacrifice to attain their goals. Such salesmen of faith are aided by the greatest of all hidden persuaders—the Divinity within man. They are motivated, and inspired and compelled to extend themselves and dedicate themselves to their mission because of their conviction that the fate and the future of the world rest upon their enthusiasm, their religious salesmanship, and their prophetic zeal. They know that they will have to overcome sales resistance, the competition of cheaper and more alluring commodities, indifference, apathy, and even violent opposition, but the difficulties will serve to intensify their persistence and challenge their capabilities.

The voice of doubt inquires: Is it possible for these devoted salesmen of hope and faith to succeed? Will they make a living for the human family or will they fail in their efforts to save mankind from destruction and moral bankruptcy? Is man capable of buying his dreams? Does man have the ability to attain his goals and make his hopes for tomorrow a reality?

Man *has* the capacity and the divine capabilities of building God's kingdom on earth. It will not be a kingdom of absolute perfection, because the finite and limited nature of fallible man does not permit even the most optimistic and the most hopeful to believe that man can create a perfect society. It is not in perfection that our hope of the future rests. It is in perfectibility and man's capacity for beauty, holiness, justice, compassion, and peace.

Man *can* build a better world. He has learned to conquer disease, wrest power from nature, construct imposing edifices, achieve almost miraculous success in mastering and utilizing technical knowledge, and in sending satellites and guided missiles into outer space as a prelude to the exploration of other planets. Man has learned to counteract and conquer gravity, and harness the forces of nature for scientific achievement. Is there any reason why we should doubt the capability of man to conquer the moral evils that beset his society, and advance to new and unexplored frontiers of spiritual, moral, and ethical progress?

Man is taking gigantic strides forward in the control of his environment. Psychology and education are offering new discoveries to enable the individual to control, sublimate, and direct his emotions creatively.

According to Judge Luther Alverson, President of the National Association of Mental Health, twenty-five years ago, a person entering a mental hospital with a severe mental disorder, had only a 30 per cent chance of leaving the hospital improved or recovered. Today, the average patient admitted to a mental hospital has better than 70 per cent chance to be discharged within six months, as partly or totally recovered. Who can predict the advances that will be made in the field of psychotherapy within the next twenty-five years?

There has been progress even in the bitter and controversial effort to implement the decision of the Supreme Court in behalf of the integration of the public schools. Newspapers have given far more news coverage to the cases of violence and disorder than to the quiet program of compliance that has been going on slowly but steadily since then.

William Peters, in *The Southern Temper*,[1] dispels the illusion of

[1] New York, Doubleday & Company, 1959.

Southern solidarity against desegregation. He points out that by June, 1959, the number of states and school districts that have complied with the Supreme Court order is impressive. Before the 1954 decision, seventeen states and the District of Columbia required separate schools for white and Negro children. Of these, the District of Columbia, Delaware, Kentucky, Maryland, Missouri, Oklahoma, Texas, and West Virginia have moved with more than deliberate speed to desegregate their schools. A second group—Arkansas, Tennessee, and North Carolina—has at least made a beginning toward compliance.

Mr. Peters asserts that the progress has been achieved through the efforts of scores of organizations in the South working toward desegregation—church groups, local chapters of national, religious, and civic organizations, chapters of the American Friends Service Committee, the Southern Regional Council with its many associated state councils, and "the women's groups—particularly the church women."

Studies in heredity, eugenics, and birth control are showing man the way to a new control of population growth. Medicine is conquering diseases that have plagued man through the centuries, and is pointing the way to health and longevity. Science is conquering the heavens and exploring new frontiers of outer space.

Dr. William C. Pickering, head of the California Institute of Technology's Jet Propulsion Laboratory, claims that within five to ten years American technology will develop a vehicle that will propel man to the moon. The noted scientist described a family of four space vehicles: Vega, Centaur, Saturn, and Nova. The last will be a 260-foot-high rocket using as its first stage a cluster of four 1.5 million-pound thrust engines now under development.

There is no limit to the potential of the human spirit to conquer and achieve. There is no power to equal the power of the human will to create and build, to persist and to prevail. To despair of man's ability to triumph over evil is to disparage the divine nature of man. The rejection of man's divine destiny is the rejection of God, and constitutes a gross blasphemy of divine purpose. It suggests a contemptuous atheism that is more than the denial of God; it constitutes a denial of God's will. Hopelessness is the product of religious infidelity. Hope is the means of nurturing man's belief in the moral possibilities of tomorrow. It enables him to progress into the future as a salesman of faith.

But faith is such a nebulous, hazy, inchoate term. If it is to have meaning, it must be concretized into particular commitments and relate to specific efforts that will contribute to the building of a moral future for mankind.

The American Dream

The faith of tomorrow will not only behold man as a totality, and quest for the wholeness of mankind, but it will recognize that man, to achieve wholeness, must advance from the particular to the universal. Consequently, every effort will be made to strengthen the particular as a means to the realization of the universal.

Before man is able to go beyond national loyalty and behold himself as a citizen of the world, a part of, and with responsibility to the whole of mankind, he must first contribute to the moral advancement of his own nation. This imposes upon American citizens the moral mandate of striving for the realization of the American dream, and implementing the principles of freedom and equal rights promulgated by the Founding Fathers of our nation and guaranteed by the Bill of Rights. This is what the poet Archibald MacLeish envisaged when he saw America as a journey toward mankind, a journey toward a realization of the hopes of men—not only the belief in the dignity of man, but a belief in the human possibility of man to make the dream a reality.

The faith of tomorrow must inspire Americans to make the American dream a sacred cause; to kindle a burning passion for the idea of America as well as the protection of America; to enable us to behold the greatness and holiness of our nation in its soul rather than in its soil.

The Communist has made a cause out of his philosophy of government. Have we? He has made a religion out of communism, and is willing to make sacrifices for the victory of his cause. To what extent are we willing to make sacrifices for our cause? The Communist sees wholeness in terms of bringing all mankind under the control of the Soviet Union, effecting by evolutionary means or revolutionary action a total commitment to the doctrines of world communism. Do we behold a vision of the American dream as the motivation for revolutionary action to commit ourselves first, and then the peoples of the world to the values of justice, freedom, brotherhood, and truth?

Harold J. Berman, Professor at Harvard Law School, has said that if we really want to defeat communism, we must construct a social order in which justice, mercy and morality take precedence over economic security, political power, and technological progress. "We must freely, thru voluntary associations, pour into that social order the same spirit of service, self-sacrifice and common purpose that under the Soviet system is induced by party discipline."

Americans must be disciples of a dream, revolutionaries dedicated to a sacred purpose, salesmen of the democratic way of life. For too long we have been devoting ourselves to the negative hatred of Russia, instead of fostering a positive love of America. Democracy must be converted into a holy and sacred cause worthy of the impassioned loyalty of its adherents. Such loyalty does not suggest a blind, jingoistic, nationalistic fervor that manifests itself by loyalty oaths, isolationistic ideology, pride in our industrial production, or the arrogation of all virtue, truth, and achievement as the exclusive monopoly of our nation. Rather must loyalty be reinterpreted as devotion to the ideas, ideals and principles of our American democracy.

The French Historian François Guizot once asked James Russell Lowell, "How long will the American republic endure?" Lowell replied, "As long as the idea and convictions of the men who founded it continue dominant."

There is some indication that we should be concerned about the future of the American dream when we review the findings of H. H. Remmers and D. H. Radler in *The American Teenager*, a book which sums up fifteen years of poll taking among 8,000 to 18,000 high-school students between grades 9 and 12. More than half of our teenage students "think the large mass of us in these United States simply aren't capable of deciding for ourselves what's right and what's wrong." Almost half are "ready to dispense with freedom of the press." A fourth "think police should be free to search your home or your person without a warrant." A third of them "believe American free speech should be denied certain people if it seems convenient." Eighty-three per cent approve of wiretapping, and 60 per cent agree that censorship of books, newspapers, and magazines is all right. Fifty-eight per cent have no objection to police use of the third degree, and more than half are ready to throw out the constitutional guarantee against self-incrimination or are uncertain about it. Thirty-seven per cent are ready to abolish the right to strike by some groups of workers. The answers to other questions indicate that an almost unquestioned value is placed on conformity and acceptance of their group. Some thirteen per cent "would restrict by law religious belief and worship."[2]

These findings prompted the *United Mine Workers Journal* to editorialize in the December 1, 1958 issue: "These statistics are frightening! They are a reflection on our whole system of education, on our churches, our clergymen, our schools, our school teachers. But most of all they are a reflection on American parents whose biases and prejudices and hatreds are passed on to their children. What we need in this country are more radical young teenagers. And we mean radical persons in the true sense, as defined by Webster: 'Of or pertaining to the root; proceeding directly from the root. . . .' "[3]

If we as Americans are to make our contribution to the future, then the salesmen of the prophetic faith must foment a new American rebellion—a rebellion that will demand a revision of our system of education, religious and secular, that will jolt our churches, our synagogues, our clergymen, our schools, our school teachers, our parents out of the smug complacency and the biases and prejudices that are transmitted to our children. The ideas, convictions, and principles of the Founding Fathers must be transvaluated into the idiom of the twentieth century, revitalized and refurbished to illumine the horizon of the American future brilliantly. If we are to sell democracy to the world, we must first activate and apply it to our nation. The love of America must inspire us to make a religion out of democracy, dedicating ourselves to its principles of justice, the dignity and worth of the individual, the civil rights of its citizens, and the uninterrupted advance toward freedom, brotherhood, and peace. The glory of the American dream must be our sacred motivation that inspires our progress into the future.

The secret of America's genius and power is not only found in pulpits flaming with righteousness; it is likewise revealed through the immortal doctrines set forth by the Founding Fathers of our nation.

Around the inner rim of the dome of the Jefferson Memorial in Washington is his deathless legend, "I Have Sworn Upon the Altar of God Eternal Hostility Against Every Form of Tyranny Over the

[2] Indianapolis, Bobbs-Merrill, 1957, pp. 16-17, 189, 194.
[3] Used by permission.

Mind of Man." On the walls are four panels that synthesize the
Jefferson philosophy:

"We hold these truths to be self-evident, That all men are created
equal, that they are endowed by their Creator with certain inalienable
rights, among these are life, liberty and the pursuit of happiness.

"Almighty God hath created the mind free. All attempts to influence it by temporal punishments or burthens are a departure from
the plan of the Holy Author of our religion.

"Commerce between Master and Slave is despotism. Nothing is
more certainly written in the book of fate than that these people are
to be free.

"As new discoveries are made, new truths discovered and manners
and opinions change, with the change of circumstances, institutions
must advance also to keep pace with the times. We might as well
require a man to wear still the coat which fitted him when a boy as
civilized society to remain ever under the regimen of their barbarous
ancestors."

This is the historic motivation for America's journey toward mankind. This is America's legacy to the future.

One Universe

If mankind is to attain maturity, the faith of the future must
emphasize the essential unity and interrelatedness of men and nations, and enable us to go beyond national sovereignty to a United
States of the world.

During World War II, Wendell Willkie wrote his *One World*.
Willkie's thesis was that the world had grown smaller and that unless
the nations could cooperate they would invite the grim alternative of
destruction. Because of the fear of internationalism and the domination of Soviet Russia, Willkie's "One World" has become an epithet
for those who object to working through the United Nations in its
efforts to work for international peace and concord.

The alternative to one world is total war. The alternative to one
universe is a struggle to the death for interplanetary supremacy.
Facing the grim possibility of future conflict, we must recognize that

the struggle for interplanetary domination will inevitably lead to the destruction of civilization. There will be co-existence or no existence.

Cardinal Richard R. Cushing has said that for centuries we've tried the power of wealth, of armies and navies, and combinations of nations, and diplomacy, and all have failed. He believes that time is running out, and that we must turn from trust in the chain reactions of exploding atoms to faith in the chain reaction of God's love: "Love—love of God and fellow men, this is God's formula for peace. Peace on earth to men of good will."

The faith of tomorrow must dispel the prejudice against internationalism and strengthen the organizations and causes that support international cooperation and the peaceful co-existence of the United Nations of the World.

The development of world law and the need for a workable World Court are requisites for the future. Consequently, the religion of tomorrow must pursue a policy of education to overcome the extreme nationalism that engenders resistance to agencies dedicated to world international cooperation and world peace.

On October 18, 1951, the following statement was inserted in the *Congressional Record* under the title "The Greatest Subversive Plot in History": "How anyone who venerates and loves Old Glory as the symbol of the deathless march of the United States through the years, to fulfil its destiny as a free and independent republic, can read this documented evidence of the greatest and most malignant plot in history, against the future of his country, and its children's children, is more than I am able to comprehend. Just how careless and unthinking can we be that we permit this band of spies and traitors to exist another day in this land we all love?"

This congressman was not describing some group plotting the overthrow of our government by force. He was talking about the United Nations Educational and Cultural Organization (UNESCO), an official body of sixty-nine nations which Soviet Russia had not joined.

Such an unfounded statement indicating a bigoted attitude toward an organization that represents a united effort in behalf of international service not only endangers the security of our nation but threatens the hope for international brotherhood and the recognition of the interrelatedness of man.

Bertrand Russell, in *Human Society in Ethics and Politics*, warned:

"If men are to escape from the consequences of their own childish cleverness, they will have to learn, in all the powerful countries of the world, or at any rate in America and Russia, to think not of separate groups of men, but of man."[4]

The hope of achieving world unity and peace is not a subversive plot. It is the sublime objective of the Judaeo-Christian religious tradition, the hope of the prophet Isaiah who dreamed of the time when peoples:

> ". . . shall beat their swords into plowshares,
> And their spears into pruning-hooks;
> Nation shall not lift up sword against nation,
> Neither shall they learn war any more" (2.4).

This aspiration toward international unity and world peace was further attested by the prophet in meaningful hyperbole when he predicted:

> "And the wolf shall dwell with the lamb,
> And the leopard shall lie down with the kid;
> And the calf and the young lion and the fatling together;
> And a little child shall lead them" (11.6).

It was to be a time when:

> "They shall not hurt nor destroy
> In all my holy mountain;
> For the earth shall be full of the knowledge of the Lord,
> As the waters cover the sea" (11.9).

There are some who interpret this to mean the time of the coming of the Messiah. They insist that world peace and international unity will be achieved only by truly miraculous and supernatural means. This is not the reasoning of the radical faith, nor is it the hope of the religion of tomorrow.

The faith of tomorrow will emphasize not the theological concept of the Messiah, but the ethical hope for the Messianic era, of God's

[4] New York, Simon and Schuster, 1955, p. 197.

kingdom on earth, the religious society created by man in co-partner-ship with God. Such a Messianic era will not be ushered in by super-natural means. It will evolve from the application of God's moral commandments to life. It will eventuate when through science and medicine, the dread diseases that afflict man will be reduced, and effectively controlled and ultimately conquered. The Messianic age will be characterized by the inclusion of economics as a component part of religion as man strives to eradicate the starvation and poverty that are now the daily lot of millions of God's children. It will accord man civil rights and liberties and enable him to fulfill his potential as a child of God. It will herald the sensitization of man to compas-sion, brotherhood, and love.

In essence, the Messianic age is not a supernatural state of existence. It is not man's realization of eternal bliss as envisaged by prophets and dreamers. The Messianic age is relative and not absolute. It is a state of mind rather than an awaited advent in time. It is man's dynamic, progressive aspiration toward perfectibility rather than the static attainment of perfection.

It is for this sacred objective that the adherents of the prophetic faith must prepare to foster a world revolution.

The Magnificent Revolution

Revolutionary procedure is not always looked upon with approval because of its semantic connotations, and yet the faith of tomorrow, the moral reconstruction of society, and the salvation of the world depend upon a magnificent revolution. To assault the bastions of ignorance and bigotry, to overthrow the moral lethargy that has governed the past, to seize and maintain control of all the vital, spiritual resources that contribute to peace, understanding, and brotherhood, necessitate a violent revolt against the prejudices and practices sanctioned by generations of indifference.

Such a moral revolution imposes solemn and sacred obligations upon its proponents. They will be summoned to subscribe to the sanctity of man and issue manifestoes declaring unceasing opposition to poverty, disease, oppression, discrimination, and war. Sensitized to the stirring appeal of Habakkuk that "the righteous shall live by his faith," they will apply to the society of the future the religious principles that we now accept in theory but reject in practice. They will be committed to follow the ethical requirements set forth by the prophet Micah, "It hath been told thee, O man"—not O Christian, not O Jew, not O Moslem, not O White, O Black, or O Brown, but, "It hath been told thee, O *man*, what is good and what the Lord doth require of thee, only to do justly, love mercy and walk humbly with God." In the words of Amos, justice will have to "well up as waters and righteousness as a mighty stream." Each citizen will have to love his neighbor as himself. Each nation will be compelled to obey the command of Jesus: "Love your enemies, bless them which despitefully use you, and persecute you." All men will be obliged to answer Malachi's question: "Have we not all one Father? Hath not one God created us?" by consecrating themselves to better understanding, good will, and the universal brotherhood of man. This is the magnificent revolution that will mobilize zealous devotees of prophetic religion to live by their faith and contribute to the building of the future brotherhood on earth.

I Seek My Brethren

The most important question of our age, then, is not "What have we accomplished?" but "What are the goals and objectives we strive to attain for the future?" The nature and character of the faith of tomorrow will be determined by the answer we give to the biblical query addressed to Joseph: "What seekest thou?" (Genesis 37.15). Moreover, the effectiveness of the magnificent revolution will be measured by the zeal with which the adherents of the prophetic faith pursue the implementation and activation of Joseph's response: "I seek my brethren."

Indian folklore tells of a patriarch who was about to die and did not know which of his four sons should receive his inheritance and be elevated to the leadership of the community. He said: "Go forth, my sons, pioneer into the unknown, and bring me back some tangible sign of how far you have progressed."

The first son started out and came to a seemingly impenetrable forest. He could not go on, and so he picked a bramble bush and returned with it to his father. The second son came to the forest and went through it until he came to a turbulent stream. He picked some moss from the bank and returned with it to his father. The third son traversed the forest and by persistent effort crossed the stream, but was stopped by a towering mountain. He picked a flower that grew at the base of the mountain and returned with it to his father. The fourth son, even more persistent, went through the forest, crossed the turbulent stream, and, confronted by the mountain, determined to make the steep ascent. He paused for a moment of prayer and then, revitalized, started up the mountainside, slowly and tortuously. He fell, but scrambled to his feet and persisted upward until, bruised and bleeding, he stood on the mountaintop. He looked up and he looked down, and then he returned to his father, saying: "I have climbed to the very top of the mountain, and O my father, I looked up and felt so close to God that I wanted to reach up to touch Him. And then I looked down and saw little specks below, and I realized that they were more than specks—they were men and women. And even more than men and women, they were my brothers and my sisters. I have brought you back nothing tangible except an exalted vision of the Fatherhood of God and the Brotherhood of all Men."

As we advance into the future, we must bring to our Heavenly Father more than tangible, material possessions and the gadgets of technical achievement. The faith of tomorrow must enable man to ascend to the mountaintop of divinity and revolutionize society to make the Fatherhood of God and the Brotherhood of Man an immediate and practical reality.

Morally sensitive men and women are sated with religious platitudes about the Fatherhood of God and the Brotherhood of Man. They are becoming impatient with pious double talk. They perceive that brotherhood is no longer a theological luxury to be enjoyed by the dedicated few. Men will have to learn to live together as brothers through the use of religion, or they will die together as enemies through the misuse of science.

It is imperative that Jews, Christians, Moslems, and those of every faith and every nationality unite and join hands for a sacred quest, and through a magnificent revolution integrate and fuse politics, science, economics, education, and religion into a moral totality and an ethically whole society that will enable man to seek and find his brethren before it is too late.

God Help Us

Man cannot successfully achieve the magnificent revolution, progress to a mature, radical, and prophetic faith for tomorrow, and build the moral society of the future without entering into a divine partnership with God.

By a divine partnership with God, we mean an identification with a divine Mystery, the sacred and supreme Reality we call God. God immanently reveals Himself in nature, in man, in the totality of everything that exists, and yet transcends the whole. This partnership of man with God is based on the conviction that man is particularly and uniquely endowed with a divine potential that elevates him above all other creatures, and enables him, through the exercise of his freedom of will, to make moral choices, to perfect himself and his society by emulating divine attributes of compassion, justice, and holiness, even though he and his society may never achieve absolute perfection. Implicit in this partnership is the belief that there is a sacred, unique relationship between man and God and God and man. Man exalts God through justice and sanctifies God through righteousness. God exalts man through the divine potential and sanctifies man by giving him the freedom of will to emulate divine attributes. Man seeks God as a source of inspiration for the realization of his quest for wholeness and holiness. God searches for man to fulfill a divine destiny, to build the moral kingdom of the future on earth. It is for this divine partnership that man must grow beyond religious infancy to attain his full potential of religious maturity. But what are the requirements of religious maturity?

The radical, prophetic, and mature faith rests on an ethical relationship to God, a moral God who requires man to emulate the attributes of justice, compassion, and holiness. It is predicated on the divinity and sanctity of the human personality, and from this premise proceeds to a program of social action to protect and promote the civil and moral rights of man. Strengthened by the divine revelation of the past, the mature faith directs itself to the application of the divine commandments to the present, even as it looks beyond the present to the attainment of its sacred objectives through the faith of tomorrow.

The mature and radical faith must be an applied faith, constantly challenging, ever disturbing, ceaselessly aspiring—with no dichotomy between religion and life. Is there a reasonable hope that man will ever achieve the religious maturity envisaged by prophet and sage, visionary and dreamer? Will man advance beyond religious infantilism to live by the precepts of the prophetic faith?

The radical faith insists that the Golden Age is not in the past; man's great future is now in the process of being created. He is on his way to the fullest and most exalted realization of all his potentialities as a human being.

As we look back upon history, we confront the awe-inspiring fact that there is something unconquerable in the human spirit. Man has advanced forward, seeking, questing, struggling—but always carrying on, fulfilling the laws of his own being.

Since man is endowed with freedom of will, his future is not predetermined, and the moral possibilities of tomorow are infinite. Through progress in science, through a better understanding of human relations and social ethics, through advances in psychological insight, the development of political and economic organization to democratic objectives, through education in the art of living together, society is taking small but determined steps in the direction of maturity.

There is truth in General Omar Bradley's statement, "Ours is a world of nuclear giants and ethical pygmies"—but man has never utilized his full potential of divinity that will enable him to increase his ethical stature and grow up to God. We have no criteria for measuring the spiritual heights that man may yet attain in the future. It is not toward the political or the scientific, but toward mature religion that mankind must look to see the dawn of universal morality break upon the horizon of tomorrow.

We measure the future of our hopes, and the hopeful possibilities of the future are infinite. It is hope that enables the salesmen of the prophetic faith to open their eyes to the divine promise in the soul of man. It is the belief that man can progress toward ethical maturity that strengthens his will to live and his determination to work and strive for moral perfection. But more than anything else, the assurance of religious progress is based on the sanctity of man. The incalculable and infinite power of God within man will yet be released to revolutionize society for the fulfillment of divine destiny. Man is not alone.

As long as man is covenanted to God in a divine partnership he will continue to grow, advance, and mature religiously for the greatest and most sublime building enterprise ever envisaged: the building of God's kingdom of the future.

This is what we should mean when we appeal, "God help us." Not that God should perform miracles in our behalf, or that our problems should be solved by the supernatural intervention of a kindergarten deity. The moral and physical laws of God are not to be changed by poignant appeals or eloquent entreaties, no matter how sincere or deserving. We must agree with Spinoza when he wrote: "By the help of God, I mean the fixed and unchangeable order of nature or the chain of natural events, for . . . the universal laws of nature according to which all things exist and are determined, are only another name for the eternal decrees of God, which always involve eternal truth and necessity, so that to say that everything happens according to natural law and to say that everything is ordained by the decree and ordinance of God, is the same thing."

God's help cannot be obtained by equating religion with liturgical formula, ceremonial act, or verbal supplication alone. It must be sought through the exploration and the liberation of the divine power within man. It must be attained through the mature prayer that enables us to commune with the holy God who is "nigh unto all who call upon Him, to all who call upon Him in truth." God's help is accessible to those who strive to emulate the moral attributes of compassion, justice, and love, who sensitize their souls to hear the still, small voice of Divinity summoning them to personal piety, moral perfectibility, and a dedication to social action in co-partnership with God.

As man lifts his eyes to the mountaintop where God may be seen, he knows that even though his world may be threatened by the pillar of fire by night and the mushroom cloud of death by day, his help cometh from God—the God who has commanded him to build His kingdom of righteousness on earth.

If the individual regards this as too abstract and, dissatisfied with this interpretation of the help of God, asks: "But what shall I do, and how shall I begin in the quest for God's help? There is so much evil in our society. How can I enter into a co-partnership with God to eradicate bigotry, ignorance, cruelty, and darkness from the world?"

he may well be reminded of a wise admonition derived from an ancient heritage.

The disciples of an eminent rabbi approached their teacher with a complaint about the prevalence of evil in the world. Intent upon driving out the forces of darkness, they requested the rabbi to counsel them. The rabbi suggested that they go down into a dark cellar, take brooms, and sweep out the darkness. The bewildered disciples applied themselves to vigorously sweeping out the darkness, but to no avail. The rabbi then advised his followers to take sticks and beat at the darkness to drive out the evil, but to no avail. He then advised them to go down into the cellar again and protest, curse the darkness. This was tried, but to no avail. The rabbi then said: "My children, let each of you meet the challenge of darkness by lighting one candle." The disciples descended into the cellar and each kindled a light. They looked, and behold! the darkness had been driven out.

When we feel overwhelmed by the malevolent forces of evil in the world and attempt to sweep out the darkness, beat at it and protest against it, we should be reminded that the most effective manner of combating darkness is through the principle of light. The admonition of the ancient sage, urgent in its appeal, may also apply to those in our generation: "Let each of you meet the challenge of darkness by kindling the candle of Divinity within, that it may light your way into the future, and enable you to grow from kindergarten religion to a mature, prophetic, and radical faith."

Man may never completely comprehend the mystery of God, but he must persist in his effort to behold glimpses and intimations of Divinity, assured by the conviction of faith that God is there. The light of God blinks and beams in luminescent splendor only to dim, fade out and recede into the shadows of history seemingly obscured by the dark vicissitudes of life, but the light of God is there. Restless, striving, persistent man, rooted in time, gropes and quests for the timeless, hungering for certainty, thirsting for truth amidst the transient movement of the years, rebuffed again and again by the timely and the transitory, but the search for the permanent and the abiding continues. The Spirit of God within man shifts and widens and expands. It shrinks, atrophies and is driven deep into the innermost recesses of his being, dormant and unfulfilled, but the Spirit of God within man is there—waiting to be brought forth and converted into a source of limitless strength, power and light for the sanctification of life and the fulfillment of human destiny.

The Voice is speaking. It is telling us something. Are we prepared to listen?

God, the Light of Divinity, the Unconquerable Spirit within man and the Voice fuse and blend into a sublime Oneness. We point our lives in the direction of Divinity, reach out to the Eternal Mystery, and ignite our souls with effervescent sparks of holiness radiating and showering from the Infinite Light. We heed and obey the Voice silently articulating the eternal summons to man to advance, to go forward to new and radical frontiers of faith, and we know that the appeal, "God help me," has been answered.